Contents

KU-311-850

TENNESSEE WILLIAMS

A Streetcar Named Desire

With commentary and notes by
PATRICIA HERN *and*
MICHAEL HOOPER

Bloomsbury Methuen Drama
An imprint of Bloomsbury Publishing Plc

BLOOMSBURY

LONDON · OXFORD · NEW YORK · NEW DELHI · SYDNEY

Bloomsbury Methuen Drama
An imprint of Bloomsbury Publishing Plc

Imprint previously known as Methuen Drama

50 Bedford Square	1385 Broadway
London	New York
WC1B 3DP	NY 10018
UK	USA

www.bloomsbury.com

BLOOMSBURY, METHUEN DRAMA and
the Diana logo are trademarks of Bloomsbury Publishing Plc

This edition first published in Great Britain in 1984 by Methuen London Ltd, by
arrangement with Secker & Warburg Ltd
Reissued with corrections 1988; reissued with a new cover design 1994;
reissued with additional material and a new cover design 2005 and 2009
Reprinted 2010 (twice), 2011, 2012, 2013, 2014, 2015 (four times), 2016

Copyright © by the Estate of the late Tennessee Williams 1947
Commentary and Notes copyright © 1984 by Methuen London Ltd,
2005, 2009 by Methuen Drama

The authors have asserted their rights under the Copyright, Designs and Patents Act, 1988,
to be identified as authors of this work.

All rights reserved. No part of this publication may be reproduced or transmitted in any form or
by any means, electronic or mechanical, including photocopying, recording, or any information
storage or retrieval system, without prior permission in writing from the publishers.

No responsibility for loss caused to any individual or organization acting on or refraining from
action as a result of the material in this publication can be accepted by Bloomsbury or the author.

All rights whatsoever in this play are strictly reserved and application for performance etc.
should be made before rehearsals by professionals to Georges Borchardt Inc., 136 East 57th
Street, New York, NY10022, USA and by amateurs to Samuel French Ltd, 52 Fitzroy Street,
London, W1P 6JR. No performance may be given unless a licence has been obtained.

No rights in incidental music or songs contained in the work are hereby granted and
performance rights for any performance/presentation whatsoever must be obtained from the
respective copyright owners.

All photographs reproduced courtesy of Warner Bros

British Library Cataloguing-in-Publication Data
A catalogue record for this book is available from the British Library

ISBN: PB: 978-1-4081-0604-4
ePDF: 978-1-4742-2531-1
ePUB: 978-1-4742-2530-4

Library of Congress Cataloging-in-Publication Data
A catalog record for this book is available from the Library of Congress

Series: Student Editions

Printed and bound in Great Britain

Tennessee Williams: 1911-1983

1911   March 26: Thomas Lanier (later Tennessee Williams) was born in Columbus, Mississippi. He had a younger brother and a younger sister, Rose, to whom he was devoted. Despite a period of serious illness, lasting nearly two years, his early childhood was happy:

> Before I was eight my life was completely unshadowed by fear. [. . .] My sister and I were gloriously happy. [. . .] And in the evenings, when the white moonlight streamed over our bed, before we were asleep, our Negro nurse Ozzie, as warm and black as a moonless Mississippi night, would lean above our bed, telling in a low, rich voice her amazing tales about foxes and bears and rabbits and wolves that behaved like human beings.
> (Edwina Dakin Williams and Lucy Freeman, *Remember Me to Tom*, Putnam's, New York, 1963, p. 19)

1919   The family moved to St. Louis, to an apartment which he later used as the model for the Wingfield home in *The Glass Menagerie*. Tom was sent to a public (state) school, where he was unhappy.

> At the age of fourteen I discovered writing as an escape from a world of reality in which I felt acutely uncomfortable. It immediately became my place of retreat, my cave, my refuge. From what? From being called a sissy by the neighbourhood kids, and 'Miss Nancy' by my father, because I would rather read books in my grandfather's large and classical library than play marbles and baseball and other normal kid games, a result of a severe childhood illness and of excessive attachment to the female members of my family, who had coaxed me back into life.
> (Foreword to *Sweet Bird of Youth*)

1927   April: an essay, 'Can a Good Wife be a Good Sport?', was published in *Smart Set*.

1928   August: a story, 'The Vengeance of Nitrocis', was accepted by *Weird Tales*.

1929   He became a student at the University of Missouri.

1931-   During the Depression his father insisted that he leave university
1934   and work with the shoe company that employed his father. Tom
        kept up his writing at night, finally making himself ill. He later
        acknowledged the value of this experience: 'I learned about
        people's lives in the little white collar job class.' (Letter to
        Kenneth Tynan, 26.7.1955.)

1935   July: a farce, called *Cairo, Shanghai, Bombay*, was produced in
        Memphis, Tennessee, where Tom was convalescing.

1936   A small theatre group, the Mummers at Washington University,
        St. Louis, produced a one-act and two longer plays: *Candles in
        the Sun* and *Fugitive Kind*. He became a student at the State
        University of Iowa, now calling himself Tennessee, instead
        of Tom.

1937   During his absence a pre-frontal lobotomy was performed on his
        sister, Rose. He felt guilty about not being at home to protect
        her; his mother blamed his father for the decision:

> Right after his [Tom's] departure, my husband and I were
> faced with a drastic decision. Rose had grown more
> withdrawn and helpless, and her fantasies of being poisoned
> and murdered more intense. Cornelius decided to commit her
> to a state mental hospital. (*Remember me to Tom*, p. 84.)

1938-   He spent several months moving about America, writing, staying
1940   in Chicago, St. Louis, New Orleans, California and Mexico.

1939   The judges of the Group Theatre Play Contest made a special
        award to Williams's *American Blues* (three one-act plays).

1940   An agent, Audrey Wood, managed to secure for him a Rockefeller
        fellowship worth $1000. Williams joined an advanced playwriting
        seminar at the New School, New York.
        December: *Battle of Angels* opened in Boston. It flopped. The
        Theatre Guild granted him $2000 to rewrite the play, justifying
        this in a letter to subscribers:

> We chose it because we felt the young author had genuine
> poetic gifts and an interesting insight into a particular
> American scene.

1940   Williams had a further, small grant from the Rockefeller
        Foundation, but eked it out by taking various short-term jobs,
        such as waiter, for nearly three years.

1943   After help from Audrey Wood, Williams was given a contract as a script writer for MGM. None of his scripts was accepted. During this time he wrote *The Glass Menagerie*.

His grandmother — a loved and powerful influence on him — died of cancer.

1944   He won an American Academy of Arts and Letters award, worth $1,000.

December: *The Glass Menagerie* opened in Chicago.

1945   March: *The Glass Menagerie* opened in New York, winning the New York Drama Critics Circle Award and the $1500 Howard Memorial Award given by the Playwrights Company.

September: *You Touched Me* had 100 performances in New York.

1946   Williams finished *27 Wagons Full of Cotton and Other Plays*.

1947   November: *A Streetcar Named Desire* opened in Boston.

December 3: *A Streetcar Named Desire* opened in New York to enthusiastic reviews; it ran for 855 performances:

> The new play is full-scale — throbbingly alive, compassionate, heart-wrenchingly human. (*New York Daily News*, 4.12.1947)

> Tennessee William's new play is a feverish, squalid, tumultuous, painful, steadily arresting and oddly touching study of feminine decay along the lower Mississippi. (*New York Post*, 4.12.1947)

There were one or two less glowing assessments:

> His play [. . .] remains largely a theatrical shocker which, while it may shock the emotions of its audience, doesn't in the slightest shock them into any spiritual education. [. . .] It is, in other words, highly successful theatre and highly successful showmanship, but considerably less than that as critically secure drama. (*New York Journal — American* 15.12.1947)

> That the play is not merely the ugly, distressing and possibly unnecessary thing which any outline must suggest is due, I suppose, in part to its sincerity, even more to that fact that the whole seems to be contemplated with genuine compassion and not, as is the case with so much modern writing about the lower depths, merely with relish. (*The Nation*, 20.12.1947)

Williams won the New York Drama Critics Circle Award for the second time, also a Pulitzer Prize.

His parents separated.

1948 He published *One Arm and Other Stories*.

October: *Summer and Smoke* opened in New York.

Williams visited Rome for the first time.

1949 Laurence Olivier directed *A Streetcar Named Desire* in London.

1950 July: *A Streetcar Named Desire* opened in Paris.

The film of *The Glass Menagerie* was released.

The Roman Spring of Mrs. Stone, a novel, was published.

1951 February: *The Rose Tattoo* opened in New York, and ran for 300 performances.

A Streetcar Named Desire was filmed, directed by Elia Kazan.

I Rise in Flame, Cried the Phoenix was published.

1952 Williams was elected to the National Institute of Arts and Letters.

1953 March: *Camino Real* opened in New York for 60 performances.

1955 March: *Cat on a Hot Tin Roof* opened in New York, winning Williams his third Drama Critics Circle Award and his second Pulitzer Price. It had 79 performances.

His grandfather died. *The Rose Tattoo* was filmed.

1956 Elia Kazan directed the film of Williams's *Baby Doll*.

1957 Williams undertook a course of psychoanalysis. His father died.

March: *Orpheus Descending* opened in New York. *The Fugitive Kind* was filmed.

1958 January: *Something Unspoken* and *Suddenly Last Summer* opened off-Broadway in New York, under the title *Garden District*.

1959 March: *Sweet Bird of Youth* opened in New York and ran for 95 performances.

Joseph L. Mankiewicz directed the film of *Suddenly Last Summer*.

1960 November: *Period of Adjustment* opened in New York and ran for 132 performances.

1961 December: *The Night of the Iguana* opened in New York and ran for 316 performances.

1962 The film of *Sweet Bird of Youth* was released.

1963 January: *The Milk Train Doesn't Stop Here Any More* opened in New York, for 69 performances.

1964 *The Night of the Iguana* was filmed.

1966 February: *Slapstick Tragedy* had seven performances in New York.

April: *Eccentricities of a Nightingale* was produced in Washington.

1968 March: *Seven Descents of Myrtle* had 29 performances in

New York.

1969   January: Williams became a Roman Catholic.

May: *In the Bar of a Tokyo Hotel* opened off-Broadway for 29 performances, winning awards from the National Institute of Arts and Letters and from the Academy of Arts and Letters.

1972   April: *Small Craft Warnings* opened off-Broadway and ran for 200 performances.

1973   March: *Out Cry* had 13 performances off-Broadway.

1975   June: *The Red Devil Battery Sign* opened in Boston.

Williams published his *Memoirs*. He was elected to a three-year term on the governing council of the Dramatists Guild.

1976   Williams was president of the jury at the Cannes Film Festival.

1977   May: *Vieux Carré* had 5 performances in New York.

1977- Williams contributed a number of articles and short stories to

1980   journals such as *Esquire*, *Time* and the *New Yorker*.

1983   March: Tennessee Williams died.

> He did have a nightmarish, tortured sense of the abyss and a smiling, compassionate complicity with those who hurtle into it. [. . .] The trouble with Williams was that, unlike the truest kind of genius, he did not grow artistically. After his best plays (of 1944 and 1947) came his good but uneven plays, after which came worse and worse ones, some still streaked with lightning flashes of splendour, some utterly lost in the murk of mechanistic iteration and self-parody. (John Simon, *New York*, 31.3.83)

Plot

Scene I

On an evening in early May, Blanche Dubois arrives at Elysian Fields in
New Orleans to find her younger sister, Stella, with whom she hopes to
stay. She is disconcerted to discover that Stella, who is married to
Stanley Kowalski, the son of Polish immigrants, has a small apartment in
a shabby house in the French Quarter (Vieux Carré). Blanche is evidently
nervous and helps herself to a drink of whisky. When Stella returns,
Blanche greets her excitedly but cannot conceal her shock at Stella's way
of life. Stella, however, is happy, fulfilled by her relationship with
Stanley. Blanche defensively confesses to the loss of Belle Reve, their
family home in Mississippi, to pay off debts accumulated, she claims,
through the dissipations and deaths of older generations of the Dubois
family. Stanley returns with two friends: Steve lives upstairs with his
assertive wife, Eunice; Mitch lives with his invalid mother. Stanley
accepts Blanche's presence with good humour but little ceremony. She is
ruffled by his lack of refinement. She reveals that she was married when
very young and that her husband died.

Scene II

The following evening, while Blanche is in the bath, Stella tells Stanley
about the loss of Belle Reve. She is unconcerned, but he suspects Blanche
of keeping to herself the profits from the sale of the estate — profits
which he believes he has a legal claim to as Stella's husband. When
Blanche appears, he demands to see the documents concerning Belle
Reve. Blanche is distressed when he snatches a bundle of papers, poems
written by her young husband, then she hands him a box full of legal
documents. He justifies his attitude on the grounds of his legal rights and
his concern for the future of the baby Stella is expecting. Blanche and
Stella go out for an evening together, leaving the apartment free for
Stanley's poker game.

Scene III

Stanley, Steve, Mitch and Pablo are still playing when Stella and Blanche
return. It is nearly 2.30 in the morning. Blanche is struck by the relative
gentleness and politeness of Mitch. Stanley grows more belligerently

drunk; finally he hurls a radio out of the window and then hits Stella, who is immediately shepherded upstairs by Blanche. Sobered by a cold shower, Stanley calls in anguish for Stella to come back to him. Slowly she descends the stairs. They embrace, then Stanley carries her into their flat. Blanche is appalled by Stella's reconciliation with Stanley, but is soothed by Mitch.

Scene IV

Next morning Stella tries to explain to Blanche the way her relationship with Stanley works. She accepts his sporadic violence as inseparable from the passion they share. Blanche hopes to persuade Stella to leave Stanley. planning a future for herself and her sister, to be financed by an old admirer who is now apparently a millionaire. Stanley overhears part of this, but, when he appears, Stella's fierce embrace demonstrates that her loyalties remain with him.

Scene V

Upstairs Steve and Eunice are brawling. On his return from bowling, Stanley frightens Blanche by asking her about a man called Shaw and a disreputable hotel called the Flamingo in Laurel, the town where Blanche was an English teacher. When he leaves, Blanche anxiously seeks reassurance from Stella that nothing unpleasant is known about her. She is expecting Mitch for a date and is desperate for him to provide her with a secure future. Between Stella's departure and Mitch's arrival, Blanche flirts with and kisses a young man who calls to collect subscriptions for a newspaper.

Scene VI

Blanche and Mitch return from an unsuccessful evening out. Blanche is coquettish but appears offended when he tries to kiss her. She complains of Stanley's hostility. Mitch talks about his mother. Blanche then speaks of her youthful and very short-lived marriage, which was destroyed when she discovered her young husband in bed with another man: she had later voiced her disgust, and her husband had rushed out and shot himself. Mitch puts his arms around her and kisses her.

Scene VII

It is September 15th, Blanche's birthday. Blanche is singing in the bath; Stella is decorating a cake. Stanley enters, armed with the destructive truth about Blanche's recent past: she has been promiscuous, slipping out at night to answer the calls of soldiers who were returning, drunk, to their barracks near Belle Reve, then, after leaving Belle Reve, she has lived like a prostitute in a cheap hotel while also teaching in the local school. Finally she lost her teaching post for trying to seduce a seventeen year-old pupil and was, effectively, driven out of Laurel. Stella tries to defend her sister, talking of the unhappiness of Blanche's early life and of her short-lived marriage. She is horrified to hear that Stanley has told Mitch all he knows. Blanche emerges happily from the bathroom but is frightened as she senses that something threatening has happened.

Scene VIII

As the birthday meal ends, in an atmosphere made tense by Mitch's non-appearance, Stanley erupts into fury when Stella criticises his manners. He presents Blanche with a bus ticket back to Laurel. She rushes out to be sick. Stella turns angrily on Stanley but suddenly feels the first movements of childbirth and asks him to take her to the hospital, leaving Blanche alone.

Scene IX

Mitch arrives, unshaven and a little drunk. He is hurt and angry at having been deceived. Blanche no longer denies but tries to excuse her disreputable past as being a refuge from her grief and guilt at the death of her husband. She asks for Mitch's protection, but he clumsily tries to rape her. He retreats in confusion when she calls out 'Fire!'

Scene X

Stanley returns from the hospital, to find Blanche dressed up in a crumpled evening dress and wearing a cheap tiara. She claims to have received a cable from the oil millionaire inviting her on a Caribbean cruise. Stanley becomes aggressive when Blanche starts to lie about Mitch's attitude to her. She tries to ward off Stanley's sexual advances with a broken bottle, but he disarms her easily and carries her off to the bed to rape her.

Scene XI

Some weeks later, Stanley and his friends are again playing poker. Stella is packing Blanche's trunk while Blanche is in the bathroom. Unbeknown to Blanche, they are awaiting the arrival of a doctor and a nurse from a State-run institution for the mentally sick, to which Stella has reluctantly agreed to have her sister committed. Stella has decided that she cannot believe Blanche's account of Stanley's assault upon her; for her own sake and that of her new baby, she must reject her sister and align herself with her husband. Blanche imagines that she is going on holiday with an admirer, but is frightened by the appearance of the nurse. However, when the doctor addresses her courteously, she goes willingly with him, leaving Stella in distress, holding her baby. Stanley tries to comfort her and starts to make love to her.

Commentary

Williams's writing: repressed self-knowledge?

In the introduction to a collection of letters from Tennessee Williams, Donald Windham wrote: 'his art sprang from his repressed self-knowledge' (*Tennessee Williams's Letters to Donald Windham*, London, Rinehart and Winston, 1972, p. vi). Windham went on to infer that Williams used his plays and stories as a way of translating himself into an acceptable fiction. Tennessee Williams himself often emphasised the close connection between his writing and the circumstances of his own life; he, however, did not describe the process as being an evasion of the truth nor an attempt to glamorise his own image. In interviews and articles written in his middle years, he was able to stand back from earlier experiences and observe the foundations of his work being laid down in his childhood and adolescence. Certain elements are clearly visible in both life and art; for example, the distress and guilt he felt at the lobotomy of his sister Rose (which was carried out when he was away at college) feature in *Suddenly Last Summer* where Catharine fights to remain intact in the face of Mrs. Venable's determination to destroy her memories and her mind. In his short story *The Resemblance between a Violin Case and a Coffin* Williams describes the shock of seeing a loved sister grow into a disturbingly separate young woman:

> I saw that it was all over, put away in a box like a doll no longer cared for, the magical intimacy of our childhood together. [. . .] And it was then, about that time, that I began to find life unsatisfactory as an explanation of itself and was forced to adopt the method of the artist of not explaining but putting the blocks together in some way that seems more significant to him. Which is a rather fancy way of saying that I started writing. (See *Remember Me to Tom*, p. 79)

The relationship between the aspiring writer and his shy, emotionally vulnerable young sister is also explored in *The Glass Menagerie*. In that play, too, the spirit of Miss Edwina, Williams's mother, finds a body and voice (although she herself always denied the relationship). Williams was

a sickly child, so his early years were spent close to his mother, an
intimacy heightened by Miss Edwina's dissatisfaction with her husband.
As the daughter of a Southern preacher — a man respected in his own
community — she was never wealthy, but enjoyed a degree of social
prestige when growing up, protected from poverty, insecurity or
harshness. As the disillusionment of marriage closed in on her, so her
youth glowed more rosily in retrospect, as she herself wrote:

> Life is as unpredictable as a dream. Once I was young and gay and
> danced night after night with beau after beau, the belle of the ball.
> Then a handsome young man from a fine family came along, fell
> in love the first time he saw me and asked my hand in marriage. How
> was I to know this charming youth would turn into a man of wrath
> and that I and my children would live by his side consumed by terror.
> (*Remember Me to Tom*, p. 88)

This insistent nostalgia and puzzled, defensive self-pity echo, too,
through the words of Amanda, the mother, in the first scene of *The Glass
Menagerie*:

> AMANDA. My callers were gentlemen — all! Among my callers were
> some of the most prominent young planters of the Mississippi Delta —
> planters and sons of planters! [. . .] There were the Cutrere brothers,
> Wesley and Bates. Bates was one of my bright particular beaux! He
> got in a quarrel with that wild Wainwright boy. They shot it out on
> the floor of Moon Lake Casino. Bates was shot through the stomach.
> Died in the ambulance on his way to Memphis. [. . .] And I could
> have been Mrs J. Fitzhugh, mind you! But — I picked your *father*!

It is interesting to note the reference here to the violent death of a young
man, his life apparently blighted by passion for the Southern belle in
whose memory he still has a picturesque existence. This idea becomes
more potent in *A Streetcar Named Desire*.

The father-figure in *The Glass Menagerie* is 'a telephone man who fell
in love with long distances', as Tom remarks in the opening monologue,
yet who once had an innocent look that fooled everybody, even Amanda's
father. He is conspicuous by his absence. This was a situation familiar
to Williams as a child for his father was then out on the road, selling
shoes. When he was promoted to a desk-job as sales manager, the rest of
his family huddled together, it seems, away from his rages and his
drinking and his angry disappointment in his wife and his eldest son —
a Stanley Kowalski in middle age, with all the shared sexual passion in
his marriage spent. When in middle age himself, Tennessee Williams was

able to view his father more objectively:

> His was not a nature that would comply with the accepted social
> moulds and patterns without a restlessness that would have driven
> him mad without the release of liquor and poker and wild weekends.
> (*Remember Me to Tom*, p. 202)

In a letter written from Rome in 1955 to Kenneth Tynan, Williams saw
his relationship with his father even more distinctly as simply one
element in his own emotional development:

> I used to have a terrific crush on the female members of my family,
> mother, sister, grandmother, and hated my father, a typical pattern
> for homosexuals. I've stopped hating my father. [. . .] He was not a
> man capable of examining his behaviour toward his family, or not
> capable of changing it. [. . .] I find him a tragic figure now, not one
> that I dislike any longer. (*Letters to Donald Windham*, p. 301)

Not only do Tennessee Williams's mother, sister and father appear
recognisably in the plays, but Williams was also acutely aware of the
effect on his own nature and creativity of his inheritance and upbringing.
His capacity for deep depression, for example:

> I have plunged into one of my period neuroses, I call them 'blue-devils',
> and it is like having wild-cats under my skin. They are a Williams
> family trait I suppose. Destroyed my sister's mind and made my
> father a raging drunkard. In me they take the form of interior storms
> that show remarkably little from the outside but which create a deep
> chasm between myself and all other people, even deeper than the
> relatively ordinary ones of homosexuality and being an artist. (*Letters
> to Donald Windham*, p. 91)

Williams's homosexuality figures large in his letters and *Memoirs*,
although – perhaps not surprisingly – his mother's account of him makes
no reference to it, recalling instead Tennessee Williams's childhood
affection for a local girl called Hazel, a relationship apparently wrecked
by his father. Miss Edwina explains her son's lack of a wife:

> Tom has said to me he never intends to marry. [. . .] 'I have no idea
> of ever marrying. I couldn't bear to make some woman unhappy. I'd
> be writing and forget all about her.' (*Remember Me to Tom*, p. 240)

Williams's letters to Donald Windham sometimes conjure up an
absurd caricature of himself as affectedly promiscuous and flighty,
particularly those letters written from Key West in Florida where there

was a bohemian colony and where homosexuality, although still illegal under state law, was tolerated by the authorities so long as it did not make itself widely conspicuous or troublesome. In the 'Vieux Carré' of New Orleans, too, he found an appealingly freewheeling way of life among artists, writers and jazz musicians in bars and brothels. He is reported to have said:

> If I can be said to have a home, it is in New Orleans where I've lived on and off since 1938 and which has provided me with more material than any other part of the country. I live near the main street of the Quarter which is named Royal. Down this street, running on the same tracks, are two streetcars, one named DESIRE and the other named CEMETERY. Their indiscourageable progress up and down Royal struck me as having some symbolic bearing of a broad nature on the life in the 'Vieux Carré' — and everywhere else for that matter. (Tischler, *Tennessee Williams: Rebellious Puritan*, Citadel Press, New York, p. 62)

He was somewhat defensive about this lifestyle on occasion, understandably so in view of Miss Edwina's carefully cultivated respectability.

> As the world grows worse, it seems more necessary to grasp what pleasure you can, to be selfish and blind, except in your work, and live just as much as you have a chance to. (*Letters to Donald Windham*, p. 22)

The urge to seek refuge from unhappiness in the pursuit of pleasure, however destructive to self and others, is an aspect of Blanche Dubois's fall from grace. Her horror at the discovery of her young husband's homosexuality perhaps reflects the kind of response Williams himself had encountered or feared. On the other hand, Blanche may be a 'cover' for a male character, a homosexual, given a female mask by Williams so as to avoid having to confront his own feelings about himself — an example of that ingenious self-preservation referred to by Donald Windham. In that case, Blanche's shock at finding her boy-husband in bed with another man echoes the intense jealousy and sense of betrayal which Tennessee Williams expresses in letters at the ending of a love affair. In an assessment of Williams, written after his death, Murray Kempton stressed the importance of Williams's homosexuality to his creativity.

> We cannot appreciate Tennessee Williams without putting his homo-eroticism into full account; and that may explain why women caught him more lovingly than men. [. . .] At bottom those plays of his that

live most vividly in the mind tell us about how men must look to
women — ogres to be appeased, small boys to be put up with, or, if
one's luck turns for the better, strangers who will accept you and
keep you safe. (*New York Book Review*, 31.3.1983)

Tennessee Williams described his writing as a cathartic or purging
process, a way of coming to terms with his life:

> In my case, I think my work is good in exact ratio to the degree of
> emotional tension which is released into it. In a sense, writing of this
> kind (lyric?) is a losing game, for steadily life takes away from you,
> bit by bit, step by step, the quality of fresh involvement, new,
> startling reactions to experience; the emotional reservoir is only rarely
> replenished, by some such crisis as I've described to you at such
> length and most of the time you are just 'paying out', drawing off.
> (*Letters to Donald Windham*, p. 306)

A Streetcar Named Desire grew out of the turbulence of Tennessee
Williams's relationships, but also out of the crisis he refers to in the letter
— the months in 1946 when he endured the terror of believing that he
was suffering from incurable pancreatic cancer. A morbid, shuddering
preoccupation with the physical ugliness and the inevitability of death
permeates the whole play.

The strong connection between the experiences and relationships of
Tennessee Williams's life and the events and characters of his plays
explains the intensity and vividness of his writing, but it has also been
seen as a limitation, not least by Williams himself:

> Frankly there must be some limitations in me as a dramatist. I can't
> handle people in routine situations. I must find characters who
> correspond to my own tensions. If these people are excessively
> melodramatic [. . .] well, a play must concentrate the events of a
> lifetime in the short span of a three-act play. Of necessity these
> events must be more violent than in life. (*Tennessee Williams:
> Rebellious Puritan*, p. 246)

An American context

The early plays of Tennessee Williams were successful in the 1940s and
1950s perhaps because they offered violence, morality, spectacle and
romance in American settings, played out by characters that often
managed to be both highly individual and representative of particular
aspects of American life and tradition. *Streetcar* draws upon at least
three of these American traditions, which had been projected effectively

for twenty years by the cinema. There was a nostalgic interest in America's past, particularly in the romance of the years before and during the Civil War. Mid-twentieth century urban Americans were intrigued and charmed by the idea of the South, by the picturesque elegance of a landed élite who flaunted their inherited wealth and their studied gentility. Morality was satisfied by the knowledge that this privileged brilliance was doomed to defeat in the Civil War and would then present an image of decorative decay. Blanche Dubois and Belle Reve belong to that tradition, crystallised for a mass audience by the highly successful film of *Gone with the Wind*, starring an English actress, Vivien Leigh, who later played Blanche in the film of *Streetcar*.

Another aspect of America's past given a wide appeal through the cinema was the folklore of the Wild West. Westerns showed home-grown heroes proving their worth in combat against savages and bandits and sticking to their friends through thick and thin — just as Stanley feels bound to protect Mitch after their time together in the army. These films also reinforced an idea of women either as child-bearers and home-makers or as whores, golden-hearted or otherwise. Stella is a home-maker and child-bearer; Blanche is neither, so might then be expected to be one of the other kind and 'no good'.

If Blanche belongs to the crumbling grandeur of the Southern plantations, Stanley is a new American, an immigrant, a man of the city. He is the one amongst his group most likely to make his mark in a world of industry and commerce, a world full of machinery like cars and locomotives. He asserts his maleness and lack of refinement; where he cannot dominate sexually he uses force. He shows, perhaps, the more acceptable face of that macho urban jungle pictured in the Hollywood gangster movies of the 1930s.

Popular entertainment, principally the cinema, offered Americans certain images of what it meant to be American. This was an idea equally important to the first or second generation immigrants from Europe as to those who thought of themselves as 'real' Americans with a pedigree reaching back to the Pilgrim Fathers or the Huguenots. Tennessee Williams's early plays dealt in familiar concepts so that even when aspects of his plots or the ideas expressed were shocking, they nonetheless were accessible to a wide audience, not only on Broadway but, later, as successful films.

Theatre, during the 1920s, 30s and 40s, changed under the impact of new techniques and forms from Europe. These influences were brought to America by touring companies, by refugees from political oppression in Europe, by the influx of avant-garde films and by Americans returning from the Continent, excited by what they had seen. In the 1920s two important theatrical groups were formed: the semi-professional Washington Square Players in New York, and the amateur Provincetown Players, who were associated with the early works of the dramatist Eugene O'Neill. The Washington Square Players developed into the wholly professional Theatre Guild which became one of the most influential organisations in the New York theatre world. The 1920s also saw the birth of various political groups; for example, those brought together in the Workers' Dramatic Council. The Federal Theatre was set up as part of Roosevelt's New Deal to encourage playwrights to use the theatre to celebrate or at least dramatise contemporary life. In 1931 Lee Strasberg, with Cheryl Crawford and Harold Clurman, founded the Group Theatre, which trained a new generation of actors and directors, Elia Kazan, for example, who later directed *Streetcar* for stage and screen. It also encouraged young dramatists with a serious social or political message, men like Clifford Odets, whose play *Waiting for Lefty* (1935) called for organised action against workers to fight against their fall in living standards. It sought 'an alliance of the men of mind, of vision, the artists, with the People, consciously working towards this creative end'. (Harold Clurman, *The Fervent Years*, London 1946, p. 79). It was the Group Theatre that gave the young Tennessee Williams significant encouragement in 1938 by giving him a special award for his collection of one-act plays, *American Blues*. A number of American dramatists were experimenting with a lyrical, heightened style of dialogue and extended speeches full of vivid imagery or highly rhythmic phrases, sometimes approaching the intensity and musicality of verse drama. This rhetorical style was complemented by non-naturalistic staging – as in Thornton Wilder's *Our Town* (1938) and *The Skin of Our Teeth* (1942), or many of Eugene O'Neill's experiments in style, of which *The Hairy Ape* (1922) will stand as an example. Here is the opening stage direction:

> The treatment of this scene, or of any other scene in the play, should by no means be naturalistic. The effect sought after is a cramped space in the bowels of a ship, imprisoned by white steel. The lines of bunks, the uprights supporting them, cross each other like the steel framework of a cage.

Thus Tennessee Williams's early plays were borne in on a swelling tide of new American drama now able to take possession of major theatres in the big cities, especially New York, and to become recognisably distinct from the European imports, while still benefiting from the new technology and the versatility demonstrated by European theatre. The need for a national identity had been sharpened by America's involvement in the two World Wars, as was the need to re-appraise the values and demands of American society. According to the critic Travis Bogard, through the twenties, thirties and forties many plays were concerned:

> with an aspect of the national past that gives them a strong emotional lever against the depressing present and the failure of the American dream. [. . .] The characters cling to their dreams tenaciously. [. . .] Their dreams are never fulfilled except in the fantasies of nostalgic romances and operettas. The sterner statements insist that the thrust of American materialism has destroyed all such dreams and left man destitute in a soulless world, a wasteland. (*The Revels History of Drama in English*, Vol. VIII, pp. 62-3)

A selection of drama reviews from the *New York Times* for the years 1945 to 1947 gives an impression of what New York audiences were being offered at the point when Tennessee Williams emerged as a significant writer. In 1945, along with *The Glass Menagerie*, there was a Rodgers and Hammerstein musical about a fairground roustabout's doomed romance with a nice all-American girl in a small fishing community. This was playing across the street from another Rodgers and Hammerstein show, *Oklahoma*, a lyrical celebration of America's mid-West where farmers and cowboys learned to live and love in energetically choreographed harmony. At the same time, Elia Kazan — first director of *A Streetcar Named Desire* — was directing *Deep Are the Roots* by Arnaud D'Usseau, a play dealing with the position of negroes in the American South. Also in production was *Home of the Brave* by Arthur Laurents about the experiences of a young Jewish soldier in the Pacific campaign of World War II. During 1946 New York saw translations of Anouilh's *Antigone*, Rostand's *Cyrano de Bergerac* and Satre's *Huis Clos*. An English company led by Laurence Olivier brought over a version by W.B. Yeats of Sophocles' *Oedipus*, as well as Sheridan's *The Critic*. There was a production of Oscar Wilde's *Lady Windermere's Fan* (described by the critic Brooks Atkinson as 'a trifle seedy') and of Shakespeare's *Henry VIII*. The most conspicuously American production was another musical — this time combining showground glamour with Wild West nostalgia — *Annie Get Your Gun* by Irving Berlin.

1947, similarly, offered home-grown musicals, such as the rather fey *Brigadoon* and *Finian's Rainbow* as well as the more serious *Street Scene*, based on a play by Elmer Rice, with music by Kurt Weill. *Street Scene* was praised by Brooks Atkinson as 'a musical play of magnificence and glory [. . .] it finds the song of humanity under the argot of the New

York streets'. As in 1946, there were several imports from Europe, but there was also the successful debut of the young American writer, Arthur Miller, whose *All My Sons*, directed by Elia Kazan, dealt with the conflict for Americans between private and public loyalties in the context of the recent war. Its characters and setting were immediately identifiable by the American audience of 1947; its action was tragic. At moments the dialogue moved from the recognisably naturalistic to a more highly charged kind of rhetoric through which the questions of morality confronting the characters were imbued with a wider significance. It was enthusiastically received:

> The theatre has acquired a genuine new talent [. . .] [The play] is a pitiless analysis of character that gathers momentum all evening and concludes with both logic and dramatic impact. (Brooks Atkinson, *New York Times*, 30.1.1947)

In December 1947 came *A Streetcar Named Desire*, another Kazan production. The play was both a commercial and a critical success:

> It reveals Mr Williams as a genuinely poetic playwright whose knowledge of people is honest and thorough and whose sympathy is profoundly human. [. . .] Out of poetic imagination and ordinary compassion he has spun a poignant and luminous story. (Brooks Atkinson, *New York Times*, 4.12.1947)

Southern Roots and European Influences

Tennessee Williams was not only carried in on a twentieth-century tide of American drama dealing with the contemporary American situation, he was also buoyed up by a strong current of specifically Southern writing, which had become powerful in the nineteenth century and was still significant. Some of this literature from the South celebrated with nostalgia the chivalry and romance associated with the landowners of the Southern States prior to the Civil War (1861-65) and the doomed gallantry which became part of the folklore of the war itself. Other plays and novels, however, saw flaws in the pre-war and post-war South, while still fascinated by the South's charisma. There was, for example, William Faulkner (1897-1962), with his series of novels set in North Mississippi (thinly disguised as Yoknapatawpha County), including *The Sound and the Fury* (1929) and *Go Down Moses* (1942). Lillian Hellman in her novels *The Little Foxes* (1939) and *Another Part of the Forest* (1946) showed treachery, greed and ambition in an Alabama family, the Hubbards, using melodrama as a vehicle for morality — it was an indictment of that materialism which she felt was corroding the once bright metal of American society.

Colouring this writing was the influence — still strong in the South — of the Scottish writer Sir Walter Scott (1771-1832), whose historical romances such as *Kenilworth*, *The Talisman* and *Ivanhoe* drew upon a picturesque notion of medieval and sixteenth-century courtliness, the chivalric clash between good and evil amidst castellated towers or the pavilions of crusading knights. Nineteenth-century European Gothic fiction (supernatural melodramas in feudal locations) found an echo in the macabre tales of the American writer Edgar Allan Poe (1809-49), such as *Fall of the House of Usher* (1839), and in Nathaniel Hawthorne's *Twice-Told Tales* (1857) and *The Scarlet Letter* (1859). Both men were still much in vogue in the twentieth century with Poe in particular being seized on by the cinema as well. The quivering horror of Tennessee Williams's Blanche Dubois in the face of the city's squalid vitality and her accounts of the sickness eating away at the splendour that had once been Belle Reve recall Poe's story of the decline of the Ushers, whose painfully acute sensibility, both physical and emotional, rendered them unfit for life outside their decaying mansion in which they too decayed with a diseased beauty.

Tennessee Williams's work grew not only out of this courtly-Gothic Southern heritage, but also out of a European culture that offered writers as attractive to him yet as diverse as the Russian playwright and story-writer, Chekhov (1860-1904), the Swedish dramatist Strindberg (1849-1912), the Norwegian playwright Ibsen (1828-1906) and the English novelist D.H. Lawrence (1885-1930). Ibsen's influence on American drama can be seen also in the early plays of Arthur Miller: tragedy moved out of the courts of princes and the heroic past, into a recognisably contemporary setting, concerning itself with the middle classes or with semi-skilled workers living in the crowded city suburbs of a money-making nation. In many of Ibsen's dramas, such as *Rosmersholm* or *Ghosts*, the action shows the eruption of some guilt, thought to be safely buried in the past, into the carefully constructed respectability of middle-class family life. The dramatic tension becomes more powerful as the audience grows more aware of the degree of pretence involved in the characters' image of themselves and senses the gradual but relentless revelation of a once-submerged horror. The climax comes when the central characters suffer the confrontation of past and present: the thing they have fled from corners them. Then they either acknowledge the justness of this and endure retribution for past guilt with the dignity traditionally associated with a tragic protagonist, or they may try to retreat even further into pretence, perhaps into madness. This tragic model was well suited to Tennessee Williams for it offered a means of dramatising through vividly characterised and recognisable individuals his sense of the South's past being still active and often destructive in modern America.

A *Streetcar Named Desire* makes it clear that for Williams the act of fleeing always becomes the act of reliving the past. Flight forces the presence of the past on his characters as the presence of what they attempted to flee. (Donald Pease in *Tennessee Williams: A Tribute*, p. 840)

A *Streetcar Named Desire* shows the conflict between traditional values: an old-world graciousness and beauty running decoratively to seed versus the thrusting, rough-edged, physically aggressive materialism of the new world. The presentation of a way of life is closely bound up with the evocation of a particular place; this 'place' both defines and explains those characters who are identified with it, and so the chopping down of a long-prized orchard or the gradual dissipation of an ancient estate gives expression to the decline of those characters themselves and of their sort of world. In this, Tennessee Williams harks back to images and emotions present in the plays of Anton Chekhov. Blanche Dubois is of the same breed as Chekhov's charming, elegantly selfish, admiration-seeking, ageing women, such as Madame Arkadina in *The Seagull* (1895) and Madame Ranevsky in *The Cherry Orchard* (1903). Interestingly Blanche explains that her name means 'White woods,' (p. 30), 'Like an orchard in spring!' But whereas Chekhov's women are still vivaciously staving off despair and the admission of defeat, Blanche is seen in her final struggles.

In *A Streetcar Named Desire* the conflict between two ways of life is concentrated within the battle between Blanche and Stanley. The old civilisation vested in Blanche is demonstrably decadent; her only means of survival in the modern world is to batten onto someone else and live off their emotional, physical and material resources, like a decorative fungus. Stanley is full of aggressive, virile energy, both contemptuous of and intrigued by the once privileged gentility of the Belle Reve world. The dramatisation of such a clash in sexual terms — the old world associated with febrile femininity, the new with a charismatic but brutal masculinity — had been tried earlier by August Strindberg. There are some interesting parallels between *Streetcar* and Strindberg's *Miss Julie* (1888). In his preface to *Miss Julie* Strindberg outlined his objectives and analysed the response he anticipated for his characters. He justified his choice of subject:

> It is still tragic to see one on whom fortune has smiled go under, much more to see a line die out. [. . .] The fact that the heroine arouses our sympathy is merely due to our weakness in not being able to resist a feeling of fear lest the same fate should befall us. [. . .] I have suggested many possible motivations for Miss Julie's unhappy fate. The passionate character of her mother; the upbringing misguidedly inflicted on her by her father; her own character; and the suggestive effect of her fiancé upon her weak and degenerate brain.

Strindberg referred to

> that innate or acquired sense of honour which the upper-classes inherit. [. . .] It is very beautiful, but nowadays it is fatal to the continuation of the species. [. . .] The servant Jean is the type who founds a species, we trace the process of differentiation.

Strindberg saw Jean's survival and strength as arising less from his class origins than from his masculinity.

> Sexually he is an aristocrat by virtue of his masculine strength, his more finely developed senses and his ability to seize the initiative. His sense of inferiority arises chiefly from the social *milieu* in which he temporarily finds himself. (Author's Preface to *Miss Julie: Strindberg: Plays One*, translated by Michael Meyer, London, Methuen, 1976, p. 92-98)

Strindberg emphasises a deliberate naturalism both in the setting of the play — the large kitchen of a Swedish manor house, on a midsummer's eve — and in its references to the routines of life. However, both Miss Julie and Jean can speak in heightened prose, using imagery and thought-associations which give the play a poetic, more universal quality. In this, too, *Streetcar* is reminiscent of *Miss Julie*:

> MISS JULIE: I have a dream which recurs from time to time, and I'm reminded of it now. I've climbed to the top of a pillar, am sitting there, and I can see no way to descend. When I look down, I become dizzy, but I must come down — but I haven't the courage to jump. [. . .]
> JEAN: No. I dream I'm lying under a high tree in a dark wood. I want to climb, up, up to the top, and look round over the bright landscape where the sun is shining — plunder the bird's nest up there where the gold eggs lie. (*Strindberg: Plays One*, translated by Michael Meyer, London, Methuen 1976, p. 116)

In *Streetcar* Stanley's syntax remains unrefined, but his words are nonetheless imaginative:

> STANLEY: I was common as dirt. You showed me the snapshot of
> the place with the columns. I pulled you down off them columns and
> how you loved it, having them coloured lights going! (p. 68)

Another writer who deals with the clash of lifestyles and moralities
often in sexual terms and in heightened language is D.H. Lawrence.
Tennessee Williams's early admiration for Lawrence was noticed and
lamented by his mother, who felt that Lawrence's writing lacked delicacy.

> One afternoon he walked in with a copy of *Lady Chatterley's Lover*.
> I picked it up for a look — Tom said I had a veritable genius for
> opening always to the most lurid pages of a book — and was shocked
> by the candour of the love scenes. [. . .] I didn't like the book or
> D.H. Lawrence as a person. [. . .] I didn't admire anything I heard
> about his character or how he treated his wife, who deserted her
> husband and children for him. The one play of Tom's I have not read
> or seen is *I Rise in Flame, Cried the Phoenix*, his poetic version of
> Lawrence's last few hours on earth. (*Remember Me to Tom*, p. 33)

It is in *Lady Chatterley's Lover* that Lawrence describes the meeting
rather than the conflict between a woman of the upper class and a man
of peasant stock (though educated and sensitive enough not to be a
prisoner of his class). The conflict is between that virile new man and the
effete aristocracy from which his mistress comes — much as Stanley
challenges Stella's family origins rather than Stella herself. Like Stella,
Constance Chatterley is happy to be pulled off her column and to have
the coloured lights going. After the gamekeeper, Mellors, has made love
to her,

> in her heart the queer wonder of him was awakened. A man! The
> strange potency of manhood upon her. [. . .] She crept nearer to him,
> nearer, only to be near to the sensual wonder of him. (*Lady
> Chatterley's Lover*, Penguin, p. 182)

Connie's sister Hilda, however, feels threatened and alienated by his
overt sexuality:

> He was looking at her with an odd, flickering smile, faintly sensual
> and appreciative.
> 'And men like you,' she said, 'ought to be segregated: justifying their
> own vulgarity and selfish lust.' (p. 256)

One justification that even Connie herself allows for the relationship is

Mellor's value as a stud, to revitalise the impotent aristocratic stock.
Similarly, Blanche sees Stanley as essentially animal, a stud:

> BLANCHE: He's just not the sort that goes for jasmine perfume! But
> maybe he's what we need to mix with our blood now that we've lost
> Belle Reve and have to go on without Belle Reve to protect us. (p. 23)

And later:

> BLANCHE: What such a man has to offer is animal force and he gave
> a wonderful exhibition of that! But the only way to live with such a
> man is to — go to bed with him! (p. 39)

In fathering Stella's child Stanley has completed his function in Blanche's
eyes, so now she feels that she and Stella can leave him behind with the
brutes and go forward to a life enriched by 'such things as art — as
poetry and music' (p. 41).

The conflict between innate sexuality and a consciously acquired
civilisation, present in *A Streetcar Named Desire*, is also a recurring
theme in Lawrence's work, often expressed in a very stylised prose full
of images drawn from nature or the elements, darkness and light, earth
and fire. Lawrence's kind of lyricism and this striving for the power of
myth through imagery infused with a sense of ritual are features observed
also in Tennessee Williams's work. For instance:

> In its sympathetic portrayal of our yearnings for transcendence, its
> realistic depiction of our inherent limitations, and its utter insistence
> on the necessity of imbuing with religious significance the rare and
> transient communion of man with his fellow, Williams's drama is a
> myth for our time. (Judith J. Thompson in *Tennessee Williams:
> A Tribute*, p. 684)

Such a response from a serious critic indicates the potency of these
images and allusions. There are many such examples of Williams's
reaching for 'religious significance':

> BLANCHE: And then the searchlight which had been turned on the
> world was turned off again and never for one moment since has there
> been any light that's stronger than this — kitchen — candle . . .
> MITCH. You need somebody. And I need somebody, too. Could it
> be — you and me, Blanche? [. . .]
> BLANCHE: Sometimes — there's God — so quickly! (p. 57)

One final instance of techniques which Lawrence and Williams share
concerns the use of 'symbolic' names. The opening passage of Lawrence's

autobiographical novel *Sons and Lovers* (1913) works on two levels: it describes the Nottinghamshire mining community in which the Morel family lives, but the names imbue the scene with the aura of myth or religious allegory:

> 'The Bottoms' succeeded to 'Hell Row'. Hell Row was a block of thatched, bulging cottages that stood by the brookside on Greenhill Lane. There lived the colliers who worked in the little gin-pits two fields away. [. . .] Mrs. Morel was not anxious to move into the Bottoms, which was already twelve years old and on the downward path, when she descended to it from Bestwood. (*Sons and Lovers*, Penguin, pp. 7-9.)

Tennessee Williams employs a similar device at the beginning of *Streetcar* when Blanche describes her journey to Stella's apartment (p. 5):

> BLANCHE: They told me to take a streetcar named Desire, and then transfer to one called Cemeteries and ride six blocks and get off at — Elysian Fields!
> EUNICE: That's where you are now.
> BLANCHE: At Elysian Fields?
> EUNICE: This here is Elysian Fields.

Structure: eleven one-act plays united by a purpose?

> The plot is simple. It moves from hope and frustration to destruction and despair. The characters themselves provide probability for every action. [. . .] Each scene is constructed like a one-act play, Williams's forte. (Tischler, pp. 140-143)

> Plot in the normal sense there is not too much of, for it is men and women in their moods of hope, despair, pretence, terror and uncertainty with whom he is concerned. Yet the play is purposeful. (Elinor Hughes, *The Boston Herald*, 4.11.1947)

> It has no plot, at least in the familiar usage of that word. It is almost unbearably tragic. (Brooks Atkinson, *New York Times*, 14.11.1947)

Plot 'in the familiar usage' implies a sequence of actions or events so organised as to give them a sense of logical progression from a beginning, through a middle, to an end that seems 'right'. What is the significance of the description of *A Streetcar Named Desire* as a collection of one-act plays? It suggests that each scene describes one situation or deals with one event fully enough for it to stand alone: with an exposition, a crisis and some kind of resolution. It is possible to approach any of the scenes in this way: scene one, for instance, introduces us to an environment, precipitates an action through the disruptive arrival into the Kowalski home of Blanche, and seems to offer a resolution in Stanley's acceptance of her. Or scene six: a man and a woman (in fact, Mitch and Blanche) return from an unsuccessful date. The audience is told why there is tension between them: he desires her, but is clumsy; she wishes to encourage him, but is anxious to preserve his respect for her. He reveals his vanities and insecurities, and gives an insight into the relationship with his mother which underpins his character. She reveals a tragedy in her past, giving an acceptably complete account of her marriage and widowing. The scene ends with them coming together — apparently a happy resolution. What welds these potentially self-sufficient segments into a cohesive play is not only the continuity of the characters, but a clear relationship between the scenes which does give a sense of progress towards the final solution and achieves a unity of subject, theme and action.

The fact that each scene contains enough information to make its action comprehensible means that certain elements recur throughout the play — the story of Blanche's past, for instance — but since their relationship to the immediate situation changes from scene to scene this does not appear merely repetitive. In the first scene, the outline of Blanche's marriage is quickly drawn as part of the initial exposition, and her extreme sensitivity to its memory demonstrated — with the symbolic sound of the polka merely a faint suggestion, having little obvious significance beyond nostalgia at that point. In scene two, the reference to Blanche's dead husband is part of her skirmishing with Stanley; it introduces the idea of her guilt but offers no further explanation. In scene six, her description of the boy she married and then destroyed, the account heightened by the now ominous strains of the polka, becomes part of the action, drawing Blanche and Mitch together for mutual support. In scene nine, Blanche offers the death of her young husband as the reason for her subsequent fall from grace, as a mitigating circumstance to lessen her guilt rather than a cause for the guilt itself. This time Mitch does not comfort her but condemns her, so her last hope of redemption by love and of future happiness — or, at least, future security — is destroyed. Each reference to the short-lived marriage strips away a layer of Blanche's protective pretence, until she is forced to stand exposed in the harsh glare of the unshaded light. When what she *really is* is then rejected, there is no other possibility left for her except retreat into an enclosed world of her dreams. The play's tension and energy come from the audience's growing awareness of the past rising inexorably to the surface where it will erupt explosively into the present; it is this which gives *Streetcar* its sense of being 'purposeful'.

The structure of the play departs from well-established theatrical practice in having no act divisions. The eleven scenes follow upon each other without any formalised arrangement into three, four or five phrases. This is appropriate to a sense of the relentless movement towards Blanche's final catastrophe. It is also, perhaps, a product of Tennessee Williams's experiences as a screen writer in Hollywood: writing for the cinema rather than the theatre most often requires the dramatist to think in terms of a sustained sequence of relatively short episodes, capitalising on the effects made possible by crisp cutting from one image or event to the next. It is worth noting that many of his plays have transferred to the screen with considerable success.

Although the play is also concerned with the relationship between Stella and Stanley, Blanche is the organising factor: the action begins with her arrival and ends as she is led away to the mental hospital. It is significant, however, that the action is confined within the Kowalski apartment and its immediate surroundings; we do not, for instance, travel with Blanche from Laurel or on to the state institution. By maintaining this 'unity of place' Williams is doing more than merely following the 'rules' laid down by Aristotle for classic drama. He is also drawing attention to the fact that *Streetcar* explores the continuing human need to secure a territory, a home, and defend it against intruders. This is a basic animal drive, well described by Konrad Lorenz in *On Aggression* (London, Methuen, 1966). Professor Lorenz progresses from a study of aggression and appeasement patterns in animals, linked to the demands of territorial possession, sexual effectiveness and self-preservation, to a view of human behaviour as displaying essentially the same patterns, although sometimes in a more oblique or sophisticated form. The rituals of threat, appeasement, sexual display, defence and retreat have the power to involve an audience because they appeal to deeply rooted responses which are universal and vigorous. The plot of *A Streetcar Named Desire* is, in part, Stanley's recognition of Blanche as a potentially dangerous invader of his territory; he cannot, as some animals might, accept her as part of his herd of brood mares, or, in human terms, as an addition to his harem. The impossibility of such an arrangement is demonstrated when he rapes her; Blanche is not shown accepting this as an initiation into a new role within Stanley's household, and Stella is prepared to cast her sister out rather than allow her to remain as a rival for Stanley's favours. Earlier on, Blanche makes a bid for possession of

Stella when she tries to persuade her sister to leave Stanley and set up a new home with her. In both phases of the struggle, Blanche is defeated.

It has been suggested that what might be regarded primarily as a plot decision — a basis for the selection and organisation of events — is more importantly the key to the playwright's intended 'message' and moral attitude. By setting the play in the Kowalskis' territory, Tennessee Williams is possibly indicating that Stella and Stanley are rightly the survivors in their world of vitality and birth, whereas Blanche's world is Belle Reve, a place of decayed gentility, of death, which must be rejected if life is to go on.

From *The Poker Night* to *Streetcar*: approaches to character

Tennessee Williams arrived at *A Streetcar Named Desire* through a series of stages, called variously *The Poker Night*, *The Primary Colors* and *The Moth*, gradually building up the plot and characters from a basic situation involving an unmarried teacher meeting a prospective husband while on a visit to her younger sister and brother-in-law. At first the action was set in Chicago, then Atlanta in Georgia, then in New Orleans. Originally the central family was Italian, then the brother-in-law became Irish while the sisters changed into Southern belles. Finally Williams settled on the Polish-American and Southern combination. Throughout all the phases, he had a fixed idea about the style of the setting:

> A symbolic link is forged between Stanley and the powerful modern engines of the railroad, and Williams once considered ending the play with Blanche throwing herself in front of the train in the freight-yards. (Vivienne Dickson in *Tennessee Williams: A Tribute*, p. 159)

Stanley's development is interesting. He begins, in the first draft, as

> 'a weakly good-looking young man. He has a playful tenderness and vivacity which would amount to effeminacy if he were not Italian'. (quoted by Vivienne Dickson, p. 163)

In his Irish phase, in *The Primary Colors*, the Stanley character — here called Ralph — becomes more assertive. Williams adds in associations with hunting and death — the character is a salesman of 'mortuary goods'. At this stage, too, Williams suggests both the character's latent femininity and his attraction to Blanche. She rejects him:

> I think you have a very wide streak of the feminine in your nature. You think you'll obscure it by acting with the greatest possible vulgarity. But what you sometimes really remind me of is a vicious

little fourteen year old girl that I've had in my class for two years.

If one remembers that view of Blanche as a disguised male, Stanley's initial effeminacy is significant in the light of Williams's homosexuality. Williams agreed in an interview that Blanche was in some ways a projection of his sense of himself; the relationship between Blanche and Stanley then becomes fraught with danger, with complications and social taboos underlying the surface conflict.

In his mature form, in *A Streetcar Named Desire*, Stanley has a force of character which has been interpreted as excitingly life-giving on the one hand, and brutally destructive on the other:

> The child of immigrants, he is the new, untamed pioneer, who brings to the South, Williams seems to be saying, a power more exuberant than destructive, a sort of power the South may have lost.
> (J.H. Adler, in *Tennessee Williams: A Tribute*, p. 41)

But:

> Stanley, in his ignorance and insensitivity, destroys both Blanche's hope and her illusion. He sees through her pose without understanding why she needs one. He thinks merely that she feels superior to him and he wishes to destroy her composure to make her recognise that she is the same as he, a sexual animal. (J.M. McGlinn in *Tennessee Williams: A Tribute*, p. 514)

Or:

> The conflict between Blanche and Stanley allegorizes the struggle between effeminate culture and masculine libido. (Robert Brustein, *America's New Cultural Hero*, 1958, p. 124)

Stanley has also been described as a twentieth-century Pan-Dionysus — that is, a modern embodiment of the ancient spirits of anarchic sexuality and the pursuit of pleasure, capable of impulsive cruelty to those who try to censor or confine them. Tennessee Williams's stage directions stress certain qualities in Stanley: his strength, his vitality, and his virility:

> *Animal joy in his being is implicit in all his movements and attitudes. Since earliest manhood the centre of his life has been pleasure with women, the giving and taking of it, not with weak indulgence, dependently, but with the power and pride of a richly feathered male bird among his hens. (p. 13)*

It would be interesting to know whether Tennessee Williams's reference to the brilliant cockerel amongst his hens contains any of the conscious irony there would be if he had in mind the old fable of Chanticleer, the subject of Chaucer's *Nun's Priest's Tale*. Chanticleer is a farmyard cock, a richly feathered male bird among his hens, whose sexuality is so rampant that it becomes absurd. For example, he longs to mate with his favourite hen, Pertelote, on their perch at night, but the beam is so narrow they would fall off. Then:

Real he was, he was namore aferd;	He was majestic, no longer afraid;
He fethered Pertelote twenty tyme,	He fondled Pertelote twenty times,
And trad as ofte, er that it was pryme.	And mated with her as often, before nine in the morning.
He looketh as it were a grym leoun	He looked like a merciless lion
An on his toos he rometh up and doun;	And roamed up and down on tiptoe;
Him deigned nat to sette his foot to ground.	Because he was too haughty to let his feet touch the ground.

The absurdity of the farmyard rooster as a sexual creature is also stressed in *A Streetcar Named Desire* by the story that Steve tells in scene three (p. 25). Tennessee Williams's decision to have Capricorn as Stanley's astronomical birth sign is similarly ambivalent: it carries pagan associations with the god-goat Pan, but the goat is also traditionally associated with low sexuality, animal lust (consider how Shakespeare's Iago uses it to denigrate Othello). Williams describes Stanley as 'the gaudy seed-bearer' and the images of his mind as 'crude' — both adjectives suggesting vulgarity and lack of refinement. On the other hand, Stanley's sexual pleasure is the 'complete and satisfying centre' of his character. Is there irony here? Does the phrase *expose* rather than simply *describe* Stanley's chief quality and indicate the limitations of his life? It is important to notice that Stanley is not wholly selfish in his sexuality; he gives as well as takes pleasure. Certainly he gives Stella enough to sustain their relationship, at least at this stage of their marriage. When he is shown as the unapologetic sexual male, Stanley often appears formidable; however, there are moments when his affectation of worldly wisdom can make him seem foolish — even to Stella:

STANLEY: I got an acquaintance that deals in this sort of merchandise. I'll have him in here to appraise it. I'm willing to bet you there's thousands of dollars invested in this stuff here!
STELLA: Don't be such an idiot, Stanley!
STANLEY: And what have we here? [. . .] A crown for an empress.

> STELLA: A rhinestone tiara she wore to a costume ball.
> STANLEY: What's rhinestone?
> STELLA: Next door to glass. (p. 18)

He is like a bull in a china shop, massively inept, in his ramsacking of Blanche's papers (pp. 21-22), whereas she here emerges with some dignity and humour. She succeeds in making him look 'somewhat sheepish', but he regains status by revealing himself as the father of Stella's expected child.

Stanley's code of morality is clear-cut and simple, ruthlessly so. He defends his territory, his wife and his friends against invasion or imposition:

> STANLEY: Mitch is a buddy of mine. We were in the same outfit together — Two-forty-first Engineers. We work in the same plant and now on the same bowling team. [. . .] I'd have that on my conscience the rest of my life if I knew all that stuff and let my best friend get caught. (p. 62)

There are areas of his self-esteem which he protects forcefully:

> STANLEY: I am not a Polack. People from Poland are Poles, not Polacks. But what I am is a one hundred per cent American, born and raised in the greatest country on earth and proud as hell of it, so don't ever call me a Polack. (p. 67)

Yet he is able to rape his wife's sister while his wife is in hospital giving birth to his child. He justifies it to himself by seeing the event as pre-determined, as if by mutual consent, like the inevitable and proper mating of animals. Blanche's terrified defiance of him with a broken bottle shatters the last fragile social taboos and, calling her 'Tiger — tiger', Stanley responds to her gesture as part of a wild mating ritual. Even at this moment there is a possible irony, a mockery beneath the dramatic intensity, in the picture of Stanley, inflated with that 'animal joy in his being', picking up Blanche's inert form and carrying it off. It offers an image familiar to any cinema-goer who has seen Hollywood classics such as the 1932 *King Kong* in which the massive ape with the sentimental heart carries Fay Wray's limp body off to his lair. When Stanley says (p. 81), 'We've had this date from the beginning', it is as if twentieth-century conventions and moralities fade away in the face of the primeval sexual drive of male to female.

It is, nonetheless, important to believe that Stanley *loves* Stella, not merely with animal desire but with deep-seated feeling which sometimes expresses itself with tenderness, sometimes with anguished need. When she retreats upstairs after he has hit her, he is racked by shuddering sobs and falls on his knees before her as she returns to him, before carrying her back into their dark apartment. After Blanche's departure at the end of the play, Stella sits sobbing on the steps, holding her new baby; Stanley leaves his card game to seek reassurance that she is still bound to him body and heart:

> STANLEY (*voluptuously, soothingly*). Now, honey. Now, love. Now, now love. (*He kneels beside her and his fingers find the opening of her blouse.*) Now, now, love. Now, love . . . (p. 89-90)

Elia Kazan's *Notebook for 'A Streetcar Named Desire'* traces his approach to the play as a director. Here he discusses Stanley's inner conflicts and dominant traits:

> He wants to knock no-one down. He only doesn't want to be taken advantage of. His code is simple and simple-minded. He is adjusted *now* . . . later, as his sexual powers die so will he; the trouble will come later, the 'problems'. [. . .] Why does he want to bring Blanche and, before her, Stella *down to his level*? . . . It's the hoodlum aristocrat. He's deeply dissatisfied, deeply hopeless, deeply cynical. [. . .] But Blanche he can't seem to do anything with. She can't come down to his level so he levels her with his sex. [. . .] Stanley is supremely indifferent to everything except his own pleasure and comfort. He is marvellously selfish, a miracle of sensuous self-centredness. (Included in *Twentieth Century Interpretations of 'A Streetcar Named Desire'*, Prentice-Hall, pp. 26-27)

Stella, according to Kazan, is driven by her determination to hold onto Stanley, so that even her sister becomes a possible enemy. In her marriage to Stanley her womanhood has flowered; she is about to move into a further stage of her life-cycle — to become a mother as well as a mate. Blanche not only appears as a rival for Stanley's favours, but tries to force Stella back into a childhood rôle, calling her 'Precious lamb!' and 'Blessed baby!' and ordering her about:

> BLANCHE: You hear me? I said stand up! (STELLA *complies reluctantly*.) You messy child, you, you've spilt something on that pretty white lace collar! (p. 9)

Blanche also tries to undermine Stella's belief in the worth and rightness of her marriage to Stanley:

> BLANCHE: I take it for granted that you still have sufficient memory of Belle Reve to find this place and these poker players impossible to live with. (p. 39)

Her challenge forces Stella to define the nature and value of her relationship with Stanley. She stands by her love for him, which, it is true, has its centre in 'things that happen between a man and a woman in the dark — that sort of make everything else seem unimportant' (p. 39-40). Blanche attempts to dismiss this as 'brutal desire', which will drag Stella back with the animals in a primitive life without beauty. Her failure is demonstrated as Stella turns to embrace Stanley 'fiercely and in full view of Blanche' (p. 41) while Stanley smiles in triumph over his wife's shoulder. Kazan suggests that Stella's commitment to her marriage costs her dear:

> Stella is a refined girl who has found a kind of salvation or realization, *but at a terrific price*. She keeps her eyes closed, even stays in bed as much as possible so that she won't realise, won't *feel* the pain of this terrific price. [. . .] She's waiting for the dark where Stanley makes her feel *only him* and she has no reminder of the price she is paying. She wants no intrusion from the other world. (*Twentieth Century Interpretations*, p. 25)

It is possible to see Stella as the crucial battleground over which Blanche and Stanley fight, possession of which ensures final victory. She is then a key figure; her changing attitudes signal the movement of the action. When she allows Blanche to lead her out of the apartment after Stanley's drunken violence, the balance of power shifts towards Blanche. When Stella chooses to return to Stanley, Blanche is left in defeat. At the end of the play it is suggested that her loyalty is now to her child, as she sits with the baby on the steps *outside* the apartment, weeping for the sister she has allowed to be taken into a kind of captivity, and neither responding to nor rejecting Stanley's advances. There are problems in accepting Stanley's and Stella's marriage, as described by Blanche in scene four. From a woman's viewpoint especially, there may be disconcerting implications:

> How did Stella ever get over those critical hurdles — Stanley's table manners, Stanley's preference in dress? [. . .] Did Stanley rape Stella, too, just by way of a how-do-you-do? Do all women burn to be raped? Is this the locker room fantasy that is Williams's version of animal purity?

It is hard to know what is more unpleasant in this image: the overt

sentimentality it expresses, or the latent brutality it masks: a
fascination with the image of the helpless creature under the physical
domination of another, accepting his favours with tears of gratitude.
(Marion Magid in *Twentieth Century Interpretations*, p. 78)

The rhetoric here is extravagant; however, it raises an important issue. In
the play, it is suggested (only to be quickly denied) that during their
courtship Stanley's lack of refinement and his forcefulness were disguised
or, perhaps, made seem acceptable by his Master Sergeant's uniform.
Stella perhaps was wise to recognise in him the best available alternative
to the decadence of Belle Reve:

STELLA: The best I could do was make my own living, Blanche.
(p. 11)

This is Stella's self-justification for what might otherwise seem a betrayal
of her family and heritage; she asserts herself at the expense of all that
Belle Reve has stood for and Blanche has tried to cling to. To some, it is
Stella's selfishness rather than her submissiveness that characterises her:

Stella ignores the needs of others and eventually adopts her own
illusion. Life with Stanley — sex with Stanley — is her highest value.
Her refusal to accept Blanche's story of the rape is a commitment to
self-preservation rather than love, and thus Stella contributes to
Blanche's disintegration. (J.M. McGlinn in *Tennessee Williams: A
Tribute*, p. 514)

Her marriage gives her a purpose. Her new motherhood ensures a
continuing rôle even if Stanley's desire for her should fade. Blanche
offers her nothing except a return to childish dependence and both
emotional and material insecurity. The final image of the play, however,
suggests that Blanche's intrusion and expulsion have irrevocably changed
the nature of Stella's relationship with her husband and her chosen way
of life.

Blanche's outstanding characteristic, according to Kazan, is
desperation; her chief motivation is the urgent need to find protection:
'The tradition of the old South says it must be through another person.'
Her problem arises from this Southern tradition,

her notion of what a woman should be. [. . .] Because this image of
herself cannot be accomplished in reality, certainly not in the South
of our day and time, it is her effort and practice to *accomplish it in
fantasy*. Everything she does in *reality* too is coloured by this
necessity, this compulsion to be *special*.

Kazan reminds any actress attempting the rôle that it requires
considerable emotional versatility — ranging from imperious self-
assertion to fluttering helplessness, from feverish gaiety to pathetic
terror. She must alternately alienate and engage the sympathy of the
audience.

> The audience at the beginning should see her bad effect on Stella,
> want Stanley to tell her off. He does. He exposes her and then
> gradually, as they see how genuinely in pain, how actually desperate
> she is, how warm, tender and loving she can be (the Mitch story), how
> freighted with need she is — then they begin to go with her. They
> begin to realize that they are sitting in at the death of something
> extraordinary [. . .] and then they feel the tragedy. (*Twentieth
> Century Interpretations*, p. 22)

The tragic flaw that undermines her herioc and admirable qualities is,
then, her need to be special, which isolates her from others. Allied to
this is her refusal to accept what is innate in her — part, that is, of her
common rather than her unique humanity — her sexuality. She denigrates
it as mere 'brutal desire', thinking of it as 'a rattle-trap streetcar, that
bangs through the Quarter, up one old narrow street and down another'
(p. 40) while she yearns for a 'Cadillac convertible, must have been a
block long' (p. 37) or 'a cruise of the Caribbean' (p. 76). She harbours
dreams of a happy-ever-after ending to her story in which she as 'a
woman of intelligence and breeding, can enrich a man's life —
immeasurably!' (p. 78). She longs to be protected against the dangers of
fading physical beauty and old age:

> BLANCHE: Physical beauty is passing. A transitory possession. But
> beauty of the mind and richness of the spirit and tenderness of the
> heart — and I have all of those things — aren't taken away, but grow!
> Increase with the years! How strange that I should be called a
> destitute woman! When I have all of these treasures locked in my
> heart. (*A choked sob comes from her.*) (p. 78)

Kazan sees *Streetcar* as resembling a classical tragedy, with Blanche like
Medea or some doomed Greek heroine, pursued to madness by the
Harpies within her own nature, with Nemesis (the spirit of retribution)
dogging her heels and baying for vengeance against her for the death of
her boy-husband and for her sinning. She is capable of exciting pity and
terror in the audience — the responses described by Aristotle as the
hallmarks of tragedy.

'Pity' implies a compassionate concern; the audience must be able to

believe in and care about the character. She must have, at least, a
dramatic reality. How is this created? She is given a past that makes sense
of her present and that makes her future fate both consistent and 'right'.
Stella refers to Blanche's upbringing and her sensitivity, in defence of
her behaviour (p. 58). She also speaks of Blanche's traumatic marriage
and widowing, 'an experience that — killed her illusions' (p. 61). Blanche
herself explains and justifies her desperate search for protection from
poverty and physical decline when she describes the squalid horror of

> All of those deaths! The long parade to the graveyard! Father,
> mother! Margaret, that dreadful way! So big with it, it couldn't be
> put in a coffin! But had to be burned like rubbish! [. . .] Which of
> them left us a fortune? Which of them left a cent of insurance even?
> Only poor Jessie — one hundred to pay for her coffin. That was all,
> Stella! And I with my pitiful salary at the school. (p. 12)

Blanche's early lessons have been bleak: gentility brought no lasting
earthly rewards; marriage brought pain and horror; material possessions
seeped away; the body swelled or shrivelled in death. As she says to
Mitch (who cannot understand her), *desire* seemed to be the opposite of
all that death, a possible antidote to the dying and the despair, so she
caught the habit, became addicted. In her final fantasies (p. 85), she
yearns for the hygienic expansiveness of the sea, for a picturesque death
without pain or disfigurement or loneliness ('my hand in the hand of
some nice-looking ship's doctor'), for a clean, bright funeral which will
be like a return to youthful romance, and the hope of eternal happiness
in heaven.

The Aristotelian 'terror' comes from the audience's recognition that
Blanche's destruction is inevitable, that she cannot free herself from the
contradictions of her own nature nor shake off the burden of guilt she
has carried ever since her husband's death. It is a tragic irony of her
situation that the only way she can attract the special attention she
craves, the protection she seems unable to survive without, is by
exploiting the sexuality she feels debases her and which ultimately
debars her from the hoped-for haven of a second marriage. She describes
her dilemma defensively, but with clarity:

> BLANCHE: I was never hard or self-sufficient enough. When people
> are soft — soft people have got to court the favour of hard ones,
> Stella. Have got to be seductive — put on soft colours, the colours of
> butterfly wings, and glow — make a little temporary magic just in
> order to pay for — one night's shelter. That's why I've been — not so
> awf'ly good lately. I've run for protection, Stella . . . protection. (p. 45)

To Mitch she admits without coquetry that her youth has suddenly vanished, that all she wants is a peaceful hiding place that is more than simply a grave, that she has lied: 'I don't tell the truth. I tell what *ought* to be the truth. And if that is sinful, then let me be damned for it!' (p. 72.). The 'if' is important; it leaves the moral issues unresolved. Blanche's morality is that of the aesthete, the dedicated seeker after beauty before all else. Like Oscar Wilde (the Anglo-Irish playwright whose life and works were designed to celebrate beauty and wit rather than more conventional moral standards), Blanche holds to the belief that 'Lying, the telling of beautiful untrue things, is the proper aim of Art' (Oscar Wilde, *Impressions*, 1891). For her, too, it is important that her life should resemble a work of art, and that art, poetry and music should be the flag she carries 'in this dark march toward whatever it is we're approaching' (p. 41). It is fitting that she should be a teacher of English. Not only does this make credible her often rather literary and poetic language, but it also fits her search for magical beauty at the expense of common-or-garden reality. It is her business 'to instil a bunch of bobby-soxers and drug-store Romeos with reverence for Hawthorne and Whitman and Poe' (p. 31). The images associated with Blanche generally imply fragile beauty, transience: an orchard in spring, its blossom bound to fall at the short season's end; a softly tinted butterfly or a moth, driven to seek warmth and brilliance from a flame that will sear its beauty then consume it.

As well as making sense in human terms, the character of Blanche has been seen as embodying a number of concepts or themes: the Soul subjected to physical existence and thus to 'the apishness and brutality of matter' (Leonard Quirino in *Tennessee Williams: A Tribute*, p. 85); a Jungian Great Mother Figure, a kind of white witch ('A Gallery of Witches' N.M. Tischler); the representation 'in her frail spirit [of] the decline and fall of a long line of decadent Southern aristocrats' (*New York Daily News*, 4.12.1947); 'beauty shipwrecked on the rock of the world's vulgarity' (*The New Republic*, 22.12.1947); 'the symbol of art and beauty, this poor flimsy creature to whom truth is mortal' (Mary McCarthy in *Twentieth Century Interpretations*, p. 99). Elia Kazan sees her, on the one hand, as a doomed dinosaur approaching extinction, and, on the other (with a male arrogance worthy of Stanley Kowalski), as:

> a heightened version, an artistic intensification of all women. That is what makes the play universal. Blanche's special relation to all women *is that she is at that critical point where the one thing above all else that she is dependent on — her attraction for men — is beginning to*

go. Blanche is like all women, dependent on a man, looking for one to hang on to: only *more so*! (*Twentieth Century Interpretations*, p. 24.)

Equally one might say that Blanche is 'an artistic intensification' of a common male conception of 'all women', and her dependency on a man is the expression of their commonly cherished hope — hence the play's universality.

Mitch is important to the plot of *Streetcar* as he represents the possibility — however pallid — of future happiness or security for Blanche, that hope which makes her ultimate catastrophe all the more poignant. He also serves to emphasise the strengths and vividness of both Stanley and Blanche by offering the contrast of his own weakness and insipidity. One feels that Blanche would have had to stoop to marry him, to confine her nature within his soft-centred mediocrity. Mitch sometimes emerges as a comic foil for Stanley; for example, his over-scrupulous concern about the way he perspires seems funny after Stanley's easy: 'My clothes're stickin' to me. Do you mind if I make myself comfortable? (*He starts to remove his shirt*.)' (p. 14). When Stanley charges after the pregnant Stella in drunken fury, Mitch's response sounds positively spinsterish: 'This is terrible' (p. 31). The way he is routed by Blanche's cries of 'Fire!' is absurd and makes Stanley's subsequent domination of her seem all the more powerful.

In the early drafts of the play, the key struggle is between Blanche and the prospective suitor, rather than between Blanche and her brother-in-law. Subsequently the character becomes weaker, but in the final stage of *A Streetcar Named Desire* Williams adds two important elements to make Mitch's rejection of Blanche more credible, since one might otherwise expect her to mould his weakness to answer her own needs. Williams emphasises Mitch's reverence for and dependence on his invalid mother, who will be outraged by Blanche's lifestyle. Also, before confronting Blanche, Mitch has tried to nerve himself by drinking more than he is accustomed to. It is difficult to be sure how sympathetic a character he is meant to be: Stanley treats him with tolerant superiority, yet feels a loyalty to him; his own gentleness and hesitancy come as a relief after Stanley's blustering towards Blanche; his concern for Stella's well-being and his courtesy towards Blanche are appealing and believable. Yet his gentleness comes out of weakness rather than strength: his advances to Blanche are hesitant because he is doubtful of his power to please; his capacity for affection and tenderness has long been absorbed by a sickly mother and a dead girl; he appears childish to his friends (p. 28); he is embarrassed by his body functions (p. 52); he lacks the experience or the insight to see through Blanche's affected demureness, and then lacks the wisdom to recognise her worth once his first illusions have been shattered. He responds to Blanche's cry for help with injured self-esteem; then his attempt to take sexual advantage of her is a fiasco; even the words of his rejection of her are weak — he doesn't *think* he wants to marry her anymore. Williams describes him as clattering awkwardly down the steps and out of sight. His inadequacy highlights the desperation that drives Blanche to say (p. 47): 'I want his respect. [. . .] I want to *rest*! I want to breathe quietly again! Yes — I *want* Mitch . . . *very badly*! Just think! If it happens! I can leave here and not be anyone's problem . . .' (p. 47). There is a truth behind the account she gives Stanley of her final encounter with Mitch:

> BLANCHE: But some things are not forgivable. Deliberate cruelty is not forgivable. It is the one unforgivable thing in my opinion and it is one thing of which I have never, never been guilty. And so I told him, I said to him, Thank you, but it was foolish of me to think we could ever adapt ourselves to each other. Our ways of life are too different. We have to be realistic about such things. (p. 78)

Is Mitch guilty of 'deliberate cruelty' in that rejection of Blanche, either in its meaning or its manner? Or, like Blanche when feeling betrayed by her boy-husband, is he simply unable to cope with this new reality, so hits out like a child then runs away?

When he reappears in the final scene, he is evidently dogged by shame and an impotent fury. He splutters with incoherent rage against Stanley, using the language of their card-playing: 'You . . . you . . . you . . . Brag . . . brag . . . bull . . . bull' (p. 82). When he hears Blanche's voice, his arm becomes nerveless and *'his gaze is dissolved into space'* (p. 83). He ducks his head, as if to hide from her, and remains hunched over the table, sullen and ashamed, when the others stand to let her pass. He cannot bear to look at her; undignified and cowardly evasion is all that is left to him. Only when Blanche is fighting for survival against the grim nurse is he stung into movement, but he is blocked by Stanley and his wild accusation merely ridiculed:

> MITCH (*wildly*): You! You done this, all o' your God damn interfering with things you —
> STANLEY. Quit the blubber! (*He pushes him aside.*)
> MITCH: I'll kill you! (*He lunges and strikes at* STANLEY.)
> STANLEY: Hold this bone-headed cry-baby! (p. 88)

Mitch collapses, sobbing helplessly over the table. He, like Blanche, will have to find some way of trying to escape from the guilt and the sense of personal failure, or he will be finished. Perhaps he will translate the whole experience into a wistful memory to keep alongside his silver cigarette case from the strange, sweet, dead girl, with its significant inscription:

And if God choose,
I shall but love thee better — after death! (p. 29)

Poet of the theatre/successful showman?

In the letter to Tynan already referred to, Tennessee Williams describes his writing as 'lyric'. This implies two important characteristics: firstly, that the writing has a musical quality rather than being prosaic or naturalistic, and, secondly, that it is an expression of the writer's personal experience or, more significantly, of his thoughts and feelings about that experience. The 'truth' or 'reality' is, therefore, highly subjective and the play's success is dependent on the dramatist's ability to present his personal perspective on life so persuasively that, for the duration of the play at least, the audience can understand and sympathise with that personal vision. Williams was, by his own admission, engrossed by his own biography, using the colourful facts of his life to create the patterns of his work and, at the same time, using that process of translation from life to literature as a means of freeing himself from emotions and memories which otherwise haunted him.

In *A Streetcar Named Desire* there are recurring themes and terrors: death, for instance. His mother recalls Tennessee Williams saying:

'We are all desperately afraid of death, much more than we dare admit even to ourselves'. (*Remember Me to Tom*, p. 252)

This terror was but one element, according to Miss Edwina, in her son's general anxiety:

Tom is so mild in looks and manner you would never suspect a violent feeling stirs in him. Yet violence is the way we fight fear and Tom has said he always had to contend with the 'adversary of fear' which gave him 'a certain tendency toward an atmosphere of hysteria and violence in my writing, an atmosphere that has existed in it from the beginning'. (*Remember Me to Tom*, p. 253)

A sense of the inexorable decay of beauty accelerated by the brutality of much of modern, urban life linked his fear of personal disintegration with his nostalgia for the tattered romance of the Old South — a nostalgia he could hardly escape, being Miss Edwina's son. She approvingly records this:

Another time he declared, 'I write out of love for the South. [. . .]
But I can't expect Southerners to realize that my writing about them
is an expression of love. It is out of regret for a South that no longer
exists that I write of the forces that have destroyed it'. (*Remember
Me to Tom*, p. 213)

The third theme dominant in much of his work, and certainly in
Streetcar, is the nature and effects of human sexuality: its voracious
energy, its disguises, the attempts made to control or domesticate it by
self-consciously civilised sections of society, the subsequent conflicts,
the relationship between love and lust, between emotional and
physical needs.

Any poet of the theatre, rather than of the study, has a vocabulary
beyond words — the three-dimensional images of the stage itself. The
first production of *Streetcar* was designed by Jo Mielziner, a man who
had come under the influence of German Expressionist stagecraft while
working in Berlin. The wish to communicate the *feeling* of the play
through its set was reflected in the sloping telegraph poles and lurid
neon lights surrounding the ornate but crumbling facade of the pale old
apartment house in Elysian Fields. Tennessee Williams's stage directions
are emotionally coloured. At the opening of the play,

> *the sky that shows round the dim white building is a peculiarly tender
> blue, almost turquoise, which invests the scene with a kind of lyricism
> and gracefully attentuates the atmosphere of decay.* (p. 3)

For scene three, *The Poker Night*, his directions are very specific,
indicating the visual tradition he is drawing on:

> *There is a picture of Van Gogh's of a billiard-parlour at night. The
> kitchen now suggests that sort of lurid nocturnal brilliance, the raw
> colours of childhood's spectrum.* (p. 24)

He stresses the relationship between the image of the set and the nature
of the characters framed within it; the card players are '*as coarse and
direct and powerful as the primary colours*', with a childlike — or
childish — lack of delicacy and sophistication, having no subtle shading
or nuances. At the end of the play, when Blanche feels like a hunted
animal finally at bay, Williams calls for her state of mind to be expressed
visually in a wholly unnaturalistic but perhaps poetic — or theatrically
shocking — way:

> *She rushes past him into the bedroom. Lurid reflections appear on
> the walls in odd, sinuous shapes.* (p. 86)

These horrid reflections of her panic fade when she is soothed by the doctor's courteous gesture. As she is led out, like someone blind, the lyricism of the surrounding turquoise sky becomes grimly ironic.

This visual projection of Blanche's inner life is complemented by the pattern of sound Williams calls for — primarily the use of music and chanted street-cries — creating a ritualistic or dreamlike feeling. The lyricism of the opening picture (p. 3) is given voice by the 'blue piano' which, Williams explains, *'expresses the spirit of the life which goes on here'*. It is eloquent of the *'infatuated fluency'* of the Old Quarter's picturesquely self-consuming culture. Later the strains of a polka become more and more insistent as the truth of Blanche's past moves closer and closer to her present refuge. At first it is faint in the distance (p. 15), then, as she speaks to Mitch of her widowing, the polka sounds more strongly, in a minor key, shifting into a major key as Mitch moves towards her with awkward compassion. When Blanche is discovered alone at the beginning of scene nine, the polka is rapid and feverish. She sits tense and hunched, no longer dressed in a near-virginal white but in a scarlet robe:

The music is in her mind; she is drinking to escape it and the sense of disaster closing in on her and she seems to whisper the words of the song. (p. 69)

It is important to remember when *reading* the play that the music in Blanche's mind is also heard by the audience in the theatre. Tennessee Williams uses a theatrical device to draw the audience into Blanche's nightmare; she and they share the same experience at this moment and so the audience may be persuaded to believe in the truth of this vision. This may be felt as the power of poetry in the theatre, or it may be seen as successful showmanship.

It is not only Blanche's passions and qualities that are expressed through emotive sounds. Stanley, for example, is associated with the powerful note of a locomotive engine — modern, brutally impressive machine-muscle. In scene four (p. 40), his invasion of the sisters' conspiracy is covered by the sound of an approaching train; so, too, is his feigned withdrawal before his victorious reclamation of Stella. It is, therefore, significant that when Blanche is telling Mitch of her marriage, the most harrowing memory is signalled by the roar of an oncoming locomotive:

She claps her hands to her ears and crouches over. The headlight of the locomotive glares into the room as it thunders past. (p. 56)

Similarly, the beginning of the last phase of the movement towards Stanley's rape of Blanche in scene ten is marked by the roar of an approaching locomotive which forces Blanche to crouch and press her fists to her ears while Stanley, grinning, waits between her and her means of escape.

Stanley has his music, too. When he is full of anguished rage at Stella's retreat upstairs, his violent gesture of hurling the telephone to the floor is accompanied by *'dissonant brass and piano sounds'* (p. 33). The transition from his howl of 'STELLAHHHHH!' to the intense sensuality of their reunion is achieved by the moaning of a low-tone clarinet. His sexual domination of Blanche in scene ten is blared out by *'the hot trumpet and drums from the Four Deuces'*.

This deliberate orchestration of the play's emotional movement is 'lyricism' in its most literal sense. When the script is read, the lyric device can be appraised intellectually as one of the several formal elements of the play as a whole. The *idea* of it is interesting. In the theatre, however, the power of these sounds is not intellectual but makes a direct appeal to or an assault upon the audience's feelings.

The language of the play is shaped by two needs: character-identification and thematic development. On a naturalistic level, the characters are placed socially and individually by the words they use and the structure of their sentences. Stanley's sentences are generally short, with a simple syntax: challenging questions are followed by single-statement answers, with key words hammered home:

> STANLEY: You know what luck is? Luck is believing you're lucky. Take at Salerno. I believed I was lucky. I figured that 4 out of 5 would not come through but I would . . . and I did. I put that down as a rule. To hold front position in this rat-race you've got to believe you are lucky. (p. 82)

His vocabulary is drawn from his day-to-day interests: card-playing and betting (p. 20), the popular culture of films and songs (p. 20), slang (p. 88), lively but hackneyed over-statement (p. 18). Nonetheless, there is a patterning of imagery, a kind of poetic rhetoric (that is, language used deliberately to create a desired effect or to make a specific point — here, this 'point' about those values and forces that Stanley embodies). The language of games-playing has not only an obvious naturalistic reference, but expresses a gambler's fatalism and his faith in his strength as someone favoured by Fortune (p. 82). It is a male-oriented philosophy: 'seven card *stud*' (p. 25), 'One-eyed *jacks* are wild' (p. 24),

'What do you two think you are? A pair of *queens*?' (p. 65). It supposes
a way of life played by a set of rules which might seem arbitrary, even
unfair, to an outsider and which must take into account the action of
forces beyond human control, where the urge to compete and conquer
is celebrated and losers may be called upon to surrender all they have.
The poker games that Stanley is seen playing are aggressive,
individualistic. Initially he is seen losing to Mitch, Blanche's most
promising ally, but by the last scene he is winning every hand (p. 82).

> Depending as it does on the skilful manipulation of the hands that
> chance deals out, the card game is used by Williams througout
> *Streetcar* as a symbol of fate and of the skilful player's ability to
> make its decrees perform in his own favour at the expense of his
> opponent's misfortune, incompetence, and horror of the game itself.
> (L. Quirino in *Tennessee Williams: A Tribute*, p. 78)

Stanley also echoes or answers images used by Blanche. Her fear of bright
light is in opposition to Stanley's delight in 'them coloured lights' that he
'gets going' with Stella. The effect of the imagery is emphasised by a
strong gesture in the final scene when Stanley speaks dismissively of
Blanche's impact on his life, then tears her paper lantern off the light:

> STANLEY: You left nothing here but spilt talcum and old empty
> perfume bottles — unless it's the paper lantern you want to take with
> you. You want the lantern? (*He crosses to dressing-table and seizes
> the paper lantern, tearing it off the light bulb, and extends it towards
> her. She cries out as if the lantern was herself . . .*) (p. 87)

Blanche's language, too, works both naturalistically and symbolically.
With her, however, the symbolism is a more conscious part of the
character's style. It is consistent with what the audience learns of her life
and of her early character that she should move from breathless flirtation
to deliberate rhetoric (p. 22) and scatter literary allusions through her
conversation (Shakespeare, Hawthorne, Whitman and Poe). But the
insistence of the motifs, like the strains of the polka, gains momentum
and demands attention: there is the image of Desire as a streetcar banging
(a word with sexual connotations) through the narrow thoroughfares of
the Old Quarter, taking Blanche first to Cemeteries then, if she is lucky,
to Elysian Fields — that area of the classical underworld reserved for the
blessed. There is a bitter irony that she who seeks happiness so fervently
should be driven out of Elysium as a sinner for whom there is no
apparent redemption. Like a moth, to which Williams compares her, she
is a creature of the night, shrinking from strong light yet fatally drawn to

the flame of passion. The songs she sings, although recognisably of the period in which the play is set, comment figuratively on her situation and make her seem not so much an individual as part of that romantic tradition of 'captive maids' brought from 'the land of the sky blue water' (p. 16) into 'a Barnum and Bailey world. Just as phony as it can be [. . .] a honky-tonk parade' (p. 60), whose promise of happiness *could* be fulfilled only 'If you believed in me!' In the final scene she seems to belong to another recognisable tradition, that of Shakespeare's Ophelia – the delicate, loving maid driven to madness by the betrayals and brutality of the world she has been unluckily born into. Unlike Ophelia, Blanche does not sing in her final defeat, but she echoes Ophelia's pathos and poignant lyricism in her dreams of a beautiful death on the water and in the refrain-like repetition of key words ('sea', 'death') and the ironic purity of the cathedral chimes. So much so, that Laertes's heart-wrung response to his sister Ophelia's madness is, perhaps, the kind of response Tennessee Williams aspires to as Blanche is led away:

> Thoughts and affliction, passion, hell itself
> She turns to favour and to prettiness.

> (*Hamlet*, IV, vi)

Production history of *A Streetcar Named Desire*

The premiere

Directed by Elia Kazan, the premiere of *A Streetcar Named Desire* was on Broadway at the Barrymore Theatre. Opening on 3 December 1947, after tryouts in Boston, New Haven and Philadelphia, it ran for an impressive eight hundred and fifty-five performances and won Tennessee Williams the Pulitzer, Donaldson and New York Drama Critics' Circle awards. Kazan, who went on to direct the 1951 film version and four other works by Tennessee Williams, was already a well-established theatre and film director when Williams's agent, Audrey Wood, and the play's producer, Irene Selznick, persuaded him to take on the project. He became a great driving force behind the play, instigating many changes to the original script (over a hundred), as he would with *Cat on a Hot Tin Roof*, and keeping detailed notes on the play's characters and themes that would later be published.

Working closely with Kazan, the Broadway production's designer, Jo Mielziner, carefully balanced the play's realism and its expressionism. Thus the set suggested both the spartan apartment in its rundown neighbourhood and the dreamy romanticism of Blanche. The latter was partly achieved through the complex series of lighting effects and the insubstantial walls of the tenement building. The production's music, composed by Alex North, followed Williams's careful layering effect – the music of the Varsouviana on top of the blue piano, for example – and included miscellaneous sound effects to capture the vibrant French Quarter.

Blanche DuBois was played by Jessica Tandy who, following Kazan's interpretation of the play, suggested that the character had already become mentally unstable at the outset. The other three principal characters were played by lesser known actors: a young, and largely unknown, Marlon Brando played Stanley Kowalski; Mitch was played by Karl Malden who had been with Brando at The Actors Studio; and Kim Hunter took the role of Stella, a character who, in Kazan's view, had to be both passionate with her husband and reflect the considerable sacrifices she has made to be with him. These last three actors would all go on to appear in the 1951 film adaptation.

The huge success of the premiere led to the play going on tour across the United States. Two companies were established, the more successful of which being the one that cast Uta Hagen as Blanche and Anthony Quinn as Stanley. Hagen, also involved with the Broadway production, was a far more physical Blanche who, contrary to Tandy, suggested that the character's madness was induced by Stanley. Quinn studied Brando's interpretation of the role closely, but, despite bringing a greater brutishness to the character through his larger frame, he was not able to match the complexity of Brando's characterisation.

Other American productions
Streetcar was revived in New York at the City Center Theater in Manhattan in February 1956. It proved to be a controversial production, Tallulah Bankhead's bold interpretation of Blanche attracting much negative criticism, even from Williams himself (he later retracted this in the *New York Times*). Bankhead's Blanche was both funny and aggressive – markedly different to Tandy and Hagen's portrayals – and, for the critic Brooks Atkinson, the comedy was out of keeping with the character. Writing in the *New York Times* on 16 February 1956, he argued that Bankhead's personality was 'worldly and sophisticated, decisive and self-sufficient: it is fundamentally comic' (cited in *The Selected Letters of Tennessee Williams, vol. II,* p. 603). In her defence, Bankhead's Southern background meant that she could bring greater realism to the role.

Four more New York productions of note were those at the Vivian Beaumont Theater in 1973, the Circle in the Square Theater in 1988, the Barrymore in 1992 and Studio 54 in 2005. The first of these, a twenty-fifth anniversary revival, was directed by Ellis Rabb and featured Rosemary Harris as Blanche and James Farentino as Stanley. Although Brendan Gill found it 'not merely a worthy successor to the original but an illuminating companion to it' (cited in Kolin, 2000, p. 93), the majority of reviewers judged it unnecessarily nostalgic and overblown: Rabb filled a large stage with noisy extras, thus detracting from the play's essential claustrophobia. There were also problems with the acting. Harris's Blanche was, paradoxically, too strong (certainly for Farentino's Stanley) and too emotional. Farentino, appearing naked at one point, sublimated some of Stanley's strength in a strong sense of being wronged.

The Circle in the Square production was directed by Nikos Psacharopoulos and starred Blythe Danner as Blanche. Psacharopoulos had already developed a reputation for directing *Streetcar* in Williamstown (Massachusetts) two years before, but, apart from Danner, the principal parts were changed for New York. Aidan Quinn took the role of Stanley and, although criticised for his lack of physical presence, he brought slyness and verbal dexterity to the part. Psacharopoulos was able to give the play greater relevance to his audience by emphasising both the importance of truth in a post-Watergate era and the role of women after the rise of feminism. The production was also notable for its staging: eschewing the proscenium, the theatre's artistic director, Theodore Mann, defended the positioning of the audience on three sides in a horseshoe effect by stating that it was easier to become part of the play.

In contrast, the highly publicised 1992 production at the Ethel Barrymore Theater attempted to recreate Kazan's more conventional set. However, the director, Gregory Mosher, was ultimately unable to capture much of the play's poetry, and Jessica Lange as Blanche failed to transfer her considerable skills as a screen actress to the stage. She was overshadowed by another film actor, Alex Baldwin, who played up Stanley's vulgarity, acknowledging the influence of Brando.

The English actress, Natasha Richardson, took the role of Blanche at Studio 54 in Manhattan in 2005. This Roundabout Theatre Company production was directed by Edward Hall and was much talked about for the casting of John C. Reilly as Stanley. To many, he was the antithesis of Brando's creation, being neither menacing nor erotic (he had previously played Mitch in Chicago, a role to which he seemed much more suited). Indeed, though Richardson was more than able to suggest the sexual experience of Blanche, there was little chemistry between the two adversaries. Amy Ryan's Stella, also unable to connect with Reilly's Stanley, was, according to Ben Brantley of the *New York Times*, the production's 'anchor of authenticity'.

Two established film stars, Faye Dunaway and John Voight, took the roles of Blanche and Stanley for another twenty-fifth anniversary production of the play at the Ahmanson Theater in Los Angeles in 1973. The director, James Bridges, tried to break with tradition, but, like Mosher, ended up draining the play of much of its poetic strength. Faye Dunaway received mixed reviews: for some, she rose above the rest of the production; however, despite being chosen by Williams, it was felt she was too young and tried to bring too much comedy to the part. Voight consciously underplayed Stanley with the result that the character lost much of his force. He was even overshadowed by Mitch, played by the very good Earl Holliman.

In 1976, Jack Gerber directed the husband and wife team of Geraldine Page and Rip Torn at the Academy Festival Theatre in Lake Forest, Illinois. This production was gritty and violent, the uncompromising set, complete with strewn rubbish and a continually burning light, being complemented by Page's robust Blanche and Torn's (overly) menacing and vulgar Stanley.

London productions
The first London *Streetcar* opened at the Aldwych Theatre in October 1949. The sold-out run lasted for 326 performances until August 1950 and was a success, despite considerable moral condemnation from members of the clergy and politicians alike. Vivien Leigh (Blanche) was directed by her husband, Laurence Olivier, and the part of Stanley was taken by Bonar Colleano; Renee Asherson was Stella and Bernard Braden was Mitch. The production drew heavily on the Broadway premiere, using the same sets and music, and Olivier even studied Kazan's notes assiduously. However, Leigh interpreted the role of Blanche differently to her American predecessors and this was underlined by a greater fidelity to Williams's notes about costume. Her role was compromised somewhat by cuts enforced by the Lord Chamberlain: for example, there was to be no reference to Allan Grey's homosexuality, a crucial aspect of her past that determines much of her subsequent behaviour. Leigh won praise for her interpretation and Colleano, intentionally more subtle than Brando, was a worthy Stanley.

The 1974 London production at the Piccadilly Theatre encountered no censorship issues. Directed by Edwin Sherin, it starred Claire

Bloom, Martin Shaw and Joss Ackland (Mitch). Arguably, Bloom's turbulent personal life prepared her well for the part of Blanche, allowing her to realise that the character's 'neediness only brings suffering' (from *Leaving a Doll's House*, cited in Kolin, 2000, p. 100). She was widely praised for a moving performance that captured both the vulnerability of the character and her determination to ensnare Mitch, and she won awards from both the *Evening Standard* and *Variety*. Shaw was an intelligent and proud Stanley, whereas Ackland offered an older Mitch, sensitive but lumbering.

The 2002 production of *A Streetcar Named Desire* at the National Theatre was directed by Trevor Nunn and starred Glenn Close as Blanche and Iain Glen as Stanley. Close's involvement was criticised by the actors' union, Equity, as depriving British talent of a chance to take the role, but she gave a consummate performance. Michael Billington, writing in the *Guardian*, said that she 'oozes fluttery condescension and coy gentility' and John Peter for the *Sunday Times* lauded the interpretation as 'thrillingly theatrical but unostentatious, and as powerful, intelligent and moving as anything I have seen on this stage'. Glen was elegant and graceful, but, for Peter, he was also 'like a matador: ruthless, confident, provocative, alert'.

Other premieres around the world

Curiously, the short Mexican premiere of *A Streetcar Named Desire* (*Un Tranvía Llamado Deseo*) in December 1948 and the follow-up run in May 1949 were the work of a Japanese director, Seki Sano. Influenced by Stanislavski, Sano had a semi-professional acting company called the Teatro de la Reforma, and it was this troupe that gave nine performances at the Palacio de Bellas Artes and then a hundred performances at the Teatro Esperanza Iris in Mexico City. Also one of the translators, Sano helped to make Williams's play both popular and respected in Mexico. María Douglas, though young and inexperienced, gave a powerful performance as Blanche, capturing, on the one hand, her arrogance and flirtatiousness and, on the other, her victimisation. Playing opposite her was an ex-boxer, Wolf Ruvinskis, who, perhaps unsurprisingly, emphasised Stanley's physical and verbal aggression.

The Italian premiere of *Streetcar* was at the Eliseo Theatre in Rome on 21 January 1949. Directed by Luchino Visconti, who would come to be known outside Italy for films like *The Leopard* (1963), the production highlighted the play's class struggle against a fussily realistic backdrop. Visconti was aided in this by his young set designer, Franco Zefferelli, the future director of the film of *Romeo and Juliet*. Zefferelli created a messy and drab apartment – simultaneously realistic and romantic – and a cacophony of sounds that reproduced both the noisy vitality of the Quarter and Blanche's breakdown. Rina Morelli played Blanche simply but effectively, concentrating on her tragic decline in a hostile world. Vittorio Gassman's Stanley was a mixture of spontaneous violence and great tenderness, while Marcello Mastroianni (also destined to be successful in the world of film) was a young and sexy Mitch, very different to Karl Malden in the Broadway premiere. Williams attended the opening night and strongly approved of the production; it ran for just over a month.

The Swedish premiere took place at the Gothenburg City Theatre on 1 March 1949, where Ingmar Bergman was the resident director. Able to benefit from a revolving stage, complete with inner and outer sections, Bergman's production added an extra building in the form of a movie theatre called Desire or the Pleasure Garden. Constantly playing *A Night in Paradise*, this cinema immediately suggested the play's main theme, while the film's title could apply to both Stanley's wedding night and his rape of Blanche; there were also echoes of the Paradise Dance Hall in *The Glass Menagerie*. An apple tree stood near the cinema – perhaps a reference to Blanche's explanation of her name as 'an orchard in spring' – visibly dropping its leaves as the play progressed. Blanche was played by Karin Kavli, an actress who impressed critics with her range of emotions; Anders Ek was a primitive but innocent Stanley.

Consistent with the Italian and Swedish premieres, the French production of *Streetcar* also involved a celebrated filmmaker: Jean Cocteau. His adaptation of the play began on 19 October 1949 and ran for 233 performances at the Théâtre Edouard VII in Paris. Cocteau's translation was rather loose in places, and his adaptation included many black extras, male and female, to help capture the spirit of New Orleans – memorably dancing in the background during the rape scene, for example. The play's set was notable for a series of transparent backdrops illuminated by important symbols or miniature scenes. Blanche was played by a comedienne, Arletty, who, at the age of forty, managed to capture all of the character's aristocratic grandeur; Yves Vincent's simian Stanley was no match for her.

The Bungakuza Dramatic Company mounted the first Asian production of *Streetcar* in Tokyo in 1953, at a time when American culture, including the already released film version of the play, was starting to have an influence. The director, Ichiro Kawaguchi, like Seki Sano in Mexico, was influenced by Stanislavski, and he made every attempt to recreate the world of the play faithfully. Blanche was played by Haruko Sugimura, a highly respected actress who went on to become identified with the role, even reviving it in 1987. Though she was prone to exaggeration in her performance, and though Japanese critics found it hard to sympathise with Blanche's character, there was considerable praise for Sugimura's interpretation, in which she captured much of the character's stature. Kazuo Kitamura (Stanley) was less successful: his inexperience was evident and he mistakenly tried to copy Brando.

Alternative productions
As well as the many international variations of *Streetcar*, there have been several productions which have foregrounded black actors or black interpretations of the play. In some cases – Jefferson City, Missouri (1953), Los Angeles (1955 and 1956), New Orleans (1984), Chicago (1987), Washington DC (1988) – the cast was all black; in other productions – West Berlin (1974) and Berkeley (1983) – only one of the parts was played by a black actor: that of Stanley. While these alternative productions have opened up the text, freeing it from conventional interpretations that may have taken the Broadway premiere as a point of departure, they have, in some cases, involved necessary amendments to the script – for example, omitting references to Stanley's Polish ancestry in the Berkeley production, or changing the number of his regiment during the war so that it faithfully denoted a black one in the New Orleans production. The Washington production at Howard University offered a different racial dimension still: Blanche was supposed to be descended from light-skinned Creoles, whereas Stanley was from the Sea Islands off the coast of South Carolina and, therefore, noticeably darker. This interpretation sought to highlight the racism that can be assimilated within gradations of colour, not just between white and black.

Gender has also proved to be an area for reinterpretation of the play. Here the collaboration of two companies, Split Britches and Bloolips, produced the parodically titled *Belle Reprieve* in 1991, a show that drew on many different styles and only really used *Streetcar* as its inspiration. Blanche was transformed into a drag queen, played by Bette Bourne, and Stanley became a butch lesbian, played by Peggy Shaw. Offering versions of some of the scenes in the original play, *Belle Reprieve* also incorporated songs, dance and a humorous script that parodied some of the serious lines of *Streetcar*. The rape, out of tune with the comic tenor of the production, was omitted. In short, the creators of *Belle Reprieve* aimed to deconstruct and question sexual roles generally, and more specifically in traditional versions of Williams's play. *Belle Reprieve* premiered at Drill Hall in London before moving to La MaMa and One Dream, two venues in New York.

Film and television adaptations
The 1951 Warner Brothers film version, directed by Elia Kazan and filmed in New Orleans, is justly famous. R. Barton Palmer explains that 'its startling differences from the standard Hollywood movie in the representation of sexual themes eminently suited Williams's play to be the source of the first Hollywood production in a new genre: the adult art film' ('Hollywood in Crisis: Tennessee Williams and the evolution of the adult film', in Roudané, 2001, p. 216). Starring three of the four main actors from the Broadway premiere (Vivien Leigh, judged to have more box-office appeal following her success with *Gone with the Wind*, replaced Jessica Tandy as Blanche), the film also used the same costume designer, Lucinda Ballard, and musical director, Alex North. Amid much critical acclaim, Leigh, Kim Hunter (Stella) and Karl Malden (Mitch) all won Oscars, but the project initially encountered significant problems with the censors, the Production Code Administration headed by Joseph Breen. Kazan and Williams were ordered to make sixty-eight cuts from the Broadway version. These included removing all reference to homosexuality and, most crucially, changing the outcome of the rape. In theatrical productions, Stanley could escape punishment; however, the film's family audience would find that this was morally unacceptable. Nevertheless, determined attempts were made to retain the spirit of the original play. The rape, for example, was suggested by showing the viewer Stanley gathering up Blanche's defeated body in a cracked mirror; the film then cuts to a cleaner hosing down a street, a crude but effective way of indicating what has happened. However, Williams could never reconcile himself to the enforced ending where Stella, clutching her baby, vows she is never going to return to Stanley.

There have been two television adaptations of *Streetcar*, both of which were made quite some time after the film. The first, broadcast on ABC on 4 March 1984, was directed by John Erman and starred Ann-Margaret as Blanche, Treat Williams as Stanley and Randy Quaid as Mitch. Without the restrictions imposed on the film, this adaptation could play up Blanche's flirtatiousness and depict the rape far more directly. Ann-Margaret was tougher than previous Blanches and did not suggest the character's madness until the rape scene. Treat Williams recreated the muscular build of Brando's Stanley, but his interpretation of the character was too one-dimensional. Beverly D'Angelo's Stella forgave her husband easily and passionately.

The second television adaptation reunited Jessica Lange and Alec Baldwin (they had appeared in the 1992 Broadway revival) and was broadcast on 29 October 1995. It was directed by Glenn Jordan and featured the comic actor, John Goodman, as Mitch. Lange's screen Blanche was considered an improvement on her stage creation, while Alec Baldwin continued to impress as Stanley.

Opera and ballet versions

Given its musical content, it is perhaps not altogether surprising that *A Streetcar Named Desire* became the inspiration for an opera performed by the San Francisco Opera Company in 1998. The score was written by André Previn, who conducted the first four performances at the War Memorial Opera House, and the libretto was written by Philip Littell. Previn steered away from the jazz that characterised Alex North's score for both the Broadway premiere and the film, choosing instead to create a modern European sound. The three acts focused strongly on Blanche, Previn firmly believing that her fate was irredeemably tragic. Consequently, Littell gave the character several arias, though the rest of the libretto had to follow Williams's play fairly closely. The set, too, reflected Blanche's centrality: with its transparent walls and the faint tilt of the apartment, it was easy to suggest the character's state of mind, particularly in the wordless rape scene where the stage split in two. Renee Fleming (Blanche) was a soprano who came to the production with an impressive reputation, and, for most, she did not disappoint, conveying the character's power and vulnerability. Rodney Gilfrey (Stanley, baritone) was imposing but subordinate to Blanche, and Elizabeth Furtel (Stella, coloratura soprano) was an effective contrast to Fleming, appropriately cast as her sister and combining well with Gilfrey.

Blanche was also intended to be the focus of a ballet based on *Streetcar* choreographed by Valerie Betis. Premiering in Montreal at Her Majesty's Theatre on 9 October 1952, before moving on to Boston, Chicago, Cleveland, St Louis and Broadway, the *Streetcar* ballet was performed by the Slavenska-Franklin troupe. Lasting a mere forty minutes, Betis' production bravely combined different dance styles, both classical and modern, culminating in a chase through several doorways (symbolising the rape) and Blanche's being led off by Death.

Betis's choreography was used again by the Dance Theatre of Harlem, an African American company, in 1981 (Montreal), 1982 (New York) and 1986 (filmed in Denmark). This ballet, initially celebrating Tennessee Williams's seventieth birthday, incorporated flashbacks in a vibrant and unconventional rendering of the original story.

Further reading

Plays and screenplays by Williams
Candles to the Sun, New York, New Directions, 2004
Fugitive Kind, New York, New Directions, 2001
The Glass Menagerie, London, Methuen, 2000
The Rose Tattoo and Other Plays (*Camino Real, Orpheus Descending*),
    Harmondsworth, Penguin, 1976
Cat on a Hot Tin Roof and Other Plays (*The Milk Train Doesn't Stop
    Here Anymore, The Night of the Iguana*), Harmondsworth, Penguin,
    1976
Baby Doll and Other Plays (*Something Unspoken, Suddenly Last
    Summer*), Harmondsworth, Penguin, 1968
Dragon Country: A Book of Plays (*In the Bar of a Tokyo Hotel, I Rise
    in Flame, Cried the Phoenix,The Mutilated, I Can't Imagine
    Tomorrow, Confessional, The Frosted Glass Coffin, The Gnädiges
    Fräulein, A Perfect Analysis Given by a Parrot*), New York, New
    Directions, 1970
The Theatre of Tennessee Williams, vol, 8 (*Vieux Carré, A Lovely
    Sunday for Creve Coeur, Clothes for a Summer Hotel, The Red Devil
    Battery Sign*), New York, New Directions, 2001
Mister Paradise and Other One-Act Plays (*These Are the Stairs You
    Got to Watch, Mister Paradise, The Palooka, Escape, Why Do You
    Smoke So Much, Lily?, Summer at the Lake, The Big Game, The Pink
    Bedroom, The Fat Man's Wife, Thank You, Kind Spirit, The
    Municipal Abattoir, Adam and Eve on a Ferry, And Tell Sad Stories
    of the Deaths of Queens*), ed. Nicholas Moschovakis and David
    Roessel, New York, New Directions, 2005
Stopped Rocking and Other Screenplays (*All Gaul is Divided, The Loss
    of a Teardrop Diamond, One Arm, Stopped Rocking*), New York,
    New Directions, 1984
The Traveling Companion and Other Plays (*The Chalky White
    Substance, The Day on Which a Man Dies, A Cavalier for Milady,
    The Pronoun 'I', The Remarkable Rooming-House of Mme Le
    Monde, Kirche, Küche, Kinder, Green Eyes, The Parade, The One
    Exception, Sunburst, Will Mr Merriwether Return from Memphis?,*

The Traveling Companion), ed. Annette J. Saddick, New York, New Directions, 2008

Prose and poetry
Collected Stories, New York, New Directions, 1994
The Roman Spring of Mrs Stone, London, Vintage, 1999
Moise and the World of Reason, New York, Simon and Schuster, 1975
The Collected Poems of Tennessee Williams, ed. David Roessel and
  Nicholas Moschovakis, New York, New Directions, 2002

Memoirs, journals, essays and letters
Memoirs, New York, Doubleday, 1975
Notebooks, ed. Margaret Bradham Thornton, New Haven, Yale
  University Press, 2006
Where I Live: Selected Essays, New York, New Directions, 1978
The Selected Letters of Tennessee Williams, vol. I, 1920–1945, ed.
  Albert J. Devlin and Nancy M. Tischler, London, Oberon Books,
  2001
The Selected Letters of Tennessee Williams, vol. II, 1945–1957, ed.
  Albert J. Devlin and Nancy M. Tischler, New York, New
  Directions, 2004

Full-length studies on Williams
Bigsby, C.W.E., *A Critical Introduction to Twentieth-Century
  American Drama, vol.2*, Cambridge, Cambridge University Press,
  1987. A biographical and critical exploration of Williams's
  development alongside studies of Arthur Miller and Edward Albee.
Boxill, Roger, *Tennessee Williams*, London, Macmillan, 1987. A short
  critical study covering the major plays.
Clum, John M., *Acting Gay: Male Homosexuality in Modern Drama*,
  New York, Columbia University Press, 1992. Contains a significant
  section on how Williams dramatises the closet.
Falk, Signi L., *Tennessee Williams*, New York, Twayne Publishers,
  1962. Divides Williams's characters into recognisable types, such as
  Southern gentlewomen and wenches. Critical of over-dependence on
  sex in the plays' plots.
Kolin, Philip C., *Williams: A Streetcar Named Desire*, Cambridge,
  Cambridge University Press, 2000. One of the Plays in Production
  series; a comprehensive account of productions across the world,
  film/television interpretations, ballet and opera versions.
Kolin, Philip C. (ed.), *The Tennessee Williams Encyclopedia*, Westport,

Greenwood Press, 2004. A useful reference guide containing
contributions from major Williams scholars.

Leverich, Lyle, *Tom: The Unknown Tennessee Williams*, New York,
W.W.Norton, 1995. The best biographical study of Williams's early
life (this goes as far as the reception of *The Glass Menagerie* in 1945).
Sadly, Leverich died before the next volume could be completed.

Paller, Michael, *Gentlemen Callers: Tennessee Williams,
Homosexuality, and Mid-Twentieth-Century Drama*, New York,
Palgrave Macmillan, 2005. A study of Williams's depiction of
homosexuality on the stage, the restrictions on this and the work of
other playwrights exploring gay themes.

Roudané, Matthew C. (ed.), *The Cambridge Companion to Tennessee
Williams*, Cambridge, Cambridge University Press, 2001. A
collection of fourteen essays by eminent scholars.

Savran, David, *Communists, Cowboys, and Queers: The Politics of
Masculinity in the Work of Arthur Miller and Tennessee Williams*,
Minneapolis, University of Minnesota Press, 1992. Both playwrights
are examined against the political background of Cold War America.

Spoto, Donald, *The Kindness of Strangers: The Life of Tennessee
Williams*, Boston, Little, Brown, 1985. The best full-length
biography.

Thompson, Judith J., *Tennessee Williams' Plays: Memory, Myth and
Symbol*, New York, Peter Lang Publishing Inc., 1987. An insight into
Williams's use of well-known myths in the major plays.

Tischler, Nancy M., *Tennessee Williams: Rebellious Puritan*, New York,
Citadel, 1961. A pioneering early study.

Vannatta, Dennis, *Tennessee Williams: A Study of the Short Fiction*,
Boston, Twayne Publishers, 1988. The only full-length publication
on Williams's short stories.

Short studies of *A Streetcar Named Desire*

Bray, Robert, 'A Streetcar Named Desire: The Political and Historical
Subtext', in Philip C. Kolin (ed.), *Confronting Tennessee Williams's* A
Streetcar Named Desire: *Essays in Critical Pluralism*, Westport,
Greenwood Press, 1993, pp. 183–98

Bray, Robert, 'A Streetcar Named *Interior: Panic*', *Tennessee Williams
Annual Review*, 9, (2007), pp. 3–5

Cardullo, Bert, 'Birth and Death in *A Streetcar Named Desire*', in
Philip C. Kolin (ed.), *Confronting Tennessee Williams's* A Streetcar
Named Desire: *Essays in Critical Pluralism*, Westport, Greenwood
Press, 1993, pp. 167–82

Kolin, Philip C., 'Eunice Hubbell and the Feminist Thematics of *A Streetcar Named Desire*', in Philip C. Kolin (ed.), *Confronting Tennessee Williams's* A Streetcar Named Desire: *Essays in Critical Pluralism*, Westport, Greenwood Press, 1993, pp. 105–20

Kolin, Philip C., '"Red Hot!" in *A Streetcar Named Desire*', *Notes on Contemporary Literature*, 19, (Sept. 1989), pp. 6–8

Londré, Felicia Hardison, 'A Streetcar Running Fifty Years', in Matthew C. Roudané (ed.), *The Cambridge Companion to Tennessee Williams*, Cambridge, Cambridge University Press, 2001, pp. 45–66

Quirino, Leonard, 'The Cards Indicate a Voyage on *A Streetcar Named Desire*', in Jac Tharpe (ed.), *Tennessee Williams: A Tribute*, Jackson, University Press of Mississippi, 1977, pp. 77–96

Vlasopolos, Anca, 'Authorizing History: Victimization in *A Streetcar Named Desire*', *Theatre Journal*, 38, (Oct. 1986), pp. 322–38

A STREETCAR NAMED DESIRE

And so it was I entered the broken world
To trace the visionary company of love, its voice
An instant in the wind [I know not whither hurled]
But not for long to hold each desperate choice.

"THE BROKEN TOWER" BY HART CRANE.

THE CHARACTERS

BLANCHE
STELLA
STANLEY
MITCH
EUNICE
STEVE
PABLO
A NEGRO WOMAN
A DOCTOR
A NURSE
A YOUNG COLLECTOR
A MEXICAN WOMAN
A TAMALE VENDOR

THE CAST

The first London production of this play was at the Aldwych Theatre on Wednesday, October 12th, 1949, with the following cast:

BLANCHE DuBOIS	*Vivien Leigh*
STELLA KOWALSKI	*Renee Asherson*
STANLEY KOWALSKI	*Bonar Colleano*
HAROLD MITCHELL [MITCH]	*Bernard Braden*
EUNICE HUBBEL	*Eileen Dale*
STEVE HUBBEL	*Lyn Evans*
PABLO GONZALES	*Theodore Bikel*
NEGRO WOMAN	*Bruce Howard*
A STRANGE MAN [DOCTOR]	*Sidney Monckton*
A STRANGE WOMAN [NURSE]	*Mona Lilian*
A YOUNG COLLECTOR	*John Forrest*
A MEXICAN WOMAN	*Eileen Way*

Directed by LAURENCE OLIVIER
Setting and lighting by JO MIELZINER
Costumes by BEATRICE DAWSON

SCENE I

The exterior of a two-storey corner building on a street in New Orleans which is named Elysian Fields and runs between the L & N tracks and the river. The section is poor but, unlike corresponding sections in other American cities, it has a raffish charm. The houses are mostly white frame, weathered grey, with rickety outside stairs and galleries and quaintly ornamented gables to the entrances of both. It is first dark of an evening early in May. The sky that shows around the dim white building is a peculiarly tender blue, almost turquoise, which invests the scene with a kind of lyricism and gracefully attenuates the atmosphere of decay. You can almost feel the warm breath of the brown river beyond the river warehouses with their faint redolences of bananas and coffee. A corresponding air is evoked by the music of Negro entertainers at a bar-room around the corner. In this part of New Orleans you are practically always just around the corner, or a few doors down the street, from a tinny piano being played with the infatuated fluency of brown fingers. This "Blue Piano" expresses the spirit of the life which goes on here.

> *Two women, one white and one coloured, are taking the air on the steps of the building. The white woman is* EUNICE, *who occupies the upstairs flat; the coloured woman a neighbour, for New Orleans is a cosmopolitan city where there is a relatively warm and easy intermingling of races in the old part of town.*
> *Above the music of the "Blue Piano" the voices of people on the street can be heard overlapping.*

NEGRO WOMAN [*to* EUNICE]: . . . she says St. Barnabas would send out his dog to lick her and when he did she'd feel an icy cold wave all up an' down her. Well, that night when——

A MAN [*to a* SAILOR]: You keep right on going and you'll find it. You'll hear them tapping on the shutters.

SAILOR [*to* NEGRO WOMAN *and* EUNICE]: Where's the Four Deuces?

VENDOR: Red hot! Red hots!

NEGRO WOMAN: Don't waste your money in that clip joint!

SAILOR: I've got a date there.

VENDOR: Re-e-ed h-o-o-t!

NEGRO WOMAN: Don't let them sell you a Blue Moon cocktail or you won't go out on your own feet!

Two men come around the corner, STANLEY KOWALSKI and MITCH. They are about twenty-eight or thirty years old, roughly dressed in blue denim work clothes. STANLEY carries his bowling jacket and a red-stained package from a butcher's.]

STANLEY [*to* MITCH]: Well, what did he say?
MITCH: He said he'd give us even money.
STANLEY: Naw! We gotta have odds!

They stop at the foot of the steps.

STANLEY [*bellowing*]: Hey, there! Stella, Baby!

STELLA comes out on the first-floor landing, a gentle young woman, about twenty-five, and of a background obviously quite different from her husband's.

STELLA [*mildly*]: Don't holler at me like that. Hi, Mitch.
STANLEY: Catch!
STELLA: What?
STANLEY: Meat!

He heaves the package at her. She cries out in protest but manages to catch it: then she laughs breathlessly. Her husband and his companion have already started back around the corner.

STELLA [*calling after him*]: Stanley! Where are you going?
STANLEY: Bowling!
STELLA: Can I come watch?
STANLEY: Come on. [*He goes out.*]
STELLA: Be over soon. [*To the white woman.*] Hello, Eunice. How are you?
EUNICE: I'm all right. Tell Steve to get him a poor boy's sandwich 'cause nothing's left here.

They all laugh; the COLOURED WOMAN does not stop. STELLA goes out.

COLOURED WOMAN: What was that package he th'ew at 'er? [*She rises from steps, laughing louder.*]
EUNICE: You hush, now!
NEGRO WOMAN: Catch *what*!

She continues to laugh. BLANCHE comes around the corner, carrying a valise. She looks at a slip of paper, then at the building, then again at the slip and again at the building. Her expression is one of shocked disbelief. Her appearance is incongruous to this setting. She is daintily dressed in a white suit with a fluffy bodice, necklace and earrings of pearl, white gloves and hat, looking as if she were arriving at a summer tea or cocktail party in the garden district. She is about five years older than STELLA. *Her delicate beauty must avoid a strong light. There is something about her uncertain manner, as well as her white clothes, that suggests a moth.*

EUNICE [*finally*]: What's the matter, honey? Are you lost?

BLANCHE [*with faintly hysterical humour*]: They told me to take a street-car named Desire, and then transfer to one called Cemeteries and ride six blocks and get off at—Elysian Fields!

EUNICE: That's where you are now.

BLANCHE: At Elysian Fields?

EUNICE: This here is Elysian Fields.

BLANCHE: They mustn't have—understood—what number I wanted . . .

EUNICE: What number you lookin' for?

BLANCHE *wearily refers to the slip of paper.*

BLANCHE: Six thirty-two

EUNICE: You don't have to look no further.

BLANCHE [*uncomprehendingly*]: I'm looking for my sister, Stella DuBois. I mean—Mrs. Stanley Kowalski.

EUNICE: That's the party.—You just did miss her, though.

BLANCHE: This—can this be—her home?

EUNICE: She's got the downstairs here and I got the up.

BLANCHE: Oh. She's—out?

EUNICE: You noticed that bowling alley around the corner?

BLANCHE: I'm—not sure I did.

EUNICE: Well, that's where she's at, watchin' her husband bowl. [*There is a pause.*] You want to leave your suitcase here an' go find her?

BLANCHE: No.

NEGRO WOMAN: I'll go tell her you come.

BLANCHE: Thanks.

NEGRO WOMAN: You welcome. [*She goes out.*]

EUNICE: She wasn't expecting you?

BLANCHE: No. No, not tonight.

EUNICE: Well, why don't you just go in and make yourself at home till they get back.

BLANCHE: How could I—do that?
EUNICE: We own this place so I can let you in.

She gets up and opens the downstairs door. A light goes on behind the blind, turning it light blue. BLANCHE slowly follows her into the downstairs flat. The surrounding areas dim out as the interior is lighted. Two rooms can be seen, not too clearly defined. The one first entered is primarily a kitchen but contains a folding bed to be used by BLANCHE. The room beyond this is a bedroom. Off this room is a narrow door to a bathroom.

EUNICE [*defensively, noticing BLANCHE'S look*]: It's sort of messed up right now but when it's clean it's real sweet.
BLANCHE: Is it?
EUNICE: Uh-huh, I think so. So you're Stella's sister?
BLANCHE: Yes. [*Wanting to get rid of her.*] Thanks for letting me in.
EUNICE: *Por nada*, as the Mexicans say, *por nada*! Stella spoke of you.
BLANCHE: Yes?
EUNICE: I think she said you taught school.
BLANCHE: Yes.
EUNICE: And you're from Mississippi, huh?
BLANCHE: Yes.
EUNICE: She showed me a picture of your home-place, the plantation.
BLANCHE: Belle Reve?
EUNICE: A great big place with white columns.
BLANCHE: Yes . . .
EUNICE: A place like that must be awful hard to keep up.
BLANCHE: If you will excuse me, I'm just about to drop.
EUNICE: Sure, honey. Why don't you set down?
BLANCHE: What I meant was I'd like to be left alone.
EUNICE [*offended*]: Aw. I'll make myself scarce, in that case.
BLANCHE: I didn't mean to be rude, but——
EUNICE: I'll drop by the bowling alley an' hustle her up. [*She goes out of the door.*

BLANCHE sits in a chair very stiffly with her shoulders slightly hunched and her legs pressed close together and her hands tightly clutching her purse as if she were quite cold. After a while the blind look goes out of her eyes and she begins to look slowly around. A cat screeches. She catches her breath with a startled gesture. Suddenly she notices something in a half opened closet. She springs up and crosses to it, and removes a whisky bottle. She pours a half tumbler of whisky and tosses it down. She carefully replaces the bottle and washes out the tumbler at the sink. Then she resumes her seat in front of the table.

BLANCHE [*faintly to herself*]: I've got to keep hold of myself!

STELLA comes quickly around the corner of the building and runs to the door of the downstairs flat.

STELLA [*calling out joyfully*]: Blanche!

For a moment they stare at each other. Then BLANCHE springs up and runs to her with a wild cry.

BLANCHE: Stella, oh, Stella, Stella! Stella for Star!

She begins to speak with feverish vivacity as if she feared for either of them to stop and think. They catch each other in a spasmodic embrace.

BLANCHE: Now, then, let me look at you. But don't you look at me, Stella, no, no, no, not till later, not till I've bathed and rested! And turn that over-light off! Turn that off! I won't be looked at in this merciless glare! [STELLA *laughs and complies.*] Come back here now! Oh, my baby! Stella! Stella for Star! [*She embraces her again.*] I thought you would never come back to this horrible place! What am I saying? I didn't mean to say that. I meant to be nice about it and say—Oh, what a convenient location and such—Ha-a-ha! Precious lamb! You haven't said a *word* to me.

STELLA: You haven't given me a chance to, honey! [*She laughs but her glance at BLANCHE is a little anxious.*]

BLANCHE: Well, now you talk. Open your pretty mouth and talk while I look around for some liquor! I know you must have some liquor on the place! Where could it be, I wonder? Oh, I spy, I spy!

She rushes to the closet and removes the bottle; she is shaking all over and panting for breath as she tries to laugh. The bottle nearly slips from her grasp.

STELLA [*noticing*]: Blanche, you sit down and let me pour the drinks. I don't know what we've got to mix with. Maybe a coke's in the icebox. Look'n see, honey, while I'm——

BLANCHE: No coke, honey, not with my nerves tonight! Where—where—where is——?

STELLA: Stanley? Bowling! He loves it. They're having a—found some soda!—tournament . . .

BLANCHE: Just water, baby, to chase it! Now don't get worried, your sister hasn't turned into a drunkard, she's just all shaken up and hot and tired and dirty! You sit down, now, and explain this place to me! What are you doing in a place like this?

STELLA: Now, Blanche——

BLANCHE: Oh, I'm not going to be hypocritical, I'm going to be honestly critical about it! Never, never, never in my worst dreams could I picture—— Only Poe! Only Mr. Edgar Allan Poe!—could do it justice! Out there I suppose is the ghoul-haunted woodland of Weir! [*She laughs.*]

STELLA: No, honey, those are the L & N tracks.

BLANCHE: No, now seriously, putting joking aside. Why didn't you tell me, why didn't you write me, honey, why didn't you let me know?

STELLA [*carefully, pouring herself a drink*]: Tell you what, Blanche?

BLANCHE: Why, that you had to live in these conditions!

STELLA: Aren't you being a little intense about it? It's not that bad at all! New Orleans isn't like other cities.

BLANCHE: This has got nothing to do with New Orleans. You might as well say—forgive me, blessed baby! [*She suddenly stops short.*] The subject is closed!

STELLA [*a little drily*]: Thanks.

During the pause, BLANCHE stares at her. She smiles at BLANCHE.

BLANCHE [*looking down at her glass, which shakes in her hand*]: You're all I've got in the world, and you're not glad to see me!

STELLA [*sincerely*]: Why, Blanche, you know that's not true.

BLANCHE: No?—I'd forgotten how quiet you were.

STELLA: You never did give me a chance to say much, Blanche. So I just got in the habit of being quiet around you.

BLANCHE [*vaguely*]: A good habit to get into . . . [*then abruptly*] You haven't asked me how I happened to get away from the school before the spring term ended.

STELLA: Well, I thought you'd volunteer that information—if you wanted to tell me.

BLANCHE: You thought I'd been fired?

STELLA: No, I—thought you might have—resigned. . . .

BLANCHE: I was so exhausted by all I'd been through my—nerves broke. [*Nervously tamping cigarette.*] I was on the verge of—lunacy, almost! So Mr. Graves—Mr. Graves is the high school superintendent—he suggested I take a leave of absence. I couldn't put all of those details into the wire. . . . [*She drinks quickly.*] Oh, this buzzes right through me and feels so *good*!

STELLA: Won't you have another?

BLANCHE: No, one's my limit.

STELLA: Sure?

BLANCHE: You haven't said a word about my appearance.

STELLA: You look just fine.

BLANCHE: God love you for a liar! Daylight never exposed so total a ruin! But you—you've put on some weight, yes, you're just as plump as a little partridge! And it's so becoming to you!

STELLA: Now, Blanche——

BLANCHE: Yes, it is, it is or I wouldn't say it! You just have to watch around the hips a little. Stand up.

STELLA: Not now.

BLANCHE: You hear me? I said stand up! [STELLA *complies reluctantly.*] You messy child, you, you've spilt something on that pretty white lace collar! About your hair—you ought to have it cut in a feather bob with your dainty features. Stella, you have a maid, don't you?

STELLA: No. With only two rooms it's——

BLANCHE: What? *Two* rooms, did you say?

STELLA: This one and—— [*She is embarrassed.*]

BLANCHE: The other one? [*She laughs sharply. There is an embarrassed silence.*] How quiet you are, you're so peaceful. Look how you sit there with your little hands folded like a cherub in choir!

STELLA [*uncomfortably*]: I never had anything like your energy, Blanche.

BLANCHE: Well, I never had your beautiful self-control. I am going to take just one little tiny nip more, sort of to put the stopper on, so to speak. . . . Then put the bottle away so I won't be tempted. [*She rises.*] I want you to look at *my* figure! [*She turns around.*] You know I haven't put on one ounce in ten years, Stella? I weigh what I weighed the summer you left Belle Reve. The summer Dad died and you left us . . .

STELLA [*a little wearily*]: It's just incredible, Blanche, how well you're looking.

BLANCHE: You see I still have that awful vanity about my looks even now that my looks are slipping! [*She laughs nervously and glances at* STELLA *for reassurance.*]

STELLA [*dutifully*]: They haven't slipped one particle.

BLANCHE: After all I've been through? You think I believe that story? Blessed child! [*She touches her forehead shakily.*] Stella, there's —only two rooms?

STELLA: And a bathroom.

BLANCHE: Oh, you do have a bathroom! First door to the right at the top of the stairs? [*They both laugh uncomfortably.*] But, Stella, I don't see where you're going to put me!

STELLA: We're going to put you in here.

BLANCHE: What kind of bed's this—one of those collapsible things? [*She sits on it.*]

STELLA: Does it feel all right?

BLANCHE [*dubiously*]: Wonderful, honey. I don't like a bed that gives much. But there's no door between the two rooms, and Stanley—will it be decent?

STELLA: Stanley is Polish, you know.

BLANCHE: Oh, yes. They're something like Irish, aren't they?

STELLA: Well——

BLANCHE: Only not so—highbrow? [*They both laugh again in the same way.*] I brought some nice clothes to meet all your lovely friends in.

STELLA: I'm afraid you won't think they are lovely.

BLANCHE: What are they like?

STELLA: They're Stanley's friends.

BLANCHE: Polacks?

STELLA: They're a mixed lot, Blanche.

BLANCHE: Heterogeneous—types?

STELLA: Oh, yes. Yes, types is right!

BLANCHE: Well—anyhow—I brought nice clothes and I'll wear them. I guess you're hoping I'll say I'll put up at a hotel, but I'm not going to put up at a hotel. I want to be *near* you, got to be *with* somebody, I *can't* be *alone*! Because—as you must have noticed— I'm—*not* very *well*. . . . [*Her voice drops and her look is frightened.*]

STELLA: You seem a little bit nervous or overwrought or something.

BLANCHE: Will Stanley like me, or will I be just a visiting in-law, Stella? I couldn't stand that.

STELLA: You'll get along fine together, if you'll just try not to— well—compare him with men that we went out with at home.

BLANCHE: Is he so—different?

STELLA: Yes. A different species.

BLANCHE: In what way; what's he like?

STELLA: Oh, you can't describe someone you're in love with! Here's a picture of him! [*She hands a photograph to* BLANCHE.]

BLANCHE: An officer?

STELLA: A Master Sergeant in the Engineers' Corps. Those are decorations!

BLANCHE: He had those on when you met him?

STELLA: I assure you I wasn't just blinded by all the brass.

BLANCHE: That's not what I——

STELLA: But of course there were things to adjust myself to later on.

BLANCHE: Such as his civilian background! [STELLA *laughs uncertainly.*] How did he take it when you said I was coming?

STELLA: Oh, Stanley doesn't know yet.

BLANCHE [*frightened*]: You—haven't told him?

STELLA: He's on the road a good deal.

BLANCHE: Oh. Travels?

STELLA: Yes.

BLANCHE: Good. I mean—isn't it?

STELLA [*half to herself*]: I can hardly stand it when he is away for a night. . . .

BLANCHE: Why, Stella?

STELLA: When he's away for a week I nearly go wild!

BLANCE: Gracious!

STELLA: And when he comes back I cry on his lap like a baby. . . . [*She smiles to herself.*]

BLANCHE: I guess that is what is meant by being in love. . . . [STELLA *looks up with a radiant smile.*] Stella——

STELLA: What?

BLANCHE [*in an uneasy rush*]: I haven't asked you the things you probably thought I was going to ask. And so I'll expect you to be understanding about what *I* have to tell *you*.

STELLA: What, Blanche? [*Her face turns anxious.*]

BLANCHE: Well, Stella—you're going to reproach me, I know that you're bound to reproach me—but before you do—take into consideration—you left! I stayed and struggled! You came to New Orleans and looked out for yourself! *I* stayed at *Belle Reve* and tried to hold it together! I'm not meaning this in any reproachful way, but *all* the burden descended on *my* shoulders.

STELLA: The best I could do was make my own living, Blanche.

BLANCHE *begins to shake again with intensity.*

BLANCHE: I know, I know. But you are the one that abandoned Belle Reve, not I! I stayed and fought for it, bled for it, almost died for it!

STELLA: Stop this hysterical outburst and tell me what's happened?
What do you mean fought and bled? What kind of——
BLANCHE: I knew you would, Stella. I knew you would take this
attitude about it!
STELLA: About—what?—please!
BLANCHE [*slowly*]: The loss—the loss . . .
STELLA: Belle Reve? Lost, is it? No!
BLANCHE: Yes, Stella.

> *They stare at each other across the yellow-checked linoleum of the
> table.* BLANCHE *slowly nods her head and* STELLA *looks slowly down
> at her hands folded on the table. The music of the "blue piano" grows
> louder.* BLANCHE *touches her handkerchief to her forehead.*

STELLA: But how did it go? What happened?
BLANCHE [*springing up*]: You're a fine one to ask me how it went!
STELLA: Blanche!
BLANCHE: You're a fine one to sit there *accusing me* of it!
STELLA: *Blanche!*
BLANCHE: I, I, *I* took the blows in my face and my body! All of
those deaths! The long parade to the graveyard! Father, mother!
Margaret, that dreadful way! So big with it, it couldn't be put in
a coffin! But had to be burned like rubbish! You just came home
in time for the funerals, Stella. And funerals are pretty compared
to deaths. Funerals are quiet, but deaths—not always. Sometimes
their breathing is hoarse, and sometimes it rattles, and sometimes
they even cry out to you, "Don't let me go!" Even the old, sometimes, say, "Don't let me go." As if you were able to stop them!
But funerals are quiet, with pretty flowers. And, oh, what gorgeous
boxes they pack them away in! Unless you were there at the bed
when they cried out, "Hold me!" you'd never suspect there was
the struggle for breath and bleeding. You didn't dream, but I
saw! Saw! Saw! And now you sit there telling me with your eyes
that I let the place go! How in hell do you think all that sickness
and dying was paid for? Death is expensive, Miss Stella! And old
Cousin Jessie's right after Margaret's, hers! Why, the Grim Reaper
had put up his tent on our doorstep! . . . Stella. Belle Reve was his
headquarters! Honey—that's how it slipped through my fingers!
Which of them left us a fortune? Which of them left a cent of
insurance even? Only poor Jessie—one hundred to pay for her coffin.
That was all, Stella! And I with my pitiful salary at the school. Yes,
accuse me! Sit there and stare at me, thinking I let the place go!

I let the place go? Where were *you*. In bed with your—Polack!

STELLA [*springing*]: Blanche! You be still! That's enough! [*She starts out.*]

BLANCHE: Where are you going?

STELLA: I'm going into the bathroom to wash my face.

BLANCHE: Oh, Stella, Stella, you're crying!

STELLA: Does that surprise you?

> STELLA *goes into the bathroom.*
> *Outside is the sound of men's voices.* STANLEY, STEVE *and* MITCH *cross to the foot of the steps.*

STEVE: And the old lady is on her way to Mass and she's late and there's a cop standin' in front of th' church an' she comes runnin' up an' says, "Officer—is Mass out yet?" He looks her over and says, "No, Lady, but y'r hat's on crooked!" [*They give a hoarse bellow of laughter.*]

STEVE: Playing poker tomorrow night?

STANLEY: Yeah—at Mitch's.

MITCH: Not at my place. My mother's still sick. [*He starts off.*]

STANLEY [*calling after him*]: All right, we'll play at my place . . . but you bring the beer.

EUNICE [*hollering down from above*]: Break it up down there! I made the spaghetti dish and ate it myself.

STEVE [*going upstairs*]: I told you and phoned you we was playing. [*To the men*] Jax beer!

EUNICE: You never phoned me once.

STEVE: I told you at breakfast—and phoned you at lunch . . .

EUNICE: Well, never mind about that. You just get yourself home here once in a while.

STEVE: You want it in the papers?

> *More laughter and shouts of parting come from the men.* STANLEY *throws the screen door of the kitchen open and comes in. He is of medium height, about five feet eight or nine, and strongly, compactly built. Animal joy in his being is implicit in all his movements and attitudes. Since earliest manhood the centre of his life has been pleasure with women, the giving and taking of it, not with weak indulgence, dependently, but with the power and pride of a richly feathered male bird among hens. Branching out from this complete and satisfying centre are all the auxiliary channels of his life, such as his heartiness with men, his appreciation of rough humour, his love of good drink and food and*

games, his car, his radio, everything that is his, that bears his emblem of the gaudy seed-bearer. He sizes women up at a glance, with sexual classifications, crude images flashing into his mind and determining the way he smiles at them.

BLANCHE [*drawing involuntarily back from his stare*]: You must be Stanley. I'm Blanche.

STANLEY: Stella's sister?

BLANCHE: Yes.

STANLEY: H'lo. Where's the little woman?

BLANCHE: In the bathroom.

STANLEY: Oh. Didn't know you were coming in town.

BLANCHE: I—uh——

STANLEY: Where you from, Blanche?

BLANCHE: Why, I—live in Laurel.

He has crossed to the closet and removed the whisky bottle.

STANLEY: In Laurel, huh? Oh, yeah. Yeah, in Laurel, that's right. Not in my territory. Liquor goes fast in hot weather. [*He holds the bottle to the light to observe its depletion.*] Have a shot?

BLANCHE: No, I—rarely touch it.

STANLEY: Some people rarely touch it, but it touches them often.

BLANCHE [*faintly*]: Ha-ha.

STANLEY: My clothes're stickin' to me. Do you mind if I make myself comfortable? [*He starts to remove his shirt.*]

BLANCHE: Please, please do.

STANLEY: Be comfortable is my motto.

BLANCHE: It's mine, too. It's hard to stay looking fresh. I haven't washed or even powdered my face and—here you are!

STANLEY: You know you can catch cold sitting around in damp things, especially when you been exercising hard like bowling is. You're a teacher, aren't you?

BLANCHE: Yes.

STANLEY: What do you teach, Blanche?

BLANCHE: English.

STANLEY: I never was a very good English student. How long you here for, Blanche?

BLANCHE: I—don't know yet.

STANLEY: You going to shack up here?

BLANCHE: I thought I would if it's not inconvenient for you all.

STANLEY: Good.

BLANCHE: Travelling wears me out.

STANLEY: Well, take it easy.

A cat screeches near the window. BLANCHE *springs up.*

BLANCHE: What's that?

STANLEY: Cats. . . . Hey, Stella!

STELLA [*faintly, from the bathroom*]: Yes, Stanley.

STANLEY: Haven't fallen in, have you? [*He grins at* BLANCHE. *She tries unsuccessfully to smile back. There is a silence.*] I'm afraid I'll strike you as being the unrefined type. Stella's spoke of you a good deal. You were married once, weren't you?

The music of the polka rises up, faint in the distance.

BLANCHE: Yes. When I was quite young.

STANLEY: What happened?

BLANCHE: The boy—the boy died. [*She sinks back down.*] I'm afraid I'm—going to be sick!

Her head falls on her arms.

SCENE II

It is six o'clock the following evening. BLANCHE *is bathing.* STELLA *is completing her toilette.* BLANCHE'S *dress, a flowered print, is laid out on* STELLA'S *bed.*

> STANLEY *enters the kitchen from outside, leaving the door open on the perpetual "blue piano" around the corner.*

STANLEY: What's all this monkey doings?

STELLA: Oh, Stan! [*She jumps up and kisses him which he accepts with lordly composure.*] I'm taking Blanche to Galatoires' for supper and then to a show, because it's your poker night.

STANLEY: How about my supper, huh? I'm not going to no Galatoire's for supper!

STELLA: I put you a cold plate on ice.

STANLEY: Well, isn't that just dandy!

STELLA: I'm going to try to keep Blanche out till the party breaks up because I don't know how she would take it. So we'll go to one of the little places in the Quarter afterwards and you'd better give me some money.

STANLEY: Where is she?

STELLA: She's soaking in a hot tub to quiet her nerves. She's terribly upset.

STANLEY: Over what?

STELLA: She's been through such an ordeal.

STANLEY: Yeah?

STELLA: Stan, we've—lost Belle Reve!

STANLEY: The place in the country?

STELLA: Yes.

STANLEY: How?

STELLA [*vaguely*]: Oh, it had to be—sacrificed or something. [*There is a pause while* STANLEY *considers.* STELLA *is changing into her dress.*] When she comes in be sure to say something nice about her appearance. And, oh! Don't mention the baby. I haven't said anything yet, I'm waiting until she gets in a quieter condition.

STANLEY [*ominously*]: So?

STELLA: And try to understand her and be nice to her, Stan.

BLANCHE [*singing in the bathroom*]:
"From the land of the sky blue water,
They brought a captive maid!"

STELLA: She wasn't expecting to find us in such a small place. You see I'd tried to gloss things over a little in my letters.

STANLEY: So?

STELLA: And admire her dress and tell her she's looking wonderful. That's important with Blanche. Her little weakness!

STANLEY: Yeah. I get the idea. Now let's skip back a little to where you said the country place was disposed of.

STELLA: Oh!—yes . . .

STANLEY: How about that? Let's have a few more details on that subject.

STELLA: It's best not to talk much about it until she's calmed down.

STANLEY: So that's the deal, huh? Sister Blanche cannot be annoyed with business details right now!

STELLA: You saw how she was last night.

STANLEY: Uh-hum, I saw how she was. Now let's have a gander at the bill of sale.

STELLA: I haven't seen any.

STANLEY: She didn't show you no papers, no deed of sale or nothing like that, huh?

STELLA: It seems like it wasn't sold.

STANLEY: Well, what in hell was it then, give away? To charity?

STELLA: Shhh! She'll hear you.

STANLEY: I don't care if she hears me. Let's see the papers!

STELLA: There weren't any papers, she didn't show any papers, I don't care about papers.

STANLEY: Have you ever heard of the Napoleonic code?

STELLA: No, Stanley, I haven't heard of the Napoleonic code and if I have, I don't see what it——

STANLEY: Let me enlighten you on a point or two, baby.

STELLA: Yes?

STANLEY: In the state of Louisiana we have the Napoleonic code according to which what belongs to the wife belongs to the husband and vice versa. For instance if I had a piece of property, or you had a piece of property——

STELLA: My head is swimming!

STANLEY: All right. I'll wait till she gets through soaking in a hot tub and then I'll inquire if *she* is acquainted with the Napoleonic code. It looks to me like you have been swindled, baby, and when you're swindled under the Napoleonic code I'm swindled *too*. And I don't like to be *swindled*.

STELLA: There's plenty of time to ask her questions later but if you do now she'll go to pieces again. I don't understand what happened to Belle Reve but you don't know how ridiculous you are being when you suggest that my sister or I or anyone of our family could have perpetrated a swindle on anyone else.

STANLEY: Then where's the money if the place was sold?

STELLA: Not sold—*lost, lost*!

He stalks into bedroom, and she follows him.

Stanley!

He pulls open the wardrobe trunk standing in middle of room and jerks out an armful of dresses.

STANLEY: Open your eyes to this stuff! You think she got them out of a teacher's pay?

STELLA: Hush!

STANLEY: Look at these feathers and furs that she come here to preen herself in! What's this here? A solid-gold dress, I believe! And this one! What is these here? Fox-pieces! [*He blows on them.*] Genuine fox fur-pieces, a half a mile long! Where are your fox-pieces, Stella? Bushy snow-white ones, no less! Where are your white fox-pieces.

STELLA: Those are inexpensive summer furs that Blanche has had a long time.

STANLEY: I got an acquaintance who deals in this sort of merchandise. I'll have him in here to appraise it. I'm willing to bet you there's thousands of dollars invested in this stuff here!

STELLA: Don't be such an idiot, Stanley!

He hurls the furs to the daybed. Then he jerks open small drawer in the trunk and pulls up a fist-full of costume jewellery.

STANLEY: And what have we here? The treasure chest of a pirate!

STELLA: Oh, Stanley!

STANLEY: Pearls! Ropes of them! What is this sister of yours, a deep-sea diver who brings up sunken treasures? Or is she the champion safe-cracker of all time! Bracelets of solid gold, too! Where are your pearls and gold bracelets?

STELLA: Shhh! Be still, Stanley!

STANLEY: And diamonds! A crown for an empress!

STELLA: A rhinestone tiara she wore to a costume ball.

STANLEY: What's rhinestone?

STELLA: Next door to glass.

STANLEY: Are you kidding? I have an acquaintance that works in a jewellery store. I'll have him in here to make an appraisal of this. Here's your plantation, or what was left of it, here!

STELLA: You have no idea how stupid and horrid you're being! Now close that trunk before she comes out of the bathroom!

He kicks the trunk partly closed and sits on the kitchen table.

STANLEY: The Kowalskis and the DuBois have different notions.

STELLA [*angrily*]: Indeed they have, thank heavens!—*I'm* going outside. [*She snatches up her white hat and gloves and crosses to the outside door.*] You come out with me while Blanche is getting dressed.

STANLEY: Since when do you give me orders?

STELLA: Are you going to stay here and insult her?

STANLEY: You're damn tootin' I'm going to stay here.

STELLA *goes out on the porch.* BLANCHE *comes out of the bathroom in a red satin robe.*

BLANCHE [*airily*]: Hello, Stanley! Here I am, all freshly bathed and scented, and feeling like a brand new human being!

He lights a cigarette.

STANLEY: That's good.

BLANCHE [*drawing the curtains at the windows*]: Excuse me while I slip on my pretty new dress!!

STANLEY: Go right ahead, Blanche.

She closes the drapes between the rooms.

BLANCHE: I understand there's to be a little card party to which we ladies are cordially *not* invited.

STANLEY [*ominously*]: Yeah?

BLANCHE *throws off her robe and slips into a flowered print dress.*

BLANCHE: Where's Stella?

STANLEY: Out on the porch.

BLANCHE: I'm going to ask a favour of you in a moment.

STANLEY: What could that be, I wonder?

BLANCHE: Some buttons in back! You may enter!

He crosses through drapes with a smouldering look.

How do I look?

STANLEY: You look all right.

BLANCHE: Many thanks! Now the buttons!

STANLEY: I can't do nothing with them.

BLANCHE: You men with your big clumsy fingers. May I have a drag on your cig?

STANLEY: Have one for yourself.

BLANCHE: Why, thanks! . . . It looks like my trunk has exploded.

STANLEY: Me an' Stella were helping you unpack.

BLANCHE: Well, you certainly did a fast and thorough job of it!

STANLEY: It looks like you raided some stylish shops in Paris.

BLANCHE: Ha-ha! Yes—clothes are my passion!

STANLEY: What does it cost for a string of fur-pieces like that?

BLANCHE: Why, those were a tribute from an admirer of mine!

STANLEY: He must have had a lot of—admiration!

BLANCHE: Oh, in my youth I excited some admiration. But look at me now! [*She smiles at him radiantly.*] Would you think it possible that I was once considered to be—attractive?

STANLEY: Your looks are okay.

BLANCHE: I was fishing for a compliment, Stanley.

STANLEY: I don't go in for that stuff.

BLANCHE: What—stuff?

STANLEY: Compliments to women about their looks. I never met a woman that didn't know if she was good-looking or not without being told, and some of them give themselves credit for more than they've got. I once went out with a doll who said to me, "I am the glamorous type, I am the glamorous type!" I said, "So what?"

BLANCHE: And what did she say then?

STANLEY: She didn't say nothing. That shut her up like a clam.

BLANCHE: Did it end the romance?

STANLEY: It ended the conversation—that was all. Some men are took in by this Hollywood glamour stuff and some men are not.

BLANCHE: I'm sure you belong in the second category.

STANLEY: That's right.

BLANCHE: I cannot imagine any witch of a woman casting a spell over you.

STANLEY: That's—right.

BLANCHE: You're simple, straightforward and honest, a little bit on the primitive side I should think. To interest you a woman would have to—— [She pauses with an indefinite gesture.]

STANLEY [slowly]: Lay . . . her cards on the table.

BLANCHE [smiling]: Yes—yes—cards on the table. . . . Well, life is too full of evasions and ambiguities, I think. I like an artist who paints in strong, bold colours, primary colours. I don't like pinks and creams and I never cared for wishy-washy people. That was why, when you walked in here last night, I said to myself—"My sister has married a man!"—Of course that was all that I could tell about you.

STANLEY [booming]: Now let's cut the re-bop!

BLANCHE [pressing hands to her ears]: Ouuuuu!

STELLA [calling from the steps]: Stanley! You come out here and let Blanche finish dressing!

BLANCHE: I'm through dressing, honey.

STELLA: Well, you come out, then.

STANLEY: Your sister and I are having a little talk.

BLANCHE [lightly]: Honey, do me a favour. Run to the drug-store and get me a lemon-coke with plenty of chipped ice in it!—Will you do that for me, Sweetie?

STELLA [uncertainly]: Yes. [She goes around the corner of the building.]

BLANCHE: The poor thing was out there listening to us, and I have an idea she doesn't understand you as well as I do. . . . All right; now, Mr. Kowalski, let us proceed without any more double-talk. I'm ready to answer all questions. I've nothing to hide. What is it?

STANLEY: There is such a thing in this State of Louisiana as the Napoleonic code, according to which whatever belongs to my wife is also mine—and vice versa.

BLANCHE: My, but you have an impressive judicial air!

She sprays herself with her atomizer; then playfully sprays him with it. He seizes the atomizer and slams it down on the dresser. She throws back her head and laughs.

STANLEY: If I didn't know that you was my wife's sister I'd get ideas about you!

BLANCHE: Such as what?

STANLEY: Don't play so dumb. You know what!—Where's the papers?

BLANCHE: Papers?

STANLEY: Papers! That stuff people write on!

BLANCHE: Oh, papers, papers! Ha-ha! The first anniversary gift, all kinds of papers!

STANLEY: I'm talking of legal papers. Connected with the plantation.

BLANCHE: There *were* some papers.

STANLEY: You mean they're no longer existing?

BLANCHE: They probably are, somewhere.

STANLEY: But not in the trunk.

BLANCHE: Everything that I own is in that trunk.

STANLEY: Then why don't we have a look for them? [*He crosses to the trunk, shoves it roughly open and begins to open compartments.*]

BLANCHE: What in the name of heaven are you thinking of! What's in the back of that little boy's mind of yours? That I am absconding with something, attempting some kind of treachery on my sister? —Let me do that! It will be faster and simpler. . . . [*She crosses to the trunk and takes out a box.*] I keep my papers mostly in this tin box. [*She opens it.*]

STANLEY: What's them underneath? [*He indicates another sheaf of paper.*]

BLANCHE: These are love-letters, yellowing with antiquity, all from one boy. [*He snatches them up. She speaks fiercely.*] Give those back to me!

STANLEY: I'll have a look at them first!

BLANCHE: The touch of your hands insults them!

STANLEY: Don't pull that stuff!

He rips off the ribbon and starts to examine them. BLANCHE snatches them from him, and they cascade to the floor.

BLANCHE: Now that you've touched them I'll burn them!

STANLEY [*staring, baffled*]: What in hell are they?

BLANCHE [*on the floor gathering them up*]: Poems a dead boy wrote. I hurt him the way that you would like to hurt me, but you can't! I'm not young and vulnerable any more. But my young husband was and I—never mind about that! Just give them back to me!

STANLEY: What do you mean by saying you'll have to burn them?

BLANCHE: I'm sorry, I must have lost my head for a moment. Everyone has something he won't let others touch because of their —intimate nature. . . .

She now seems faint with exhaustion and she sits down with the strong box and puts on a pair of glasses and goes methodically through a large stack of papers.

Ambler & Ambler. Hmmmmm. . . . Crabtree. . . . More Ambler & Ambler.

STANLEY: What is Ambler & Ambler?

BLANCHE: A firm that made loans on the place.

STANLEY: Then it *was* lost on a mortgage?

BLANCHE [*touching her forehead*]: That must've been what happened.

STANLEY: I don't want no ifs, ands or buts! What's all the rest of them papers?

She hands him the entire box. He carries it to the table and starts to examine the papers.

BLANCHE [*picking up a large envelope containing more papers*]: There are thousands of papers, stretching back over hundreds of years, affecting Belle Reve as, piece by piece, our improvident grand-fathers and father and uncles and brothers exchanged the land for their epic fornications—to put it plainly! [*She removes her glasses with an exhausted laugh.*] Till finally all that was left—and Stella can verify that!—was the house itself and about twenty acres of ground, including a graveyard, to which now all but Stella and I have retreated. [*She pours the contents of the envelope on the table.*] Here all of them are, all papers! I hereby endow you with them! Take them, peruse them—commit them to memory, even! I think it's wonderfully fitting that Belle Reve should finally be this bunch of old papers in your big, capable hands! . . . I wonder if Stella's come back with my lemon-coke. . . .

She leans back and closes her eyes.

STANLEY: I have a lawyer acquaintance who will study these out.

BLANCHE: Present them to him with a box of aspirin tablets.

STANLEY [*becoming somewhat sheepish*]: You see, under the Napoleonic code—a man has to take an interest in his wife's affairs—especially now that she's going to have a baby.

BLANCHE *opens her eyes. The "blue piano" sounds louder.*

BLANCHE: Stella? Stella going to have a baby? [*Dreamily.*] I didn't know she was going to have a baby!

She gets up and crosses to the outside door. Stella appears around the corner with a carton from the drug-store.
Stanley goes into the bedroom with the envelope and the box. The inner rooms fade to darkness and the outside wall of the house is visible.
BLANCHE *meets* STELLA *at the foot of the steps to the sidewalk.*

BLANCHE: Stella, Stella for Star! How lovely to have a baby! [*She embraces her sister.* STELLA *returns the embrace with a convulsive sob.* BLANCHE *speaks softly.*] Everything is all right; we thrashed it out. I feel a bit shaky, but I think I handled it nicely. I laughed and treated it all as a joke, called him a little boy and laughed—and flirted! Yes—I was flirting with your husband, Stella!

STEVE *and* PABLO *appear carrying a case of beer.*

The guests are gathering for the poker party.

The two men pass between them, and with a short, curious stare at BLANCHE, *they enter the house.*

STELLA: I'm sorry he did that to you.

BLANCHE: He's just not the sort that goes for jasmine perfume! But maybe he's what we need to mix with our blood now that we've lost Belle Reve and have to go on without Belle Reve to protect us. . . . How pretty the sky is! I ought to go there on a rocket that never comes down.

A TAMALE VENDOR *calls out as he rounds the corner.*

VENDOR: Red hots! Red hots!

BLANCHE *utters a sharp, frightened cry and shrinks away; then she laughs breathlessly again.*

BLANCHE: Which way do we—go now—Stella?

VENDOR: Re-e-d ho-o-ot!

BLANCHE: The blind are—leading the blind!

> *They disappear around the corner, BLANCHE'S desperate laughter*
> *ringing out once more.*
> *Then there is a bellowing laugh from the interior of the flat.*
> *Then the "blue piano" and the hot trumpet sound louder.*

SCENE III

The Poker Night.
There is a picture of Van Gogh's of a billiard-parlour at night. The kitchen
now suggests that sort of lurid nocturnal brilliance, the raw colours of child-
hood's spectrum. Over the yellow linoleum of the kitchen table hangs an
electric bulb with a vivid green glass shade. The poker players—STANLEY,
STEVE, MITCH and PABLO—wear coloured shirts, solid blues, a purple,
a red-and-white check, a light green, and they are men at the peak of their
physical manhood, as coarse and direct and powerful as the primary colours.
There are vivid slices of watermelon on the table, whisky bottles and glasses.
The bedroom is relatively dim with only the light that spills between the
portières and through the wide window on the street.

> *For a moment there is absorbed silence as a hand is dealt.*

STEVE: Anything wild this deal?
PABLO: One-eyed jacks are wild.
STEVE: Give me two cards.
PABLO: You, Mitch?
MITCH: I'm out.
PABLO: One.
MITCH: Anyone want a shot?
STANLEY: Yeah. Me.
PABLO: Why don't somebody go to the Chinaman's and bring
    back a load of chop suey?
STANLEY: When I'm losing you want to eat! Ante up! Openers?
    Openers! Get off the table, Mitch. Nothing belongs on a poker
    table but cards, chips and whisky.

> *He lurches up and tosses some watermelon rinds to the floor.*

MITCH: Kind of on your high horse, ain't you?

STANLEY: How many?

STEVE: Give me three.

STANLEY: One.

MITCH: I'm out again. I oughta go home pretty soon.

STANLEY: Shut up.

MITCH: I gotta sick mother. She don't go to sleep until I come in at night.

STANLEY: Then why don't you stay home with her?

MITCH: She says to go out, so I go, but I don't enjoy it. All the while I keep wondering how she is.

STANLEY: Aw, for God's sake, go home, then!

PABLO: What've you got?

STEVE: Spade flush.

MITCH: You all are married. But I'll be alone when she goes.— I'm going to the bathroom.

STANLEY: Hurry back and we'll fix you a sugar-tit.

MITCH: Aw, lay off. [*He crosses through the bedroom into the bathroom.*]

STEVE [*dealing a hand*]: Seven card stud. [*Telling his joke as he deals.*] This ole nigger is out in back of his house sittin' down th'owing corn to the chickens when all at once he hears a loud cackle and this young hen comes lickety split around the side of the house with the rooster right behind her and gaining on her fast.

STANLEY [*impatient with the story*]: Deal!

STEVE: But when the rooster catches sight of the nigger th'owing the corn he puts on the brakes and lets the hen get away and starts pecking corn. And the old nigger says, "Lord God, I hopes I never gits *that* hongry!"

> STEVE *and* PABLO *laugh. The sisters appear around the corner of the building.*

STELLA: The game is still going on.

BLANCHE: How do I look?

STELLA: Lovely, Blanche.

BLANCHE: I feel so hot and frazzled. Wait till I powder before you open the door. Do I look done in?

STELLA: Why no. You are as fresh as a daisy.

BLANCHE: One that's been picked a few days.

> STELLA *opens the door and they enter.*

STELLA: Well, well, well. I see you boys are still at it!

STANLEY: Where you been?

STELLA: Blanche and I took in a show. Blanche, this is Mr. Gonzales and Mr. Hubbel.

BLANCHE: Please don't get up.

STANLEY: Nobody's going to get up, so don't be worried.

STELLA: How much longer is this game going to continue?

STANLEY: Till we get ready to quit.

BLANCHE: Poker is so fascinating. Could I kibitz?

STANLEY: You could not. Why don't you women go up and sit with Eunice?

STELLA: Because it is nearly two-thirty. [BLANCHE *crosses into the bedroom and partially closes the portières.*] Couldn't you call it quits after one more hand?

A chair scrapes. STANLEY *gives a loud whack of his hand on her thigh.*

STELLA [*sharply*]: That's not fun, Stanley.

The men laugh. STELLA *goes into the bedroom.*

STELLA: It makes me so mad when he does that in front of people.

BLANCHE: I think I will bathe.

STELLA: Again?

BLANCHE: My nerves are in knots. Is the bathroom occupied?

STELLA: I don't know.

BLANCHE *knocks.* MITCH *opens the door and comes out, still wiping his hands on a towel.*

BLANCHE: Oh!—good evening.

MITCH: Hello. [*He stares at her.*]

STELLA: Blanche, this is Harold Mitchell. My sister, Blanche DuBois.

MITCH [*with awkward courtesy*]: How do you do, Miss DuBois.

STELLA: How is your mother now, Mitch?

MITCH: About the same, thanks. She appreciated your sending over that custard.—Excuse me, please.

He crosses slowly back into the kitchen, glancing back at BLANCHE *and coughing a little shyly. He realizes he still has the towel in his hands and with an embarrassed laugh hands it to* STELLA. BLANCHE *looks after him with a certain interest.*

BLANCHE: That one seems—superior to the others.

STELLA: Yes, he is.

BLANCHE: I thought he had a sort of sensitive look.

STELLA: His mother is sick.

BLANCHE: Is he married?

STELLA: No.

BLANCHE: Is he a wolf?

STELLA: Why, Blanche! [BLANCHE *laughs.*] I don't think he would be.

BLANCHE: What does—what does he do?

She is unbuttoning her blouse.

STELLA: He's on the precision bench in the spare parts department. At the plant Stanley travels for.

BLANCHE: Is that something much?

STELLA: No. Stanley's the only one of his crowd that's likely to get anywhere.

BLANCHE: What makes you think Stanley will?

STELLA: Look at him.

BLANCHE: I've looked at him.

STELLA: Then you should know.

BLANCHE: I'm sorry, but I haven't noticed the stamp of genius even on Stanley's forehead.

She takes off the blouse and stands in her pink silk brassière and white skirt in the light through the portières. The game has continued in undertones.

STELLA: It isn't on his forehead and it isn't genius.

BLANCHE: Oh. Well, what is it, and where? I would like to know.

STELLA: It's a drive that he has. You're standing in the light, Blanche!

BLANCHE: Oh, am I!

She moves out of the yellow streak of light. STELLA has removed her dress and put on a light blue satin kimono.

STELLA [*with girlish laughter*]: You ought to see their wives.

BLANCHE [*laughingly*]: I can imagine. Big, beefy things, I suppose.

STELLA: You know that one upstairs? [*More laughter.*] One time [*laughing*] the plaster—[*laughing*] cracked——

STANLEY: You hens cut out that conversation in there!

STELLA: You can't hear us.

STANLEY: Well, you can hear me and I said to hush up!

STELLA: This is my house and I'll talk as much as I want to!

BLANCHE: Stella, don't start a row.

STELLA: He's half drunk!—I'll be out in a minute

She goes into the bathroom. BLANCHE *rises and crosses leisurely to a small white radio and turns it on.*

STANLEY: Awright, Mitch, you in?
MITCH: What? Oh!—No, I'm out!

BLANCHE *moves back into the streak of light. She raises her arms and stretches, as she moves indolently back to the chair.*
Rhumba music comes over the radio. MITCH *rises at the table.*

STANLEY: Who turned that on in there?
BLANCHE: I did. Do you mind?
STANLEY: Turn it off!
STEVE: Aw, let the girls have their music.
PABLO: Sure, that's good, leave it on!
STEVE: Sounds like Xavier Cugat!

STANLEY *jumps up and, crossing to the radio, turns it off. He stops short at sight of* BLANCHE *in the chair. She returns his look without flinching. Then he sits again at the poker table.*
Two of the men have started arguing hotly.

STEVE: I didn't hear you name it.
PABLO: Didn't I name it, Mitch?
MITCH: I wasn't listenin'.
PABLO: What were you doing, then?
STANLEY: He was looking through them drapes. [*He jumps up and jerks roughly at curtains to close them.*] Now deal the hand over again and let's play cards or quit. Some people get ants when they win.

MITCH *rises as* STANLEY *returns to his seat.*

STANLEY [*yelling*]: Sit down!
MITCH: I'm going to the "head". Deal me out.
PABLO: Sure he's got ants now. Seven five-dollar bills in his pants pocket folded up tight as spitballs.
STEVE: Tomorrow you'll see him at the cashier's window getting them changed into quarters.
STANLEY: And when he goes home he'll deposit them one by one in a piggy bank his mother give him for Christmas [*Dealing.*] This game is Spit in the Ocean.

MITCH *laughs uncomfortably and continues through the portières. He stops just inside.*

BLANCHE [*softly*]: Hello! The Little Boys' Room is busy right now.

MITCH: We've—been drinking beer.

BLANCHE: I hate beer.

MITCH: It's—a hot weather drink.

BLANCHE: Oh, I don't think so; it always makes me warmer. Have you got any cigs? [*She has slipped on the dark red satin wrapper.*]

MITCH: Sure.

BLANCHE: What kind are they?

MITCH: Luckies.

BLANCHE: Oh, good. What a pretty case. Silver?

MITCH: Yes. Yes; read the inscription.

BLANCHE: Oh, is there an inscription? I can't make it out. [*He strikes a match and moves closer.*] Oh! [*reading with feigned difficulty*]
> "And if God choose,
> I shall but love thee better—after—death!"

Why, that's from my favourite sonnet by Mrs. Browning!

MITCH: You know it?

BLANCHE: Certainly I do!

MITCH: There's a story connected with that inscription.

BLANCHE: It sounds like a romance.

MITCH: A pretty sad one.

BLANCHE: Oh?

MITCH: The girl's dead now.

BLANCHE [*in a tone of deep sympathy*]: *Oh!*

MITCH: She knew she was dying when she give me this. A very strange girl, very sweet—very!

BLANCHE: She must have been fond of you. Sick people have such deep, sincere attachments.

MITCH: That's right, they certainly do.

BLANCHE: Sorrow makes for sincerity, I think.

MITCH: It sure brings it out in people.

BLANCHE: The little there is belongs to people who have experienced some sorrow.

MITCH: I believe you are right about that.

BLANCHE: I'm positive that I am. Show me a person who hasn't known any sorrow and I'll show you a shuperficial—— Listen to me! My tongue is a little—thick! You boys are responsible for it. The show let out at eleven and we couldn't come home on account of the poker game so we had to go somewhere and drink. I'm not accustomed to having more than one drink. Two is the limit—and *three*! [*She laughs.*] Tonight I had three.

STANLEY: Mitch!

MITCH: Deal me out. I'm talking to Miss——

BLANCHE: DuBois.

MITCH: Miss DuBois?

BLANCHE: It's a French name. It means woods and Blanche means white, so the two together mean white woods. Like an orchard in spring! You can remember it by that.

MITCH: You're French?

BLANCHE: We are French by extraction. Our first American ancestors were French Huguenots.

MITCH: You are Stella's sister, are you not?

BLANCHE: Yes, Stella is my precious little sister. I call her little in spite of the fact she's somewhat older than I. Just slightly. Less than a year. Will you do something for me?

MITCH: Sure. What?

BLANCHE: I bought this adorable little coloured paper lantern at a Chinese shop on Bourbon. Put it over the light bulb! Will you, please?

MITCH: Be glad to.

BLANCHE: I can't stand a naked light bulb, any more than I can a rude remark or a vulgar action.

MITCH [*adjusting the lantern*]: I guess we strike you as being a pretty rough bunch.

BLANCHE: I'm very adaptable—to circumstances.

MITCH: Well, that's a good thing to be. You are visiting Stanley and Stella?

BLANCHE: Stella hasn't been so well lately, and I came down to help her for a while. She's very run down.

MITCH: You're not——?

BLANCHE: Married? No, no. I'm an old maid schoolteacher!

MITCH: You may teach school but you're certainly not an old maid.

BLANCHE: Thank you, sir! I appreciate your gallantry!

MITCH: So you are in the teaching profession?

BLANCHE: Yes. Ah, yes . . .

MITCH: Grade school or high school or——

STANLEY [*bellowing*]: *Mitch!*

MITCH: *Coming!*

BLANCHE: Gracious, what lung-power! . . . I teach high school. In Laurel.

MITCH: What do you teach? What subject?

BLANCHE: Guess!

MITCH: I bet you teach art or music? [BLANCHE *laughs delicately.*]
   Of course I could be wrong. You might teach arithmetic.

BLANCHE: Never arithmetic, sir; never arithmetic! [*with a laugh*]
   I don't even know my multiplication tables! No, I have the misfortune of being an English instructor. I attempt to instil a bunch
   of bobby-soxers and drug-store Romeos with reverence for Hawthorne and Whitman and Poe!

MITCH: I guess that some of them are more interested in other
   things.

BLANCHE: How very right you are! Their literary heritage is not
   what most of them treasure above all else! But they're sweet
   things! And in the spring, it's touching to notice them making
   their first discovery of love! As if nobody had ever known it
   before!

   The bathroom door opens and STELLA *comes out.* BLANCHE *continues talking to* MITCH.

Oh! Have you finished? Wait—I'll turn on the radio.

   She turns the knobs on the radio and it begins to play "*Wien, Wien,
   nur du allein.*" BLANCHE *waltzes to the music with romantic gestures.*
   MITCH *is delighted and moves in awkward imitation like a dancing
   bear.*
   STANLEY *stalks fiercely through the portières into the bedroom.
   He crosses to the small white radio and snatches it off the table. With
   a shouted oath, he tosses the instrument out of the window.*

STELLA: *Drunk—drunk—animal thing, you!* [*She rushes through to
   the poker table.*] All of you—please go home! If any of you have
   one spark of decency in you——

BLANCHE: [*wildly*]: Stella, watch out, he's——

   STANLEY *charges after* STELLA.

MEN [*feebly*]: Take it easy, Stanley. Easy, fellow.—Let's all——

STELLA: You lay your hands on me and I'll——

   *She backs out of sight. He advances and disappears. There is the
   sound of a blow.* STELLA *cries out.* BLANCHE *screams and runs
   into the kitchen. The men rush forward and there is grappling and
   cursing. Something is overturned with a crash.*

BLANCHE [*shrilly*]: My sister is going to have a baby!

MITCH: This is terrible.

BLANCHE: Lunacy, absolute lunacy!
MITCH: Get him in here, men.

> STANLEY *is forced, pinioned by the two men, into the bedroom. He nearly throws them off. Then all at once he subsides and is limp in their grasp.*
> *They speak quietly and lovingly to him and he leans his face on one of their shoulders.*

STELLA [*in a high, unnatural voice, out of sight*]: I want to go away, I want to go away!
MITCH: Poker shouldn't be played in a house with women.

> BLANCHE *rushes into the bedroom.*

BLANCHE: I want my sister's clothes! We'll go to that woman's upstairs!
MITCH: Where is the clothes?
BLANCHE [*opening the closet*]: I've got them! [*She rushes through to* STELLA.] Stella, Stella, precious! Dear, dear little sister, don't be afraid!

> With her arms around STELLA, BLANCHE *guides her to the outside doors and upstairs.*

STANLEY [*dully*]: What's the matter; what's happened?
MITCH: You just blew your top, Stan.
PABLO: He's okay, now.
STEVE: Sure, my boy's okay!
MITCH: Put him on the bed and get a wet towel.
PABLO: I think coffee would do him a world of good, now.
STANLEY [*thickly*]: I want water.
MITCH: Put him under the shower!

> *The men talk quietly as they lead him to the bathroom.*

STANLEY: Let go of me, you sons of bitches!

> *Sounds of blows are heard. The water goes on full tilt.*

STEVE: Let's get quick out of here!

> *They rush to the poker table and sweep up their winnings on their way out.*

MITCH [*sadly but firmly*]: Poker should not be played in a house with women.

The door closes on them and the place is still. The Negro entertainers in the bar around the corner play "Paper Doll" slow and blue. After a moment STANLEY *comes out of the bathroom dripping water and still in his clinging wet polka dot drawers.*

STANLEY: Stella! [*There is a pause.*] My baby doll's left me!

He breaks into sobs. Then he goes to the phone and dials, still shuddering with sobs.

Eunice? I want my baby! [*He waits a moment; then he hangs up and dials again.*] Eunice! I'll keep on ringin' until I talk with my baby!

An indistinguishable shrill voice is heard. He hurls phone to floor. Dissonant brass and piano sounds as the rooms dim out to darkness and the outer walls appear in the night light. The "blue piano" plays for a brief interval.
Finally, STANLEY *stumbles half-dressed out to the porch and down the wooden steps to the pavement before the building. There he throws back his head like a baying hound and bellows his wife's name: "Stella! Stella, sweetheart! Stella!"*

STANLEY: Stell-*lahhhhh*!
EUNICE [*calling down from the door of her upper apartment*]: Quit that howling out there an' go back to bed!
STANLEY: I want my baby down here. Stella, Stella!
EUNICE: She ain't comin' down so you quit! Or you'll git th' law on you!
STANLEY: Stella!
EUNICE: You can't beat on a woman an' then call 'er back! She won't come! And her goin' t' have a baby! . . . You stinker! You whelp of a Polack, you! I hope they do haul you in and turn the fire hose on you, same as the last time!
STANLEY [*humbly*]: Eunice, I want my girl to come down with me!
EUNICE: Hah! [*She slams her door.*]
STANLEY [*with heaven-splitting violence*]: *STELL-LAHHHHHH!*

The low-tone clarinet moans. The door upstairs opens again. STELLA *slips down the rickety stairs in her robe. Her eyes are glistening with tears and her hair loose about her throat and shoulders. They stare at each other. Then they come together with low, animal moans. He falls to his knees on the steps and presses his face to her belly, curving a little with maternity. Her eyes go blind with tenderness as she catches*

his head and raises him level with her. He snatches the screen door open and lifts her off her feet and bears her into the dark flat.
BLANCHE *comes out on the upper landing in her robe and slips fearfully down the steps.*

BLANCHE: Where is my little sister? Stella? Stella?

She stops before the dark entrance of her sister's flat. Then catches her breath as if struck. She rushes down to the walk before the house. She looks right and left as if for sanctuary.
The music fades away. MITCH *appears from around the corner.*

MITCH: Miss DuBois?
BLANCHE: Oh!
MITCH: All quiet on the Potomac now?
BLANCHE: She ran downstairs and went back in there with him.
MITCH: Sure she did.
BLANCHE: I'm terrified!
MITCH: Ho-ho! There's nothing to be scared of. They're crazy about each other.
BLANCHE: I'm not used to such——
MITCH: Naw, it's a shame this had to happen when you just got here. But don't take it serious.
BLANCHE: Violence! Is so——
MITCH: Set down on the steps and have a cigarette with me.
BLANCHE: I'm not properly dressed.
MITCH: That's don't make no difference in the Quarter.
BLANCHE: Such a pretty silver case.
MITCH: I showed you the inscription, didn't I?
BLANCHE: Yes. [*During the pause, she looks up at the sky.*] There's so much—so much confusion in the world. . . . [*He coughs diffidently.*] Thank you for being so kind! I need kindness now.

SCENE IV

It is early the following morning. There is a confusion of street cries like a choral chant.

STELLA *is lying down in the bedroom. Her face is serene in the early morning sunlight. One hand rests on her belly, rounding slightly with new maternity. From the other dangles a book of coloured comics. Her*

*eyes and lips have that almost narcotized tranquillity that is in the
faces of Eastern idols.*

*The table is sloppy with remains of breakfast and the debris of the
preceding night, and* STANLEY'S *gaudy pyjamas lie across the thres-
hold of the bathroom. The outside door is slightly ajar on a sky of
summer brilliance.*

BLANCHE *appears at this door. She has spent a sleepless night and
her appearance entirely contrasts with* STELLA'S. *She presses her
knuckles nervously to her lips as she looks through the door, before
entering.*

BLANCHE: Stella?
STELLA [*stirring lazily*]: Hmmh?

> BLANCHE *utters a moaning cry and runs into the bedroom, throwing
> herself down beside* STELLA *in a rush of hysterical tenderness.*

BLANCHE: Baby, my baby sister!
STELLA [*drawing away from her*]: Blanche, what is the matter with
you?

> BLANCHE *straightens up slowly and stands beside the bed looking down
> at her sister with knuckles pressed to her lips.*

BLANCHE: He's left?
STELLA: Stan? Yes.
BLANCHE: Will he be back?
STELLA: He's gone to get the car greased. Why?
BLANCHE: Why! I've been half crazy, Stella! When I found out
you'd been insane enough to come back in here after what happened
—I started to rush in after you!
STELLA: I'm glad you didn't.
BLANCHE: What were you thinking of? [STELLA *makes an indefinite
gesture.*] Answer me! What? What?
STELLA: Please, Blanche! Sit down and stop yelling.
BLANCHE: All right, Stella. I will repeat the question quietly now.
How could you come back in this place last night? Why, you must
have slept with him!

> STELLA *gets up in a calm and leisurely way.*

STELLA: Blanche, I'd forgotten how excitable you are. You're
making much too much fuss about this.
BLANCHE: Am I?
STELLA: Yes, you are, Blanche. I know how it must have seemed

to you and I'm awful sorry it had to happen, but it wasn't anything as serious as you seem to take it. In the first place, when men are drinking and playing poker anything can happen. It's always a powder-keg. He didn't know what he was doing. . . . He was as good as a lamb when I came back and he's really very, very ashamed of himself.

BLANCHE: And that—that makes it all right?

STELLA: No, it isn't all right for anybody to make such a terrible row, but—people do sometimes. Stanley's always smashed things. Why, on our wedding night—soon as we came in here—he snatched off one of my slippers and rushed about the place smashing the light-bulbs with it.

BLANCHE: He did—*what*?

STELLA: He smashed all the light-bulbs with the heel of my slipper! [*She laughs.*]

BLANCHE: And you—you *let* him? Didn't *run*, didn't *scream*?

STELLA: I was—sort of—thrilled by it. [*She waits for a moment.*] Eunice and you had breakfast?

BLANCHE: Do you suppose I wanted any breakfast?

STELLA: There's some coffee left on the stove.

BLANCHE: You're so—matter of fact about it, Stella.

STELLA: What other can I be? He's taken the radio to get it fixed. It didn't land on the pavement so only one tube was smashed.

BLANCHE: And you are standing there smiling!

STELLA: What do you want me to do?

BLANCHE: Pull yourself together and face the facts.

STELLA: What are they, in your opinion?

BLANCHE: In my opinion? You're married to a madman!

STELLA: No!

BLANCHE: Yes, you are, your fix is worse than mine is! Only you're not being sensible about it. I'm going to *do* something. Get hold of myself and make myself a new life!

STELLA: Yes?

BLANCHE: But you've given in. And that isn't right, you're not old! You can get out.

STELLA [*slowly and emphatically*]: I'm not in anything I want to get out of.

BLANCHE [*incredulously*]: What—Stella?

STELLA: I said I am not in anything that I have a desire to get out of. Look at the mess in this room! And those empty bottles! They went through two cases last night! He promised this morning that he was going to quit having these poker parties, but you know how long such a promise is going to keep. Oh, well, it's his pleasure, like mine is movies and bridge. People have got to tolerate each other's habits, I guess.

BLANCHE: I don't understand you. [STELLA *turns toward her.*] I don't understand your indifference. Is this a Chinese philosophy you've—cultivated?

STELLA: Is what—what?

BLANCHE: This—shuffling about and mumbling—"One tube smashed—beer-bottles—mess in the kitchen"—as if nothing out of the ordinary has happened! [STELLA *laughs uncertainly and picking up the broom, twirls it in her hands.*]

BLANCHE: Are you deliberately shaking that thing in my face?

STELLA: No.

BLANCHE: Stop it. Let go of that broom. I won't have you cleaning up for him!

STELLA: Then who's going to do it? Are you?

BLANCHE: I? I!

STELLA: No, I didn't think so.

BLANCHE: Oh, let me think, if only my mind would function! We've got to get hold of some money, that's the way out!

STELLA: I guess that money is always nice to get hold of.

BLANCHE: Listen to me. I have an idea of some kind. [*Shakily she twists a cigarette into her holder.*] Do you remember Shep Huntleigh? [STELLA *shakes her head.*] Of course you remember Shep Huntleigh. I went out with him at college and wore his pin for a while. Well——

STELLA: Well?

BLANCHE: I ran into him last winter. You know I went to Miami during the Christmas holidays?

STELLA: No.

BLANCHE: Well, I did. I took the trip as an investment, thinking I'd meet someone with a million dollars.

STELLA: Did you?

BLANCHE: Yes. I ran into Shep Huntleigh—I ran into him on Biscayne Boulevard, on Christmas Eve, about dusk . . . getting into his car—Cadillac convertible; must have been a block long!

STELLA: I should think it would have been—inconvenient in traffic!

BLANCHE: You've heard of oil-wells?

STELLA: Yes—remotely.

BLANCHE: He has them, all over Texas. Texas is literally spouting gold in his pockets.

STELLA: My, my.

BLANCHE: Y'know how indifferent I am to money. I think of money in terms of what it does for you. But he could do it, he could certainly do it!

STELLA: Do what, Blanche?

BLANCHE: Why—set us up in a—shop!

STELLA: What kind of a shop?

BLANCHE: Oh, a—shop of some kind! He could do it with half what his wife throws away at the races.

STELLA: He's married?

BLANCHE: Honey, would I be here if the man weren't married? [STELLA *laughs a little.* BLANCHE *suddenly springs up and crosses to phone. She speaks shrilly.*] How do I get Western Union?—Operator! Western Union!

STELLA: That's a dial phone, honey.

BLANCHE: I can't dial, I'm too——

STELLA: Just dial O.

BLANCHE: O?

STELLA: Yes, "O" for Operator! [BLANCHE *considers a moment; then she puts the phone down.*]

BLANCHE: Give me a pencil. Where is a slip of paper? I've got to write it down first—the message, I mean . . .

She goes to the dressing-table, and grabs up a sheet of Kleenex and an eyebrow pencil for writing equipment.

Let me see now . . . [*She bites the pencil.*] "Darling Shep. Sister and I in desperate situation."

STELLA: I beg your pardon!

BLANCHE: "Sister and I in desperate situation. Will explain details later. Would you be interested in——?" [*She bites the pencil again.*] "Would you be—interested—in . . ." [*She smashes the pencil on the table and springs up.*] You never get anywhere with direct appeals!

STELLA [*with a laugh*]: Don't be so ridiculous, darling!

BLANCHE: But I'll think of something, I've *got* to think of—something! Don't, don't laugh at me, Stella! Please, please don't—I—I want you to look at the contents of my purse! Here's what's in it! [*She snatches her purse open.*] Sixty-five measly cents in coin of the realm!

STELLA [*crossing to bureau*]: Stanley doesn't give me a regular allowance, he likes to pay bills himself, but—this morning he gave me ten dollars to smooth things over. You take five of it, Blanche, and I'll keep the rest.

BLANCHE: Oh, no. No, Stella.

STELLA [*insisting*]: I know how it helps your morale just having a little pocket-money on you.

BLANCHE: No, thank you—I'll take to the streets!

STELLA: Talk sense! How did you happen to get so low on funds?

BLANCHE: Money just goes—it goes places. [*She rubs her forehead.*] Sometime today I've got to get hold of a bromo!

STELLA: I'll fix you one now.

BLANCHE: Not yet—I've got to keep thinking!

STELLA: I wish you'd just let things go, at least for a—while . . .

BLANCHE: Stella, I can't live with him! You can, he's your husband. But how could I stay here with him, after last night, with just those curtains between us?

STELLA: Blanche, you saw him at his worst last night.

BLANCHE: On the contrary, I saw him at his best! What such a man has to offer is animal force and he gave a wonderful exhibition of that! But the only way to live with such a man is to—go to bed with him! And that's your job—not mine!

STELLA: After you've rested a little, you'll see it's going to work out. You don't have to worry about anything while you're here. I mean—expenses . . .

BLANCHE: I have to plan for us both, to get us both—out!

STELLA: You take it for granted that I am in something that I want to get out of.

BLANCHE: I take it for granted that you still have sufficient memory of Belle Reve to find this place and these poker players impossible to live with.

STELLA: Well, you're taking entirely too much for granted.

BLANCHE: I can't believe you're in earnest.

STELLA: No?

BLANCHE: I understand how it happened—a little. You saw him in uniform, an officer, not here but——

STELLA: I'm not sure it would have made any difference where I saw him.

BLANCHE: Now don't say it was one of those mysterious electric things between people! If you do I'll laugh in your face.

STELLA: I am not going to say anything more at all about it!

BLANCHE: All right, then, don't!

STELLA: But there are things that happen between a man and a

woman in the dark—that sort of make everything else seem—
unimportant. [*Pause.*]

BLANCHE: What you are talking about is brutal desire—just—
Desire!—the name of that rattle-trap street-car that bangs through
the Quarter, up one old narrow street and down another . . .

STELLA: Haven't you ever ridden on that street-car?

BLANCHE: It brought me here.—Where I'm not wanted and where
I'm ashamed to be . . .

STELLA: Then don't you think your superior attitude is a bit out
of place?

BLANCHE: I am not being or feeling at all superior, Stella. Believe
me I'm not! It's just this. This is how I look at it. A man like that is
someone to go out with—once—twice—three times when the
devil is in you. But live with! Have a child by?

STELLA: I have told you I love him.

BLANCHE: Then I *tremble* for you! I just—*tremble* for you. . . .

STELLA: I can't help your trembling if you insist on trembling!

There is a pause.

BLANCHE: May I—speak—*plainly?*

STELLA: Yes, do. Go ahead. As plainly as you want to.

Outside, a train approaches. They are silent till the noise subsides.
They are both in the bedroom.
Under cover of the train's noise STANLEY *enters from outside. He*
stands unseen by the women, holding some packages in his arms, and
overhears their following conversation. He wears an undershirt and
grease-stained seersucker pants.

BLANCHE: Well—if you'll forgive me—he's *common!*

STELLA: Why, yes, I suppose he is.

BLANCHE: Suppose! You can't have forgotten that much of our
bringing up, Stella, that you just *suppose* that any part of a gentleman's in his nature! *Not one particle, no!* Oh, if he was just—*ordinary!*
Just *plain*—but good and wholesome, but—*no*. There's something
downright—*bestial*—about him! You're hating me saying this,
aren't you?

STELLA [*coldly*]: Go on and say it all, Blanche.

BLANCHE: He acts like an animal, has an animal's habits! Eats like
one, moves like one, talks like one! There's even something—
sub-human—something not quite to the stage of humanity yet!
Yes, something—ape-like about him, like one of those pictures

I've seen in—anthropological studies! Thousands and thousands
of years have passed him right by, and there he is—Stanley Kowalski
—survivor of the stone age! Bearing the raw meat home from the
kill in the jungle! And you—*you* here—*waiting* for him! Maybe
he'll strike you or maybe grunt and kiss you! That is, if kisses have
been discovered yet! Night falls and the other apes gather! There
in the front of the cave, all grunting like him, and swilling and
gnawing and hulking! His poker night!—you call it—this party of
apes! Somebody growls—some creature snatches at something—
the fight is on! *God!* Maybe we are a long way from being made in
God's image, but Stella—my sister—there has been *some* progress
since then! Such things as art—as poetry and music—such kinds of
new light have come into the world since then! In some kinds of
people some tenderer feelings have had some little beginning!
That we have got to make *grow!* And *cling* to, and hold as our flag!
In this dark march toward whatever it is we're approaching. . .
Don't—don't hang back with the brutes!

Another train passes outside. STANLEY *hesitates, licking his lips.
Then suddenly he turns stealthily about and withdraws through front
door. The women are still unaware of his presence. When the train has
passed he calls through the closed front door.*

STANLEY: Hey! Hey, Stella!
STELLA [*who has listened gravely to* BLANCHE]: Stanley!
BLANCHE: Stell, I——

But STELLA *has gone to the front door.* STANLEY *enters casually
with his packages.*

STANLEY: Hiyuh, Stella, Blanche back?
STELLA: Yes, she's back.
STANLEY: Hiyuh, Blanche. [*He grins at her.*]
STELLA: You must've got under the car.
STANLEY: Them darn mechanics at Fritz's don't know their can
from third base!

STELLA *has embraced him with both arms, fiercely, and full in the
view of* BLANCHE. *He laughs and clasps her head to him. Over her
head he grins through the curtains at* BLANCHE.
*As the lights fade away, with a lingering brightness on their embrace,
the music of the* "*blue piano*" *and trumpet and drums is heard.*

SCENE V

BLANCHE *is seated in the bedroom fanning herself with a palm leaf as she reads over a just completed letter. Suddenly she bursts into a peal of laughter.* STELLA *is dressing in the bedroom.*

STELLA: What are you laughing at, honey?

BLANCHE: Myself, myself, for being such a liar! I'm writing a letter to Shep. [*She picks up the letter.*] "Darling Shep. I am spending the summer on the wing, making flying visits here and there. And who knows, perhaps I shall take a sudden notion to *swoop* down on *Dallas!* How would you feel about that? Ha-ha! [*She laughs nervously and brightly, touching her throat as if actually talking to* SHEP.] Forewarned is forearmed, as they say!"—How does that sound?

STELLA: Uh-huh . . .

BLANCHE [*going on nervously*]: "Most of my sister's friends go north in the summer but some have homes on the Gulf and there has been a continued round of entertainments, teas, cocktails, and luncheons——"

A disturbance is heard upstairs at the HUBBELS' *apartment.*

STELLA [*crossing to the door*]: Eunice seems to be having some trouble with Steve.

EUNICE'S *voice shouts in terrible wrath.*

EUNICE: I heard about you and that blonde!

STEVE: That's a damn lie!

EUNICE: You ain't pulling the wool over my eyes! I wouldn't mind if you'd stay down at the Four Deuces, but you always going up.

STEVE: Who ever seen me up?

EUNICE: I seen you chasing her 'round the balcony—I'm gonna call the vice squad!

STEVE: Don't you throw that at me!

EUNICE [*shrieking*]: You hit me! I'm gonna call the police!

A clatter of aluminium striking a wall is heard, followed by a man's angry roar, shouts and overturned furniture. There is a crash; then a relative hush.

BLANCHE [*brightly*]: Did he *kill* her?

EUNICE appears on the steps in daemonic disorder.

STELLA: No! She's coming downstairs.

EUNICE: Call the police, I'm going to call the police! [*She rushes around the corner.*

STELLA [*returning from the door*]: Some of your sister's friends have stayed in the city.

They laugh lightly. STANLEY comes around the corner in his green and scarlet silk bowling shirt. He trots up the steps and bangs into the kitchen. BLANCHE registers his entrance with nervous gestures.

STANLEY: What's a matter with Eun-uss?

STELLA: She and Steve had a row. Has she got the police?

STANLEY: Naw. She's gettin' a drink.

STELLA: That's much more practical!

STEVE comes down nursing a bruise on his forehead and looks in the door.

STEVE: *She here?*

STANLEY: Naw, naw. At the Four Deuces.

STEVE: That hunk! [*He looks around the corner a bit timidly, then turns with affected boldness and runs after her.*]

BLANCHE: I must jot that down in my notebook. Ha-ha! I'm compiling a notebook of quaint little words and phrases I've picked up here.

STANLEY: You won't pick up nothing here you ain't heard before.

BLANCHE: Can I count on that?

STANLEY: You can count on it up to five hundred.

BLANCHE: That's a mighty high number. [*He jerks open the bureau drawer, slams it shut and throws shoes in a corner. At each noise BLANCHE winces slightly. Finally she speaks.*] What sign were you born under?

STANLEY [*while he is dressing*]: Sign?

BLANCHE: Astrological sign. I bet you were born under Aries. Aries people are forceful and dynamic. They dote on noise! They love to bang things around! You must have had lots of banging around in the army, and now that you're out, you make up for it by treating inanimate objects with such a fury!

STELLA has been going in and out of closet during this scene. Now she pops her head out of the closet.

STELLA: Stanley was born just five minutes after Christmas.

BLANCHE: Capricorn—the Goat!

STANLEY: What sign were *you* born under?

BLANCHE: Oh, my birthday's next month, the fifteenth of September; that's under Virgo.

STANLEY: What's Virgo?

BLANCHE: Virgo is the Virgin.

STANLEY [*contemptuously*]: *Hah!* [*He advances a little as he knots his tie.*] Say, do you happen to know somebody named Shaw?

Her face expresses a faint shock. She reaches for the cologne bottle and dampens her handkerchief as she answers carefully.

BLANCHE: Why, everybody knows somebody named Shaw!

STANLEY: Well, this somebody named Shaw is under the impression he met you in Laurel, but I figure he must have got you mixed up with some other party because this other party is someone he met at a hotel called the Flamingo.

BLANCHE *laughs breathlessly as she touches the cologne-dampened handkerchief to her temples.*

BLANCHE: I'm afraid he does have me mixed up with this "other party". The Hotel Flamingo is not the sort of establishment I would dare to be seen in!

STANLEY: You know of it?

BLANCHE: Yes, I've seen it and smelled it.

STANLEY: You must've got pretty close if you could smell it.

BLANCHE: The odour of cheap perfume is penetrating.

STANLEY: That stuff you use is expensive?

BLANCHE: Twenty-five dollars an ounce! I'm nearly out. That's just a hint if you want to remember my birthday! [*She speaks lightly but her voice has a note of fear.*]

STANLEY: Shaw must've got you mixed up. He goes in and out of Laurel all the time, so he can check on it and clear up any mistake.

He turns away and crosses to the portières. BLANCHE *closes her eyes as if faint. Her hand trembles as she lifts the handkerchief again to her forehead.*

STEVE *and* EUNICE *come around corner.* STEVE'S *arm is around* EUNICE'S *shoulder and she is sobbing luxuriously and he is cooing love-words. There is a murmur of thunder as they go slowly upstairs in a tight embrace.*

STANLEY [*to* STELLA]: I'll wait for you at the Four Deuces!
STELLA: Hey! Don't I rate one kiss?
STANLEY: Not in front of your sister.

> *He goes out.* BLANCHE *rises from her chair. She seems faint; looks about her with an expression of almost panic.*

BLANCHE: Stella! What have you heard about me?
STELLA: Huh?
BLANCHE: What have people been telling you about me?
STELLA: Telling?
BLANCHE: You haven't heard any—unkind—gossip about me?
STELLA: Why, no, Blanche, of course not!
BLANCHE: Honey, there was—a good deal of talk in Laurel.
STELLA: About *you*, Blanche?
BLANCHE: I wasn't so good the last two years or so, after Belle Reve had started to slip through my fingers.
STELLA: All of us do things we——
BLANCHE: I never was hard or self-sufficient enough. When people are soft—soft people have got to court the favour of hard ones, Stella. Have got to be seductive—put on soft colours, the colours of butterfly wings, and glow—make a little—temporary magic just in order to pay for—one night's shelter! That's why I've been —not so awf'ly good lately. I've run for protection, Stella, from under one leaky roof to another leaky roof—because it was storm —all storm, and I was—caught in the centre. . . . People don't see you—*men* don't—don't even admit your existence unless they are making love to you. And you've got to have your existence admitted by someone, if you're going to have someone's protection. And so the soft people have got to—shimmer and glow—put a —paper lantern over the light. . . . But I'm scared now—awf'ly scared. I don't know how much longer I can turn the trick. It isn't enough to be soft. You've got to be soft *and attractive*. And I—I'm fading now!

> *The afternoon has faded to dusk.* STELLA *goes into the bedroom and turns on the light under the paper lantern. She holds a bottled soft drink in her hand.*

Have you been listening to me?
STELLA: I don't listen to you when you are being morbid! [*She advances with the bottled coke.*]
BLANCHE [*with abrupt change to gaiety*]: Is that coke for me?

STELLA: Not for anyone else!

BLANCHE: Why, you precious thing, you! Is it just coke?

STELLA [*turning*]: You mean you want a shot in it!

BLANCHE: Well, honey, a shot never does a coke any harm! Let me? You mustn't wait on me!

STELLA: I like to wait on you, Blanche. It makes it seem more like home. [*She goes into the kitchen, finds a glass and pours a shot of whisky into it.*]

BLANCHE: I have to admit I love to be waited on. . . .

> She rushes into the bedroom. STELLA goes to her with the glass. BLANCHE suddenly clutches STELLA'S free hand with a moaning sound and presses the hand to her lips. STELLA is embarrassed by her show of emotion. BLANCHE speaks in a choked voice.

You're—you're—so *good* to me! And I——

STELLA: Blanche.

BLANCHE: I know, I won't! You hate me to talk sentimental. But honey, *believe* I feel things more than I *tell* you! I *won't* stay long! I won't, I *promise* I——

STELLA: Blanche!

BLANCHE [*hysterically*]: I won't, I promise, *I'll* go! Go *soon*! I will *really*! I *won't* hang around until he—throws me out. . . .

STELLA: Now will you stop talking foolish?

BLANCHE: Yes, honey. Watch how you pour—that fizzy stuff foams over!

> BLANCHE *laughs shrilly and grabs the glass, but her hand shakes so it almost slips from her grasp.* STELLA *pours the coke into the glass. It foams over and spills.* BLANCHE *gives a piercing cry.*

STELLA [*shocked by the cry*]: Heavens!

BLANCHE: Right on my pretty white skirt!

STELLA: Oh. . . . Use my hanky. Blot gently.

BLANCHE [*slowly recovering*]: I know—gently—gently . . .

STELLA: Did it stain?

BLANCHE: Not a bit. Ha-ha! Isn't that lucky? [*She sits down shakily, taking a grateful drink. She holds the glass in both hands and continues to laugh a little.*]

STELLA: Why did you scream like that?

BLANCHE: I don't know why I screamed! [*Continuing nervously.*] Mitch—Mitch is coming at seven. I guess I am just feeling nervous about our relations. [*She begins to talk rapidly and breathlessly.*] He hasn't gotten a thing but a goodnight kiss, that's all I have given him, Stella. I want his respect. And men don't want anything they get too easy. But on the other hand men lose interest quickly. Especially when the girl is over—thirty. They think a girl over thirty ought to—the vulgar term is—"put out." . . . And I—I'm not "putting out." Of course he—he doesn't know—I mean I haven't informed him—of my real age!

STELLA: Why are you sensitive about your age?

BLANCHE: Because of hard knocks my vanity's been given. What I mean is—he thinks I'm sort of—prim and proper, you know! [*She laughs out sharply.*] I want to *deceive* him enough to make him—want me. . . .

STELLA: Blanche, do you want *him*?

BLANCHE: I want to *rest*! I want to breathe quietly again! Yes—I *want* Mitch . . . *very badly*! Just think! If it happens! I can leave here and not be anyone's problem. . . .

STANLEY *comes around the corner with a drink under his belt.*

STANLEY [*bawling*]: Hey, Steve! Hey, Eunice! Hey, Stella!

There are joyous calls from above. Trumpet and drums are heard from around the corner.

STELLA [*kissing* BLANCHE *impulsively*]: It *will* happen!

BLANCHE [*doubtfully*]: It will?

STELLA: It *will*! [*She goes across into the kitchen, looking back at* BLANCHE.] It will, honey, *it will*. . . . But don't take another drink! [*Her voice catches as she goes out of the door to meet her husband.*]

BLANCHE *sinks faintly back in her chair with her drink.* EUNICE *shrieks with laughter and runs down the steps.* STEVE *bounds after her with goat-like screeches and chases her around corner.* STANLEY *and* STELLA *twine arms as they follow, laughing.*
Dusk settles deeper. The music from the Four Deuces is slow and blue.

BLANCHE: Ah, me, ah, me, ah, me . . .

Her eyes fall shut and the palm leaf drops from her fingers. She slaps her hand on the chair arm a couple of times; then she raises herself wearily to her feet and picks up the hand mirror.
There is a little glimmer of lightning about the building.
The NEGRO WOMAN, *cackling hysterically, swaying drunkenly, comes around the corner from the Four Deuces. At the same time, a*

Young Man enters from the opposite direction. The Negro Woman snaps her fingers before his belt.

NEGRO WOMAN: Hey! Sugar!

She says something indistinguishable. The Young Man shakes his head violently and edges hastily up the steps. He rings the bell. Blanche puts down the mirror. The Negro Woman has wandered down the street.

BLANCHE: Come in.

The Young Man appears through the portières. She regards him with interest.

BLANCHE: Well, well! What can I do for *you*?
YOUNG MAN: I'm collecting for *The Evening Star*.
BLANCHE: I didn't know that stars took up collections.
YOUNG MAN: It's the paper.
BLANCHE: I know, I was joking—feebly! Will you—have a drink?
YOUNG MAN: No, ma'am. No, thank you. I can't drink on the job.
BLANCHE: Oh, well, now, let's see. . . . No, I don't have a dime! I'm not the lady of the house. I'm her sister from Mississippi. I'm one of those poor relations you've heard about.
YOUNG MAN: That's all right. I'll drop by later. [*He starts to go out. She approaches a little.*]
BLANCHE: Hey! [*He turns back shyly. She puts a cigarette in a long holder.*] Could you give me a light? [*She crosses toward him. They meet at the door between the two rooms.*]
YOUNG MAN: Sure. [*He takes out a lighter.*] This doesn't always work.
BLANCHE: It's temperamental? [*It flares.*] Ah! Thank you.
YOUNG MAN: Thank *you*! [*He starts away again.*]
BLANCHE: Hey! [*He turns again, still more uncertainly. She goes close to him.*] What time is it?
YOUNG MAN: Fifteen of seven.
BLANCHE: So late? Don't you just love these long rainy afternoons in New Orleans when an hour isn't just an hour—but a little bit of Eternity dropped in your hands—and who knows what to do with it?
YOUNG MAN: Yes, ma'am.

In the ensuing pause, the "blue piano" is heard. It continues through the rest of this scene and the opening of the next. The Young Man clears his throat and looks glancingly at the door.

BLANCHE: You—uh—didn't get wet in the shower?

YOUNG MAN: No, ma'am. I stepped inside.

BLANCHE: In a drug-store? And had a soda?

YOUNG MAN: Uhhuh.

BLANCHE: Chocolate?

YOUNG MAN: No, ma'am. Cherry.

BLANCHE: Mmmm!

YOUNG MAN: A cherry soda!

BLANCHE: You make my mouth water.

YOUNG MAN: Well, I'd better be——

BLANCHE: Young man! Young, young, young, young—man! Has anyone ever told you that you look like a young prince out of the Arabian Nights?

YOUNG MAN: No, ma'am.

The YOUNG MAN *laughs uncomfortably and stands like a bashful kid.* BLANCHE *speaks softly to him.*

BLANCHE: Well, you do, honey lamb. Come here! Come on over here like I told you! I want to kiss you—just once—softly and sweetly on your mouth. [*Without waiting for him to accept, she crosses quickly to him and presses her lips to his.*] Run along now! It would be nice to keep you, but I've got to be good and keep my hands off children. Adios!

YOUNG MAN: Huh?

He stares at her a moment. She opens the door for him and blows a kiss to him as he goes down the steps with a dazed look. She stands there a little dreamily after he has disappeared. Then MITCH *appears around the corner with a bunch of roses.*

BLANCHE: Look who's coming! My Rosenkavalier! Bow to me first! Now present them.

He does so. She curtsies low.

Ahhh! Merciiii!

SCENE VI

It is about two a.m. the same night. The outer wall of the building is visible. BLANCHE *and* MITCH *come in. The utter exhaustion which only a neurasthenic personality can know is evident in* BLANCHE'S *voice and manner.* MITCH *is stolid but depressed. They have probably been out to the amusement park on Lake Pontchartrain, for* MITCH *is bearing, upside down, a plaster statuette of Mae West, the sort of prize won at shooting-galleries and carnival games of chance.*

BLANCHE [*stopping lifelessly at the steps*]: Well——

    MITCH *laughs uneasily.*

Well . . .

MITCH: I guess it must be pretty late—and you're tired.

BLANCHE: Even the hot tamale man has deserted the street, and he hangs on till the end. [MITCH *laughs uneasily again.*] How will you get home?

MITCH: I'll walk over to Bourbon and catch an owl-car.

BLANCHE [*laughing grimly*]: Is that street-car named Desire still grinding along the tracks at this hour?

MITCH [*heavily*]: I'm afraid you haven't gotten much fun out of this evening, Blanche.

BLANCHE: I spoiled it for *you*.

MITCH: No, you didn't, but I felt all the time that I wasn't giving you much—entertainment.

BLANCHE: I simply couldn't rise to the occasion. That was all. I don't think I've ever tried so hard to be gay and made such a dismal mess of it. I get ten points for trying!—I *did* try.

MITCH: Why did you try if you didn't feel like it, Blanche?

BLANCHE: I was just obeying the law of nature.

MITCH: Which law is that?

BLANCHE: The one that says the lady must entertain the gentleman—or no dice! See if you can locate my door-key in this purse. When I'm so tired my fingers are all thumbs!

MITCH [*rooting in her purse*]: This it?

BLANCHE: No, honey, that's the key to my trunk which I must soon be packing.

MITCH: You mean you are leaving here soon?

BLANCHE: I've outstayed my welcome.

MITCH: This it?

The music fades away.

BLANCHE: Eureka! Honey, you open the door while I take a last look at the sky. [*She leans on the porch rail. He opens the door and stands awkwardly behind her.*] I'm looking for the Pleiades, the Seven Sisters, but these girls are not out tonight. Oh, yes they are, there they are! God bless them! All in a bunch going home from their little bridge party. . . . Y' get the door open? Good boy! I guess you —want to go now . . .

He shuffles and coughs a little.

MITCH: Can I—uh—kiss you—good night?

BLANCHE: Why do you always ask me if you may?

MITCH: I don't know whether you want me to or not.

BLANCHE: Why should you be so doubtful?

MITCH: That night when we parked by the lake and I kissed you, you——

BLANCHE: Honey, it wasn't the kiss I objected to. I liked the kiss very much. It was the other little—familiarity—that I—felt obliged to—discourage. . . . I didn't resent it! Not a bit in the world! In fact, I was somewhat flattered that you—desired me! But, honey, you know as well as I do that a single girl, a girl alone in the world, has got to keep a firm hold on her emotions or she'll be lost!

MITCH [*solemnly*]: Lost?

BLANCHE: I guess you are used to girls that like to be lost. The kind that get lost immediately, on the first date!

MITCH: I like you to be exactly the way that you are, because in all my—experience—I have never known anyone like you.

BLANCHE *looks at him gravely; then she bursts into laughter and then claps a hand to her mouth.*

MITCH: Are you laughing at me?

BLANCHE: No, honey. The lord and lady of the house have not yet returned, so come in. We'll have a night-cap. Let's leave the lights off. Shall we?

MITCH: You just—do what you want to.

BLANCHE *precedes him into the kitchen. The outer wall of the building disappears and the interiors of the two rooms can be dimly seen.*

BLANCHE [*remaining in the first room*]: The other room's more comfortable—go on in. This crashing around in the dark is my search for some liquor.

MITCH: You want a drink?

BLANCHE: I want *you* to have a drink! You have been so anxious and solemn all evening, and so have I; we have both been anxious and solemn and now for these few last remaining moments of our lives together—I want to create—*joie de vivre*! I'm lighting a candle.

MITCH: That's good.

BLANCHE: We are going to be very Bohemian. We are going to pretend that we are sitting in a little artists' cafe on the Left Bank in Paris! [*She lights a candle stub and puts it in a bottle.*] *Je suis la Dame aux Camellias! Vous êtes—Armand!* Understand French?

MITCH [*heavily*]: Naw. Naw, I——

BLANCHE: *Voulez-vous couchez avec moi ce soir? Vous ne comprenez pas? Ah, quel dommage!*—I mean it's a damned good thing. . . . I've found some liquor! Just enough for two shots without any dividends, honey . . .

MITCH [*heavily*]: That's—good.

She enters the bedroom with the drinks and the candle.

BLANCHE: Sit down! Why don't you take off your coat and loosen your collar?

MITCH: I better leave it on.

BLANCHE: No. I want you to be comfortable.

MITCH: I am ashamed of the way I perspire. My shirt is sticking to me.

BLANCHE: Perspiration is healthy. If people didn't perspire they would die in five minutes. [*She takes his coat from him.*] This is a nice coat. What kind of material is it?

MITCH: They call that stuff alpaca.

BLANCHE: Oh. Alpaca.

MITCH: It's very light weight alpaca.

BLANCHE: Oh. Light weight alpaca.

MITCH: I don't like to wear a wash-coat even in summer because I sweat through it.

BLANCHE: Oh.

MITCH: And it don't look neat on me. A man with a heavy build has got to be careful of what he puts on him so he don't look too clumsy.

BLANCHE: You are not too heavy.

MITCH: You don't think I am?

BLANCHE: You are not the delicate type. You have a massive bone-structure and a very imposing physique.

MITCH: Thank you. Last Christmas I was given a membership to the New Orleans Athletic Club.

BLANCHE: Oh, good.

MITCH: It was the finest present I ever was given. I work out there with the weights and I swim and I keep myself fit. When I started there, I was getting soft in the belly but now my belly is hard. It is so hard that now a man can punch me in the belly and it don't hurt me. Punch me! Go on! See? [*She pokes lightly at him.*]

BLANCHE: Gracious. [*Her hand touches her chest.*]

MITCH: Guess how much I weigh, Blanche?

BLANCHE: Oh, I'd say in the vicinity of—one hundred and eighty?

MITCH: Guess again.

BLANCHE: Not that much?

MITCH: No. More.

BLANCHE: Well, you're a tall man and you can carry a good deal of weight without looking awkward.

MITCH: I weigh two hundred and seven pounds and I'm six feet one and one half inches tall in my bare feet—without shoes on. And that is what I weigh stripped.

BLANCHE: Oh, my goodness, me! It's awe-inspiring.

MITCH [*embarrassed*]: My weight is not a very interesting subject to talk about. [*He hesitates for a moment.*] What's yours?

BLANCHE: My weight?

MITCH: Yes.

BLANCHE: Guess!

MITCH: Let me lift you.

BLANCHE: Samson! Go on, lift me. [*He comes behind her and puts his hand on her waist and raises her lightly off the ground.*] Well?

MITCH: You are light as a feather.

BLANCHE: Ha-ha! [*He lowers her but keeps his hands on her waist. BLANCHE speaks with an affectation of demureness.*] You may release me now.

MITCH: Huh?

BLANCHE [*gaily*]: I said unhand me, sir. [*He fumblingly embraces her. Her voice sounds gently reproving.*] Now, Mitch. Just because Stanley and Stella aren't at home is no reason why you shouldn't behave like a gentleman.

MITCH: Just give me a slap whenever I step out of bounds.

BLANCHE: That won't be necessary. You're a natural gentleman, one of the very few that are left in the world. I don't want you to think that I am severe and old maid school-teacherish or anything like that. It's just—well——

MITCH: Huh?

BLANCHE: I guess it is just that I have—old-fashioned ideals! [*She rolls her eyes, knowing he cannot see her face.* MITCH *goes to the front door. There is a considerable silence between them.* BLANCHE *sighs and* MITCH *coughs self-consciously.*]

MITCH [*finally*]: Where's Stanley and Stella tonight?

BLANCHE: They have gone out. With Mr. and Mrs. Hubbel upstairs.

MITCH: Where did they go?

BLANCHE: I think they were planning to go to a midnight prevue at Loew's State.

MITCH: We should all go out together some night.

BLANCHE: No. That wouldn't be a good plan.

MITCH: Why not?

BLANCHE: You are an old friend of Stanley's?

MITCH: We was together in the Two-forty-first.

BLANCHE: I guess he talks to you frankly?

MITCH: Sure.

BLANCHE: Has he talked to you about me?

MITCH: Oh—not very much.

BLANCHE: The way you say that, I suspect that he has.

MITCH: No, he hasn't said much.

BLANCHE: But what he *has* said. What would you say his attitude toward me was?

MITCH: Why do you want to ask that?

BLANCHE: Well——

MITCH: Don't you get along with him?

BLANCHE: What do you think?

MITCH: I don't think he understands you.

BLANCHE: That is putting it mildly. If it weren't for Stella about to have a baby, I wouldn't be able to endure things here.

MITCH: He isn't—nice to you?

BLANCHE: He is insufferably rude. Goes out of his way to offend me.

MITCH: In what way, Blanche?

BLANCHE: Why, in every conceivable way.

MITCH: I'm surprised to hear that.

BLANCHE: Are you?

MITCH: Well, I—don't see how anybody could be rude to you.

BLANCHE: It's really a pretty frightful situation. You see, there's no privacy here. There's just these portières between the two rooms at night. He stalks through the rooms in his underwear at night. And I have to ask him to close the bathroom door. That sort of commonness isn't necessary. You probably wonder why I don't move out. Well, I'll tell you frankly. A teacher's salary is barely sufficient for her living-expenses. I didn't save a penny last year and so I had to come here for the summer. That's why I have to put up with my sister's husband. And he has to put up with me, apparently so much against his wishes. . . . Surely he must have told you how much he hates me!

MITCH: I don't think he hates you.

BLANCHE: He hates me. Or why would he insult me? Of course there is such a thing as the hostility of—perhaps in some perverse kind of way he—No! To think of it makes me . . . [*She makes a gesture of revulsion. Then she finishes her drink. A pause follows.*]

MITCH: Blanche——

BLANCHE: Yes, honey?

MITCH: Can I ask you a question?

BLANCHE: Yes. What?

MITCH: How old are you?

She makes a nervous gesture.

BLANCHE: Why do you want to know?

MITCH: I talked to my mother about you and she said, "How old is Blanche?" And I wasn't able to tell her. [*There is another pause.*]

BLANCHE: You talked to your mother about me?

MITCH: Yes.

BLANCHE: Why?

MITCH: I told my mother how nice you were, and I liked you.

BLANCHE: Were you sincere about that?

MITCH: You know I was.

BLANCHE: Why did your mother want to know my age?

MITCH: Mother is sick.

BLANCHE: I'm sorry to hear it. Badly?

MITCH: She won't live long. Maybe just a few months.

BLANCHE: Oh.

MITCH: She worries because I'm not settled.

BLANCHE: Oh.

MITCH: She wants me to be settled down before she—— [*His voice is hoarse and he clears his throat twice, shuffling nervously around with his hands in and out of his pockets.*]

BLANCHE: You love her very much, don't you?

MITCH: Yes.

BLANCHE: I think you have a great capacity for devotion. You will be lonely when she passes on, won't you? [MITCH *clears his throat and nods.*] I understand what that is.

MITCH: To be lonely?

BLANCHE: I loved someone, too, and the person I loved I lost.

MITCH: Dead? [*She crosses to the window and sits on the sill, looking out. She pours herself another drink.*] A man?

BLANCHE: He was a boy, just a boy, when I was a very young girl. When I was sixteen, I made the discovery—love. All at once and much, much too completely. It was like you suddenly turned a blinding light on something that had always been half in shadow, that's how it struck the world for me. But I was unlucky. Deluded. There was something different about the boy, a nervousness, a softness and tenderness which wasn't like a man's, although he wasn't the least bit effeminate looking—still—that thing was there. . . . He came to me for help. I didn't know that. I didn't find out anything till after our marriage when we'd run away and come back and all I knew was I'd failed him in some mysterious way and wasn't able to give the help he needed but couldn't speak of! He was in the quicksands and clutching at me—but I wasn't holding him out, I was slipping in with him! I didn't know that. I didn't know anything except I loved him unendurably but without being able to help him or help myself. Then I found out. In the worst of all possible ways. By coming suddenly into a room that I thought was empty—which wasn't empty, but had two people in it . . .

> *A locomotive is heard approaching outside. She claps her hands to her ears and crouches over. The headlight of the locomotive glares into the room as it thunders past. As the noise recedes she straightens slowly and continues speaking.*

Afterwards we pretended that nothing had been discovered. Yes, the three of us drove out to Moon Lake Casino, very drunk and laughing all the way.

Polka music sounds, in a minor key faint with distance.

We danced the Varsouviana! Suddenly in the middle of the dance the boy I had married broke away from me and ran out of the casino. A few moments later—a shot!

The Polka stops abruptly.
BLANCHE rises stiffly. Then the Polka resumes in a major key.

I ran out—all did!—all ran and gathered about the terrible thing at the edge of the lake! I couldn't get near for the crowding. Then somebody caught my arm. "Don't go any closer! Come back! You don't want to see!" See? See what! Then I heard voices say—Allan! Allan! The Grey boy! He'd stuck the revolver into his mouth, and fired—so that the back of his head had been— blown away!

She sways and covers her face.

It was because—on the dance-floor—unable to stop myself—I'd suddenly said—"I know! I know! You disgust me . . ." And then the searchlight which had been turned on the world was turned off again and never for one moment since has there been any light that's stronger than this—kitchen—candle. . . .

MITCH gets up awkwardly and moves towards her a little. The Polka music increases. MITCH stands beside her.

MITCH [*drawing her slowly into his arms*]: You need somebody. And I need somebody, too. Could it be—you and me, Blanche?

She stares at him vacantly for a moment. Then with a soft cry huddles in his embrace. She makes a sobbing effort to speak but the words won't come. He kisses her forehead and her eyes and finally her lips. The Polka tune fades out. Her breath is drawn and released in long, grateful sobs.

BLANCHE: Sometimes—there's God—so quickly!

SCENE VII

It is late afternoon in mid-September.
*The portières are open and a table is set for a birthday supper, with cake
and flowers.*
     STELLA *is completing the decorations as* STANLEY *comes in.*

STANLEY: What's all this stuff for?

STELLA: Honey, it's Blanche's birthday.

STANLEY: She here?

STELLA: In the bathroom.

STANLEY [*mimicking*]: "Washing out some things"?

STELLA: I reckon so.

STANLEY: How long she been in there?

STELLA: All afternoon.

STANLEY [*mimicking*]: "Soaking in a hot tub"?

STELLA: Yes.

STANLEY: Temperature 100 on the nose, and she soaks herself in a
     hot tub.

STELLA: She says it cools her off for the evening.

STANLEY: And you run out an' get her cokes, I suppose? And serve
     'em to Her Majesty in the tub? [STELLA *shrugs.*] Set down here a
     minute.

STELLA: Stanley, I've got things to do.

STANLEY: Set down! I've got th' dope on your big sister, Stella.

STELLA: Stanley, stop picking on Blanche.

STANLEY: That girl calls *me* common!

STELLA: Lately you been doing all you can think of to rub her the
     wrong way, Stanley, and Blanche is sensitive and you've got to
     realize that Blanche and I grew up under very different circum-
     stances than you did.

STANLEY: So I been told. And told and told and told! You know
     she's been feeding us a pack of lies here?

STELLA: No, I don't, and——

STANLEY: Well, she has, however. But now the cat's out of the
     bag! I found out some things!

STELLA: What—things?

STANLEY: Things I already suspected. But now I got proof from the most reliable sources—which I have checked on!

BLANCHE *is singing in the bathroom a saccharine popular ballad which is used contrapunctally with* STANLEY'S *speech.*

STELLA [*to* STANLEY]: Lower your voice!

STANLEY: Some canary-bird, huh!

STELLA: Now please tell me quietly what you think you've found out about my sister.

STANLEY: Lie Number One: All this squeamishness she puts on! You should just know the line she's been feeding to Mitch. He thought she had never been more than kissed by a fellow! But Sister Blanche is no lily! Ha-ha! Some lily she is!

STELLA: What have you heard and who from?

STANLEY: Our supply-man down at the plant has been going through Laurel for years and he knows all about her and everybody else in the town of Laurel knows all about her. She is as famous in Laurel as if she was the President of the United States, only she is not respected by any party! This supply-man stops at a hotel called the Flamingo.

BLANCHE [*singing blithely*]:
    "Say, it's only a paper moon, Sailing over a cardboard sea
    —But it wouldn't be make-believe If you believed in me!"

STELLA: What about the—Flamingo?

STANLEY: She stayed there, too.

STELLA: My sister lived at Belle Reve.

STANLEY: This is after the home-place had slipped through her lily-white fingers! She moved to the Flamingo! A second-class hotel which has the advantage of not interfering in the private social life of the personalities there! The Flamingo is used to all kinds of goings-on. But even the management of the Flamingo was impressed by Dame Blanche! In fact they were so impressed by Dame Blanche that they requested her to turn in her room-key —for permanently! This happened a couple of weeks before she showed here.

BLANCHE [*singing*]:
    "It's a Barnum and Bailey world, Just as phony as it can be—
    But it wouldn't be make-believe If you believed in me!"

STELLA: What—contemptible—lies!

STANLEY: Sure, I can see how you would be upset by this. She pulled the wool over your eyes as much as Mitch's!

STELLA: It's pure invention! There's not a word of truth in it and if I were a man and this creature had dared to invent such things in my presence——

BLANCHE [singing]:

> "Without your love,
> It's a honky-tonk parade!
> Without your love,
> It's a melody played In a penny arcade . . ."

STANLEY: Honey, I told you I thoroughly checked on these stories! Now wait till I finished. The trouble with Dame Blanche was that she couldn't put on her act any more in Laurel! They got wised up after two or three dates with her and then they quit, and she goes on to another, the same old lines, same old act, some old hooey! But the town was too small for this to go on forever! And as time went by she became a town character. Regarded as not just different but downright loco—nuts.

STELLA *draws back.*

And for the last year or two she has been washed up like poison. That's why she's here this summer, visiting royalty, putting on all this act—because she's practically told by the mayor to get out of town! Yes, did you know there was an army camp near Laurel and your sister's was one of the places called "Out-of-Bounds"?

BLANCHE:

> "It's only a paper moon, Just as phony as it can be—
> But it wouldn't be make-believe If you believed in me!"

STANLEY: Well, so much for her being such a refined and particular type of girl. Which brings us to Lie Number Two.

STELLA: I don't want to hear any more!

STANLEY: She's not going back to teach school! In fact I am willing to bet you that she never had no idea of returning to Laurel! She didn't resign temporarily from the high school because of her nerves! No, siree, Bob! She didn't. They kicked her out of that high school before the spring term ended—and I hate to tell you the reason that step was taken! A seventeen-year-old boy—she'd gotten mixed up with!

BLANCHE:

> "It's a Barnum and Bailey world, Just as phony as it can be——"

In the bathroom the water goes on loud; little breathless cries and peals of laughter are heard as if a child were frolicking in the tub.

STELLA: This is making me—sick!

STANLEY: The boy's dad learned about it and got in touch with the high school superintendent. Boy, oh, boy, I'd like to have been in that office when Dame Blanche was called on the carpet! I'd like to have seen her trying to squirm out of that one! But they had her on the hook good and proper that time and she knew that the jig was all up! They told her she better move on to some fresh territory. Yep, it was practickly a town ordinance passed against her!

The bathroom door is opened and BLANCHE *thrusts her head out holding a towel about her hair.*

BLANCHE: Stella!

STELLA [*faintly*]: Yes, Blanche?

BLANCHE: Give me another bath-towel to dry my hair with. I've just washed it.

STELLA: Yes, Blanche. [*She crosses in a dazed way from the kitchen to the bathroom door with a towel.*]

BLANCHE: What's the matter, honey?

STELLA: Matter? Why?

BLANCHE: You have such a strange expression on your face!

STELLA: Oh—— [*She tries to laugh.*] I guess I'm a little tired!

BLANCHE: Why don't you bathe, too, soon as I get out?

STANLEY [*calling from the kitchen*]: How soon is that going to be?

BLANCHE: Not so terribly long! Possess your soul in patience!

STANLEY: It's not my soul I'm worried about!

BLANCHE *slams the door.* STANLEY *laughs harshly.* STELLA *comes slowly back into the kitchen.*

STANLEY: Well, what do you think of it?

STELLA: I don't believe all of those stories and I think your supply-man was mean and rotten to tell them. It's possible that some of the things he said are partly true. There are things about my sister I don't approve of—things that caused sorrow at home. She was always—flighty!

STANLEY: Flighty is some word for it!

STELLA: But when she was young, very young, she had an experience that—killed her illusions!

STANLEY: What experience was that?

STELLA: I mean her marriage, when she was—almost a child! She married a boy who wrote poetry. . . . He was extremely good-looking. I think Blanche didn't just love him but worshipped the ground he walked on! Adored him and thought him almost too fine to be human! But then she found out——

STANLEY: What?

STELLA: This beautiful and talented young man was a degenerate. Didn't your supply-man give you that information?

STANLEY: All we discussed was recent history. That must have been a pretty long time ago.

STELLA: Yes, it was—a pretty long time ago. . . .

> STANLEY *comes up and takes her by the shoulders rather gently. She gently withdraws from him. Automatically she starts sticking little pink candles in the birthday cake.*

STANLEY: How many candles you putting in that cake?

STELLA: I'll stop at twenty-five.

STANLEY: Is company expected?

STELLA: We asked Mitch to come over for cake and ice-cream.

> STANLEY *looks a little uncomfortable. He lights a cigarette from the one he has just finished.*

STANLEY: I wouldn't be expecting Mitch over tonight.

> STELLA *pauses in her occupation with candles and looks slowly around at* STANLEY.

STELLA: *Why?*

STANLEY: Mitch is a buddy of mine. We were in the same outfit together—Two-forty-first Engineers. We work in the same plant and now on the same bowling team. You think I could face him if——

STELLA: Stanley Kowalski, did you—did you repeat what that——?

STANLEY: You're goddam right I told him! I'd have that on my conscience the rest of my life if I knew all that stuff and let my best friend get caught!

STELLA: Is Mitch through with her?

STANLEY: Wouldn't you be if——?

STELLA: I said, *Is Mitch through with her?*

> BLANCHE'S *voice is lifted again, serenely as a bell. She sings* "But it wouldn't be make-believe If you believed in me."

STANLEY: No, I don't think he's necessarily through with her—just wised up!

STELLA: Stanley, she thought Mitch was—going to—going to marry her. I was hoping so, too.

STANLEY: Well, he's not going to marry her. Maybe he *was*, but he's not going to jump in a tank with a school of sharks—now! [*He rises.*] Blanche! Oh, Blanche! Can I please get in my bathroom? [*There is a pause.*]

BLANCHE: Yes, indeed, sir! Can you wait one second while I dry?

STANLEY: Having waited one hour I guess one second ought to pass in a hurry.

STELLA: And she hasn't got her job? Well, what will she do!

STANLEY: She's not stayin' here after Tuesday. You know that, don't you? Just to make sure I bought her ticket myself. A bus-ticket!

STELLA: In the first place, Blanche wouldn't go on a bus.

STANLEY: She'll go on a bus and like it.

STELLA: No, she won't, no, she won't, Stanley!

STANLEY: *She'll go!* Period. P.S. She'll go *Tuesday*!

STELLA [*slowly*]: What'll—she—do? What on earth will she—*do*!

STANLEY: Her future is mapped out for her.

STELLA: What do you mean?

BLANCHE *sings*.

STANLEY: Hey, canary bird! Toots! Get *OUT* of the *BATH-ROOM*! Must I speak more plainly?

The bathroom door flies open and BLANCHE *emerges with a gay peal of laughter, but as* STANLEY *crosses past her, a frightened look appears in her face, almost a look of panic. He doesn't look at her but slams the bathroom door shut as he goes in.*

BLANCHE [*snatching up a hair-brush*]: Oh, I feel so good after my long, hot bath, I feel so good and cool and—rested!

STELLA [*sadly and doubtfully from the kitchen*]: Do you, Blanche?

BLANCHE [*brushing her hair vigorously*]: Yes, I do, so refreshed. [*She tinkles her highball glass.*] A hot bath and a long, cold drink always gives me a brand new outlook on life! [*She looks through the portières at* STELLA, *standing between them, and slowly stops brushing.*] Something has happened!—What is it?

STELLA [*turning quickly away*]: Why, nothing has happened, Blanche.

BLANCHE: You're lying! Something has!

She stares fearfully at STELLA, *who pretends to be busy at the table. The distant piano goes into a hectic breakdown.*

SCENE VIII

Three-quarters of an hour later.
The view through the big windows is fading gradually into a still-golden dusk. A torch of sunlight blazes on the side of a big water-tank or oil-drum across the empty lot toward the business district which is now pierced by pin-points of lighted windows or windows reflecting the sunset.

> *The three people are completing a dismal birthday supper.* STANLEY *looks sullen.* STELLA *is embarrassed and sad.*
> BLANCHE *has a tight, artificial smile on her drawn face. There is a fourth place at the table which is left vacant.*

BLANCHE [*suddenly*]: Stanley, tell us a joke, tell us a funny story to make us all laugh. I don't know what's the matter, we're all so solemn. Is it because I've been stood up by my beau?

> STELLA *laughs feebly.*

It's the first time in my entire experience with men, and I've had a good deal of all sorts, that I've actually been stood up by anybody! Ha-ha! I don't know how to take it. . . . Tell us a funny little story, Stanley! Something to help us out.

STANLEY: I didn't think you liked my stories, Blanche.

BLANCHE: I like them when they're amusing but not indecent.

STANLEY: I don't know any refined enough for your taste.

BLANCHE: Then let me tell one.

STELLA: Yes, you tell one, Blanche. You used to know lots of good stories.

> *The music fades.*

BLANCHE: Let me see, now. . . . I must run through my repertoire! Oh, yes—I love parrot stories! Do you all like parrot stories? Well, this one's about the old maid and the parrot. This old maid, she had a parrot that cursed a blue streak and knew more vulgar expressions than Mr. Kowalski!

STANLEY: Huh.

BLANCHE: And the only way to hush the parrot up was to put the cover back on its cage so it would think it was night and go back to sleep. Well, one morning the old maid had just uncovered the parrot for the day—when who should she see coming up the front walk but the preacher! Well, she rushed back to the parrot and slipped the cover back on the cage and then she let in the preacher. And the parrot was perfectly still, just as quiet as a mouse, but just as she was asking the preacher how much sugar he wanted in his coffee—the parrot broke the silence with a loud—(*she whistles*) —and said—"God *damn*, but that was a short day!"

> *She throws back her head and laughs.* STELLA *also makes an ineffectual effort to seem amused.* STANLEY *pays no attention to the story but reaches way over the table to spear his fork into the remaining chop which he eats with his fingers.*

BLANCHE: Apparently Mr. Kowalski was not amused.

STELLA: Mr. Kowalski is too busy making a pig of himself to think of anything else!

STANLEY: That's right, baby.

STELLA: Your face and your fingers are disgustingly greasy. Go and wash up and then help me clear the table.

> *He hurls a plate to the floor.*

STANLEY: That's how I'll clear the table! [*He seizes her arm.*] Don't ever talk that way to me! "Pig—Polack—disgusting—vulgar—greasy!"—them kind of words have been on your tongue and your sister's too much around here! What do you two think you are? A pair of queens? Remember what Huey Long said—"Every Man is a King!" And I am the king around here, so don't forget it! [*He hurls a cup and saucer to the floor.*] My place is cleared! You want me to clear your places?

> STELLA *begins to cry weakly.* STANLEY *stalks out on the porch and lights a cigarette.*
> *The Negro entertainers around the corner are heard.*

BLANCHE: What happened while I was bathing? What did he tell you, Stella?

STELLA: Nothing, nothing, nothing!

BLANCHE: I think he told you something about Mitch and me! You know why Mitch didn't come but you won't tell me! [STELLA *shakes her head helplessly.*] I'm going to call him!

STELLA: I wouldn't call him, Blanche.

BLANCHE: I am, I'm going to call him on the phone.

STELLA [*miserably*]: I wish you wouldn't.

BLANCHE: I intend to be given some explanation from someone!

She rushes to the phone in the bedroom. STELLA *goes out on the porch and stares reproachfully at her husband. He grunts and turns away from her.*

STELLA: I hope you're pleased with your doings. I never had so much trouble swallowing food in my life, looking at the girl's face and the empty chair. [*She cries quietly.*]

BLANCHE [*at the phone*]: Hello. Mr. Mitchell, please. . . . Oh. . . . I would like to leave a number if I may. Magnolia 9047. And say it's important to call. . . . Yes, very important. . . . Thank you. [*She remains by the phone with a lost, frightened look.*]

STANLEY *turns slowly back towards his wife and takes her clumsily in his arms.*

STANLEY: Stell, it's gonna be all right after she goes and after you've had the baby. It's gonna be all right again between you and me the way that it was. You remember that way that it was? Them nights we had together? God, honey, it's gonna be sweet when we can make noise in the night the way that we used to and get the coloured lights going with nobody's sister behind the curtains to hear us!

Their upstairs neighbours are heard in bellowing laughter at something. STANLEY *chuckles.*

Steve an' Eunice . . .

STELLA: Come on back in. [*She returns to the kitchen and starts lighting the candles on the white cake.*] Blanche?

BLANCHE: Yes. [*She returns from the bedroom to the table in the kitchen.*] Oh, those pretty, pretty little candles! Oh, don't burn them, Stella.

STELLA: I certainly will.

STANLEY *comes back in.*

BLANCHE: You ought to save them for baby's birthdays. Oh, I hope candles are going to glow in his life and I hope that his eyes are going to be like candles, like two blue candles lighted in a white cake!

STANLEY [*sitting down*]: What poetry!

BLANCHE: His Auntie knows candles aren't safe, that candles burn out in little boys' and girls' eyes, or wind blows them out and after that happens, electric light bulbs go on and you see too plainly . . . [*She pauses reflectively for a moment.*] I shouldn't have called him.

STELLA: There's lots of things could have happened.

BLANCHE: There's no excuse for it, Stella. I don't have to put up with insults. I won't be taken for granted.

STANLEY: Goddamn, it's hot in here with the steam from the bathroom.

BLANCHE: I've said I was sorry three times. [*The piano fades out.*] I take hot baths for my nerves. Hydro-therapy, they call it. You healthy Polack, without a nerve in your body, of course you don't know what anxiety feels like!

STANLEY: I am not a Polack. People from Poland are Poles, not Polacks. But what I am is a one hundred per cent. American, born and raised in the greatest country on earth and proud as hell of it, so don't ever call me a Polack.

The phone rings. BLANCHE *rises expectantly.*

BLANCHE: Oh, that's for me, I'm sure.

STANLEY: *I'm* not sure. Keep your seat. [*He crosses leisurely to phone.*] H'lo. Aw, yeh, hello, Mac.

He leans against wall, staring insultingly in at BLANCHE. *She sinks back in her chair with a frightened look.* STELLA *leans over and touches her shoulder.*

BLANCHE: Oh, keep your hands off me, Stella. What is the matter with you? Why do you look at me with that pitying look?

STANLEY [*bawling*]: QUIET IN THERE!—We've got a noisy woman on the place.—Go on, Mac. At Riley's? No, I don't wanta bowl at Riley's. I had a little trouble with Riley last week. I'm the team-captain, ain't I? All right, then, we're not gonna bowl at Riley's, we're gonna bowl at the West Side or the Gala! All right, Mac. See you!

He hangs up and returns to the table. BLANCHE *fiercely controls herself, drinking quietly from her tumbler of water. He doesn't look at her but reaches in a pocket. Then he speaks slowly and with false amiability.*

Sister Blanche, I've got a little birthday remembrance for you.

BLANCHE: Oh, have you, Stanley? I wasn't expecting any, I—I don't know why Stella wants to observe my birthday! I'd much

rather forget it—when you—reach twenty-seven! Well—age is a
subject that you'd prefer to—ignore!

STANLEY: Twenty-seven?

BLANCHE [quickly]: What is it? Is it for me?

He is holding a little envelope towards her.

STANLEY: Yes, I hope you like it!

BLANCHE: Why, why—— Why, it's a——

STANLEY: Ticket! Back to Laurel! On the Greyhound! Tuesday!

The Varsouviana music steals in softly and continues playing. STELLA
rises abruptly and turns her back. BLANCHE tries to smile. Then she
tries to laugh. Then she gives both up and springs from the table and
runs into the next room. She clutches her throat and then runs into the
bathroom. Coughing, gagging sounds are heard.

Well!

STELLA: You didn't need to do that.

STANLEY: Don't forget all that I took off her.

STELLA: You needn't have been so cruel to someone alone as she is.

STANLEY: Delicate piece she is.

STELLA: She is. She was. You didn't know Blanche as a girl. Nobody, nobody, was tender and trusting as she was. But people like
you abused her, and forced her to change.

He crosses into the bedroom, ripping off his shirt, and changes into a
brilliant silk bowling shirt. She follows him.

Do you think you're going bowling now?

STANLEY: Sure.

STELLA: You're not going bowling. [*She catches hold of his shirt.*] Why
did you do this to her?

STANLEY: I done nothing to no one. Let go of my shirt. You've torn
it.

STELLA: I want to know why. Tell me why.

STANLEY: When we first met, me and you, you thought I was
common. How right you was, baby. I was common as dirt. You
showed me the snapshot of the place with the columns. I pulled
you down off them columns and how you loved it, having them
coloured lights going! And wasn't we happy together, wasn't it
all okay till she showed here?

STELLA makes a slight movement. Her look goes suddenly inward

*as if some interior voice had called her name. She begins a slow,
shuffling progress from the bedroom to the kitchen, leaning and resting
on the back of the chair and then on the edge of a table with a blind
look and listening expression.* STANLEY, *finishing with his shirt,
is unaware of her reaction.*

And wasn't we happy together? Wasn't it all okay? Till she showed
here. Hoity-toity, describing me as an ape. [*He suddenly notices the
change in* STELLA.] Hey, what is it, Stel? [*He crosses to her.*]
STELLA [*quietly*]: Take me to the hospital.

*He is with her now, supporting her with his arm, murmuring in-
distinguishably as they go outside. The "Varsouviana" is heard,
its music rising with sinister rapidity as the bathroom door opens slightly.*
BLANCHE *comes out twisting a washcloth. She begins to whisper the
words as the light fades slowly.*

BLANCHE: *El pan de mais, el pan de mais,*
            El pan de mais sin sal.
            El pan de mais, el pan de mais,
            El pan de mais sin sal . . .

SCENE IX

A while later that evening. BLANCHE *is seated in a tense hunched position
in a bedroom chair that she has re-covered with diagonal green and white
stripes. She has on her scarlet satin robe. On the table beside chair is a bottle
of liquor and a glass. The rapid, feverish polka tune, the "Varsouviana,"
is heard. The music is in her mind; she is drinking to escape it and the sense
of disaster closing in on her, and she seems to whisper the words of the song.
An electric fan is turning back and forth across her.*

  MITCH *comes around the corner in work clothes: blue denim shirt and
  pants. He is unshaven. He climbs the steps to the door and rings.*
  BLANCHE *is startled*

BLANCHE: Who is it, please?
MITCH [*hoarsely*]: Me. Mitch.

  The polka tune stops.

BLANCHE: Mitch!—Just a minute.

She rushes about frantically, hiding the bottle in a closet, crouching at the mirror and dabbing her face with cologne and powder. She is so excited that her breath is audible as she dashes about. At last she rushes to the door in the kitchen and lets him in.

MITCH!—Y'know, I really shouldn't let you in after the treatment I have received from you this evening! So utterly uncavalier! But hello, beautiful!

She offers him her lips. He ignores it and pushes past her into the flat. She looks fearfully after him as he stalks into the bedroom.

My, my, what a cold shoulder! And a face like a thundercloud! And such uncouth apparel! Why, you haven't even shaved! The unforgivable insult to a lady! But I forgive you. I forgive you because it's such a relief to see you. You've stopped that polka tune that I had caught in my head. Have you ever had anything caught in your head? Some words, a piece of music? That goes relentlessly on and on in your head? No, of course you haven't, you dumb angel-puss, you'd never get anything awful caught in your head!

He stares at her while she follows him while she talks. It is obvious that he has had a few drinks on the way over.

MITCH: Do we have to have that fan on?
BLANCHE: No!
MITCH: I don't like fans.
BLANCHE: Then let's turn it off, honey. I'm not partial to them!

She presses the switch and the fan nods slowly off. She clears her throat uneasily as MITCH plumps himself down on the bed in the bedroom and lights a cigarette.

I don't know what there is to drink. I—haven't investigated.
MITCH: I don't want Stan's liquor.
BLANCHE: It isn't Stan's. Everything here isn't Stan's. Some things on the premises are actually mine! How is your mother? Isn't your mother well?
MITCH: Why?
BLANCHE: Something's the matter tonight, but never mind. I won't cross-examine the witness. I'll just—— [*She touches her forehead vaguely. The polka tune starts up again.*]—pretend I don't notice anything different about you! That—music again . . .
MITCH: What music?

BLANCHE: The "Varsouviana"? The polka tune they were playing when Allan——— Wait!

A distant revolver shot is heard, BLANCHE *seems relieved.*

There now, the shot! It always stops after that.

The polka music dies out again.

Yes, now it's stopped.

MITCH: Are you boxed out of your mind?

BLANCHE: I'll go and see what I can find in the way of——— [*She crosses into the closet, pretending to search for the bottle.*] Oh, by the way, excuse me for not being dressed. But I'd practically given you up! Had you forgotten your invitation to supper?

MITCH: I wasn't going to see you any more.

BLANCHE: Wait a minute. I can't hear what you're saying and you talk so little that when you do say something, I don't want to miss a single syllable of it. . . . What am I looking around here for? Oh, yes—liquor! We've had so much excitement around here this evening that I *am* boxed out of my mind! [*She pretends suddenly to find the bottle. He draws his foot up on the bed and stares at her contemptuously.*] Here's something. Southern Comfort! What is that, I wonder?

MITCH: If you don't know, it must belong to Stan.

BLANCHE: Take your foot off the bed. It has a light cover on it. Of course you boys don't notice things like that. I've done so much with this place since I've been here.

MITCH: I bet you have.

BLANCHE: You saw it before I came. Well, look at it now! This room is almost—dainty! I want to keep it that way. I wonder if this stuff ought to be mixed with something? Ummm, it's sweet, so sweet! It's terribly, terribly sweet! Why, it's a *liqueur*, I believe! Yes, that's what it *is*, a liqueur! [MITCH *grunts.*] I'm afraid you won't like it, but try it, and maybe you will.

MITCH: I told you already I don't want none of his liquor and I mean it. You ought to lay off his liquor. He says you been lapping it up all summer like a wild-cat!

BLANCHE: What a fantastic statement! Fantastic of him to say it, fantastic of you to repeat it! I won't descend to the level of such cheap accusations to answer them, even!

MITCH: Huh.

BLANCHE: What's in your mind? I see something in your eyes!

MITCH [*getting up*]: It's dark in here.

BLANCHE: I like it dark. The dark is comforting to me.

MITCH: I don't think I ever seen you in the light. [BLANCHE *laughs breathlessly.*] That's a fact!

BLANCHE: Is it?

MITCH: I've never seen you in the afternoon.

BLANCHE: Whose fault is that?

MITCH: You never want to go out in the afternoon.

BLANCHE: Why, Mitch, you're at the plant in the afternoon!

MITCH: Not Sunday afternoon. I've asked you to go out with me sometimes on Sundays but you always make an excuse. You never want to go out till after six and then it's always some place that's not lighted much.

BLANCHE: There is some obscure meaning in this but I fail to catch it.

MITCH: What it means is I've never had a real good look at you, Blanche.

BLANCHE: What are you leading up to?

MITCH: Let's turn the light on here.

BLANCHE [*fearfully*]: Light? Which light? What for?

MITCH: This one with the paper thing on it. [*He tears the paper lantern off the light bulb. She utters a frightened gasp.*]

BLANCHE: What did you do that for?

MITCH: So I can take a look at you good and plain!

BLANCHE: Of course you don't really mean to be insulting!

MITCH: No, just realistic.

BLANCHE: I don't want realism.

MITCH: Naw, I guess not.

BLANCHE: I'll tell you what I want. Magic! [MITCH *laughs.*] Yes, yes, magic! I try to give that to people. I misrepresent things to them. I don't tell truth, I tell what *ought* to be truth. And if that is sinful, then let me be damned for it!—*Don't turn the light on!*

MITCH *crosses to the switch. He turns the light on and stares at her. She cries out and covers her face. He turns the light off again.*

MITCH [*slowly and bitterly*]: I don't mind you being older than what I thought. But all the rest of it—God! That pitch about your ideals being so old-fashioned and all the malarkey that you've dished out all summer. Oh, I knew you weren't sixteen any more. But I was a fool enough to believe you was straight.

BLANCHE: Who told you I wasn't—"straight"? My loving brother-in-law. And you believed him.

MITCH: I called him a liar at first. And then I checked on the story. First I asked our supply-man who travels through Laurel. And then I talked directly over long-distance to this merchant.

BLANCHE: Who is the merchant?

MITCH: Kiefaber.

BLANCHE: The merchant Kiefaber of Laurel! I know the man. He whistled at me. I put him in his place. So now for revenge he makes up stories about me.

MITCH: Three people, Kiefaber, Stanley and Shaw, swore to them!

BLANCHE: Rub-a-dub-dub, three men in a tub! And such a filthy tub!

MITCH: Didn't you stay at a hotel called The Flamingo?

BLANCHE: Flamingo? No! Tarantula was the name of it! I stayed at a hotel called The Tarantula Arms!

MITCH [stupidly]: Tarantula?

BLANCHE: Yes, a big spider! That's where I brought my victims. [She pours herself another drink.] Yes, I had many intimacies with strangers. After the death of Allan—intimacies with strangers was all I seemed able to fill my empty heart with. . . . I think it was panic, just panic, that drove me from one to another, hunting for some protection—here and there, in the most—unlikely places —even, at last, in a seventeen-year-old boy but—somebody wrote the superintendent about it—"This woman is morally unfit for her position!"

She throws back her head with convulsive, sobbing laughter.
Then she repeats the statement, gasps, and drinks.

True? Yes, I suppose—unfit somehow—anyway. . . . So I came here. There was nowhere else I could go. I was played out. You know what played out is? My youth was suddenly gone up the water-spout, and—I met you. You said you needed somebody. Well, I needed somebody, too. I thanked God for you, because you seemed to be gentle—a cleft in the rock of the world that I could hide in! The poor man's Paradise—is a little peace. . . . But I guess I was asking, hoping—too much! Kiefaber, Stanley and Shaw have tied an old tin can to the tail of the kite.

There is a pause. MITCH stares at her dumbly.

MITCH: You lied to me, Blanche.

BLANCHE: Don't say I lied to you.

MITCH: Lies, lies, inside and out, all lies.

BLANCHE: Never inside, I didn't lie in my heart. . . .

A Vendor comes around the corner. She is a blind MEXICAN WOMAN *in a dark shawl, carrying bunches of those gaudy tin flowers that lower class Mexicans display at funerals and other festive occasions. She is calling barely audibly. Her figure is only faintly visible outside the building.*

MEXICAN WOMAN: *Flores. Flores. Flores para los muertos. Flores. Flores.*

BLANCHE: What? Oh! Somebody outside. . . . I—I lived in a house where dying old women remembered their dead men . . .

MEXICAN WOMEN: *Flores. Flores para los muertos . . .*

The polka tune fades in.

BLANCHE [*as if to herself*]: Crumble and fade and—regrets—re-criminations . . . "If you'd done this, it wouldn't've cost me that!"

MEXICAN WOMAN: *Corones para los muertos. Corones . . .*

BLANCHE: Legacies! Huh. . . . And other things such as blood-stained pillow-slips—"Her linen needs changing"—"Yes Mother. But couldn't we get a coloured girl to do it?" No, we couldn't of course. Everything gone but the——

MEXICAN WOMAN: *Flores.*

BLANCHE: Death—I used to sit here and she used to sit over there and death was as close as you are. . . . We didn't dare even admit we had ever heard of it!

MEXICAN WOMAN: *Flores para los muertos, flores—flores . . .*

BLANCHE: The opposite is desire. So do you wonder? How could you possibly wonder! Not far from Belle Reve, before we had lost Belle Reve, was a camp where they trained young soldiers. On Saturday nights they would go in town to get drunk——

MEXICAN WOMAN [*softly*]: *Corones . . .*

BLANCHE: —and on the way back they would stagger on to my lawn and call—"Blanche! Blanche!"—The deaf old lady remaining suspected nothing. But sometimes I slipped outside to answer their calls. . . . Later the paddy-wagon would gather them up like daisies . . . the long way home . . .

The MEXICAN WOMAN *turns slowly and drifts back off with her soft mournful cries.* BLANCHE *goes to the dresser and leans forward on it. After a moment,* MITCH *rises and follows her purposefully. The polka music fades away. He places his hands on her waist and tries to turn her about.*

BLANCHE: What do you want?

MITCH [*fumbling to embrace her*]: What I been missing all summer.

BLANCHE: Then marry me, Mitch!

MITCH: I don't think I want to marry you any more.

BLANCHE: No?

MITCH [*dropping his hands from her waist*]: You're not clean enough to bring in the house with my mother.

BLANCHE: Go away, then. [*He stares at her.*] Get out of here quick before I start screaming fire! [*Her throat is tightening with hysteria.*] Get out of here quick before I start screaming fire.

He still remains staring. She suddenly rushes to the big window with its pale blue square of the soft summer light and cries wildly.

Fire! Fire! Fire!

With a startled gasp, MITCH turns and goes out of the outer door, clatters awkwardly down the steps and around the corner of the building. BLANCHE staggers back from the window and falls to her knees. The distant piano is slow and blue.

SCENE X

It is a few hours later that night.

BLANCHE *has been drinking fairly steadily since* MITCH *left. She has dragged her wardrobe trunk into the centre of the bedroom. It hangs open with flowery dresses thrown across it. As the drinking and packing went on, a mood of hysterical exhilaration came into her and she has decked herself out in a somewhat soiled and crumpled white satin evening gown and a pair of scuffed silver slippers with brilliants set in their heels.*

Now she is placing the rhinestone tiara on her head before the mirror of the dressing-table and murmuring excitedly as if to a group of spectral admirers.

BLANCHE: How about taking a swim, a moonlight swim at the old rock-quarry? If anyone's sober enough to drive a car! Ha-Ha! Best way in the world to stop your head buzzing! Only you've got to be careful to dive where the deep pool is—if you hit a rock you don't come up till tomorrow. . . .

Tremblingly she lifts the hand mirror for a closer inspection. She catches her breath and slams the mirror face down with such violence that the glass cracks. She moans a little and attempts to rise.

STANLEY *appears around the corner of the building. He still has on the vivid green silk bowling shirt As he rounds the corner the honky-tonk music is heard. It continues softly throughout the scene.*

He enters the kitchen, slamming the door. As he peers in at BLANCHE, *he gives a low whistle. He has had a few drinks on the way and has brought some quart beer bottles home with him.*

BLANCHE: How is my sister?

STANLEY: She is doing okay.

BLANCHE: And how is the baby?

STANLEY [*grinning amiably*]: The baby won't come before morning so they told me to go home and get a little shut-eye.

BLANCHE: Does that mean we are to be alone in here?

STANLEY: Yep. Just me and you, Blanche. Unless you got somebody hid under the bed. What've you got on those fine feathers for?

BLANCHE: Oh, that's right. You left before my wire came.

STANLEY: You got a wire?

BLANCHE: I received a telegram from an old admirer of mine.

STANLEY: Anything good?

BLANCHE: I think so. An invitation.

STANLEY: What to? A fireman's ball?

BLANCHE [*throwing back her head*]: A cruise of the Caribbean on a yacht!

STANLEY: Well, well. What do you know?

BLANCHE: I have never been so surprised in my life.

STANLEY: I guess not.

BLANCHE: It came like a bolt from the blue!

STANLEY: Who did you say it was from?

BLANCHE: An old beau of mine.

STANLEY: The one that give you the white fox-pieces?

BLANCHE: Mr. Shep Huntleigh. I wore his ATO pin my last year at college. I hadn't seen him again until last Christmas. I ran in to him on Biscayne Boulevard. Then—just now—this wire—inviting me on a cruise of the Caribbean! The problem is clothes. I tore into my trunk to see what I have that's suitable for the tropics!

STANLEY: And come up with that—gorgeous—diamond—tiara?

BLANCHE: This old relic! Ha-ha! It's only rhinestones.

STANLEY: Gosh. I thought it was Tiffany diamonds. [*He unbuttons his shirt.*]

BLANCHE: Well, anyhow, I shall be entertained in style.

STANLEY: Uh-huh. It goes to show, you never know what is coming.

BLANCHE: Just when I thought my luck had begun to fail me——

STANLEY: Into the picture pops this Miami millionaire.

BLANCHE: This man is not from Miami. This man is from Dallas.

STANLEY: This man is from Dallas?

BLANCHE: Yes, this man is from Dallas where gold spouts out of the ground!

STANLEY: Well, just so he's from somewhere! [*He starts removing his shirt.*]

BLANCHE: Close the curtains before you undress any further.

STANLEY [*amiably*]: This is all I'm going to undress right now. [*He rips the sack off a quart beer-bottle.*] Seen a bottle-opener?

> *She moves slowly towards the dresser, where she stands with her hands knotted together.*

I used to have a cousin who could open a beer-bottle with his teeth. [*Pounding the bottle cap on the corner of table.*] That was his only accomplishment, all he could do—he was just a human bottle-opener. And then one time, at a wedding party, he broke his front teeth off! After that he was so ashamed of himself he used t' sneak out of the house when company came . . .

> *The bottle cap pops off and a geyser of foam shoots up.* STANLEY *laughs happily, holding up the bottle over his head.*

Ha-ha! Rain from heaven! [*He extends the bottle towards her.*] Shall we bury the hatchet and make it a loving-cup? Huh?

BLANCHE: No, thank you.

STANLEY: Well, it's a red letter night for us both. You having an oil-millionaire and me having a baby.

> *He goes to the bureau in the bedroom and crouches to remove something from the bottom drawer.*

BLANCHE [*drawing back*]: What are you doing in here?

STANLEY: Here's something I always break out on special occasions like this! The silk pyjamas I wore on my wedding night!

BLANCHE: Oh.

STANLEY: When the telephone rings and they say, "You've got a son!" I'll tear this off and wave it like a flag! [*He shakes out a brilliant pyjama coat.*] I guess we are both entitled to put on the dog. [*He goes back to the kitchen with the coat over his arm.*]

BLANCHE: When I think of how divine it is going to be to have such a thing as privacy once more—I could weep with joy!

STANLEY: This millionaire from Dallas is not going to interfere with your privacy any?

BLANCHE: It won't be the sort of thing you have in mind. This man is a gentleman and he respects me. [*Improvising feverishly.*] What he wants is my companionship. Having great wealth sometimes makes people lonely!

STANLEY: I wouldn't know about that.

BLANCHE: A cultivated woman, a woman of intelligence and breeding, can enrich a man's life—immeasurably! I have those things to offer, and this doesn't take them away. Physical beauty is passing. A transitory possession. But beauty of the mind and richness of the spirit and tenderness of the heart—and I have all of those things —aren't taken away, but grow! Increase with the years! How strange that I should be called a destitute woman! When I have all of these treasures locked in my heart. [*A choked sob comes from her.*] I think of myself as a very, very rich woman! But I have been foolish—casting my pearls before swine!

STANLEY: Swine, huh?

BLANCHE: Yes, swine! Swine! And I'm thinking not only of you but of your friend, Mr. Mitchell. He came to see me tonight. He dared to come here in his work-clothes! And to repeat slander to me, vicious stories that he had gotten from you! I gave him his walking papers . . .

STANLEY: You did, huh?

BLANCHE: But then he came back. He returned with a box of roses to beg my forgiveness! He implored my forgiveness. But some things are not forgivable. Deliberate cruelty is not forgivable. It is the one unforgivable thing in my opinion and it is the one thing of which I have never, never been guilty. And so I told him, I said to him, "Thank you," but it was foolish of me to think that we could ever adapt ourselves to each other. Our ways of life are too different. Our attitudes and our backgrounds are incompatible. We have to be realistic about such things. So farewell, my friend! And let there be no hard feelings . . .

STANLEY: Was this before or after the telegram came from the Texas oil millionaire?

BLANCHE: What telegram? No! No, after! As a matter of fact, the wire came just as——

STANLEY: As a matter of fact there wasn't no wire at all!

BLANCHE: Oh, oh!

STANLEY: There isn't no millionaire! And Mitch didn't come back
with roses 'cause I know where he is——

BLANCHE: Oh!

STANLEY: There isn't a goddam thing but imagination!

BLANCHE: Oh!

STANLEY: And lies and conceit and tricks!

BLANCHE: Oh!

STANLEY: And look at yourself! Take a look at yourself in that
worn-out Mardi Gras outfit, rented for fifty cents from some rag-
picker! And with the crazy crown on! What queen do you think
you are!

BLANCHE: Oh—God ...

STANLEY: I've been on to you from the start! Not once did you pull
any wool over this boy's eyes! You come in here and sprinkle the
place with powder and spray perfume and cover the light-bulb
with a paper lantern, and lo and behold the place has turned into
Egypt and you are the Queen of the Nile! Sitting on your throne
and swilling down my liquor! I say—*Ha—Ha!* Do you hear me?
Ha—ha—ha! [*He walks into the bedroom.*]

BLANCHE: Don't come in here!

> *Lurid reflections appear on the walls around* BLANCHE. *The shadows
> are of a grotesque and menacing form. She catches her breath, crosses
> to the phone and jiggles the hook.* STANLEY *goes into the bathroom
> and closes the door.*

Operator, operator! Give me long-distance, please. ... I want to
get in touch with Mr. Shep Huntleigh of Dallas. He's so well-
known he doesn't require any address. Just ask anybody who——
Wait!—No, I couldn't find it right now. . . . Please understand,
I—No! No, wait! . . . One moment! Someone is—Nothing!
Hold on, please!

> *She sets the phone down and crosses warily into the kitchen.*
> *The night is filled with inhuman voices like cries in a jungle.*
> *The shadows and lurid reflections move sinuously as flames along the
> wall spaces.*
> *Through the back wall of the rooms, which have become transparent,
> can be seen the sidewalk. A prostitute has rolled a drunkard. He pursues
> her along the walk, overtakes her and there is a struggle. A policeman's
> whistle breaks it up. The figures disappear.*

Some moments later the NEGRO WOMAN *appears around the corner with a sequined bag which the prostitute had dropped on the walk. She is rooting excitedly through it.*

BLANCHE *presses her knuckles to her lips and returns slowly to the phone. She speaks in a hoarse whisper.*

Operator! Operator! Never mind long-distance. Get Western Union. There isn't time to be—Western—Western Union!
She waits anxiously.

Western Union? Yes! I—want to—— Take down this message! "In desperate, desperate circumstances! Help me! Caught in a trap. Caught in——" *Oh!*

The bathroom door is thrown open and STANLEY *comes out in the brilliant silk pyjamas. He grins at her as he knots the tasselled sash about his waist. She gasps and backs away from the phone. He stares at her for a count of ten. Then a clicking becomes audible from the telephone, steady and rasping.*

STANLEY: You left th' phone off th' hook.

He crosses to it deliberately and sets it back on the hook. After he has replaced it, he stares at her again, his mouth slowly curving into a grin, as he waves between BLANCHE *and the outer door.*
The barely audible "blue piano" begins to drum up louder. The sound of it turns into the roar of an approaching locomotive. BLANCHE *crouches, pressing her fists to her ears until it has gone by.*

BLANCHE [*finally straightening*]: Let me—let me get by you!
STANLEY: Get by me? Sure. Go ahead. [*He moves back a pace in the doorway.*]
BLANCHE: You—you stand over there! [*She indicates a further position.*]
STANLEY [*grinning*]: You got plenty of room to walk by me now.
BLANCHE: Not with you there! But I've got to get out somehow!
STANLEY: You think I'll interfere with you? Ha-ha!

The "blue piano" goes softly. She turns confusedly and makes a faint gesture. The inhuman jungle voices rise up. He takes a step towards her, biting his tongue which protrudes between his lips.

STANLEY [*softly*]: Come to think of it—maybe you wouldn't be bad to—interfere with . . .

BLANCHE *moves backward through the door into the bedroom.*

BLANCHE: Stay back! Don't you come towards me another step or I'll——

STANLEY: What?

BLANCHE: Some awful thing will happen! It will!

STANLEY: What are you putting on now?

They are now both inside the bedroom.

BLANCHE: I warn you, don't, I'm in danger!

He takes another step. She smashes a bottle on the table and faces him, clutching the broken top.

STANLEY: What did you do that for?

BLANCHE: So I could twist the broken end in your face!

STANLEY: I bet you would do that!

BLANCHE: I would! I will if you——

STANLEY: Oh! So you want some rough-house! All right, let's have some rough-house!

He springs towards her, overturning the table. She cries out and strikes at him with the bottle top but he catches her wrist.

Tiger—tiger! Drop the bottle-top! Drop it! We've had this date with each other from the beginning!

She moans. The bottle-top falls. She sinks to her knees. He picks up her inert figure and carries her to the bed. The hot trumpet and drums from the Four Deuces sound loudly.

SCENE XI

It is some weeks later. STELLA is packing BLANCHE's things. Sound of water can be heard running in the bathroom.
The portières are partly open on the poker players—STANLEY, STEVE, MITCH and PABLO—who sit around the table in the kitchen. The atmosphere of the kitchen is now the same raw, lurid one of the disastrous poker night.
The building is framed by the sky of turquoise. STELLA has been crying as she arranges the flowery dresses in the open trunk.
EUNICE *comes down the steps from her flat above and enters the kitchen. There is another burst from the poker table.*

STANLEY: Drew to an inside straight and made it, by God.

PABLO: *Maldita sea tu suerto!*

STANLEY: Put it in English, greaseball.

PABLO: I am cursing your goddam luck.

STANLEY [*prodigiously elated*]: You know what luck is? Luck is believing you're lucky. Take at Salerno. I believed I was lucky. I figured that 4 out of 5 would not come through but I would . . . and I did. I put that down as a rule. To hold front position in this rat-race you've got to believe you are lucky.

MITCH: You . . . you . . . you. . . . Brag . . . brag . . . bull . . . bull.

STELLA *goes into the bedroom and starts folding a dress.*

STANLEY: What's the matter with him?

EUNICE [*walking past the table*]: I always did say that men are callous things with no feelings, but this does beat anything. Making pigs of yourselves. [*She comes through the portières into the bedroom.*]

STANLEY: What's the matter with her?

STELLA: How is my baby?

EUNICE: Sleeping like a little angel. Brought you some grapes. [*She puts them on a stool and lowers her voice.*] Blanche?

STELLA: Bathing.

EUNICE: How is she?

STELLA: She wouldn't eat anything but asked for a drink.

EUNICE: What did you tell her?

STELLA: I—just told her that—we'd made arrangements for her to rest in the country. She's got it mixed in her mind with Shep Huntleigh.

BLANCHE *opens the bathroom door slightly.*

BLANCHE: Stella.

STELLA: Yes, Blanche?

BLANCHE: If anyone calls while I'm bathing take the number and tell them I'll call right back.

STELLA: Yes.

BLANCHE: That cool yellow silk—the bouclé. See if it's crushed. If it's not too crushed I'll wear it and on the lapel that silver and turquoise pin in the shape of a seahorse. You will find them in the heart-shaped box I keep my accessories in. And Stella . . . Try and locate a bunch of artificial violets in that box, too, to pin with the seahorse on the lapel of the jacket.

She closes the door. STELLA *turns to* EUNICE.

STELLA: I don't know if I did the right thing.

EUNICE: What else could you do?

STELLA: I couldn't believe her story and go on living with Stanley.

EUNICE: Don't ever believe it. Life has got to go on. No matter what happens, you've got to keep on going.

The bathroom door opens a little.

BLANCHE [*looking out*]: Is the coast clear?

STELLA: Yes, Blanche. [*To* EUNICE.] Tell her how well she's looking.

BLANCHE: Please close the curtains before I come out.

STELLA: They're closed.

STANLEY: —How many for you

PABLO: Two.—

STEVE: —Three.

BLANCHE appears in the amber light of the door. She has a tragic radiance in her red satin robe following the sculptural lines of her body. The "Varsouviana" rises audibly as BLANCHE *enters the bedroom.*

BLANCHE [*with faintly hysterical vivacity*]: I have just washed my hair.

STELLA: Did you?

BLANCHE: I'm not sure I got the soap out.

EUNICE: Such fine hair!

BLANCHE [*accepting the compliment*]: It's a problem. Didn't I get a call?

STELLA: Who from, Blanche?

BLANCHE: Shep Huntleigh . . .

STELLA: Why, not yet, honey!

BLANCHE: How strange! I——

At the sound of BLANCHE'S *voice* MITCH'S *arm supporting his cards has sagged and his gaze is dissolved into space.* STANLEY *slaps him on the shoulder.*

STANLEY: Hey, Mitch, come to!

The sound of this new voice shocks BLANCHE. *She makes a shocked gesture, forming his name with her lips.* STELLA *nods and looks quickly away.* BLANCHE *stands quite still for some moments—the silverbacked mirror in her hand and a look of sorrowful perplexity as though all human experience shows on her face.* BLANCHE *finally speaks with sudden hysteria.*

BLANCHE: What's going on here?

She turns from STELLA *to* EUNICE *and back to* STELLA. *Her rising voice penetrates the concentration of the game.* MITCH *ducks his head lower but* STANLEY *shoves back his chair as if about to rise.* STEVE *places a restraining hand on his arm.*

BLANCHE [*continuing*]: What's happened here? I want an explanation of what's happened here.

STELLA [*agonizingly*]: Hush! Hush!

EUNICE: Hush! Hush! Honey.

STELLA: Please, Blanche.

BLANCHE: Why are you looking at me like that? Is something wrong with me?

EUNICE: You look wonderful, Blanche. Don't she look wonderful?

STELLA: Yes.

EUNICE: I understand you are going on a trip.

STELLA: Yes, Blanche *is*. She's going on vacation.

EUNICE: I'm green with envy.

BLANCHE: Help me, help me get dressed!

STELLA [*handing her dress*]: Is this what you——

BLANCHE: Yes, it will do! I'm anxious to get out of here—this place is a trap!

EUNICE: What a pretty blue jacket.

STELLA: It's lilac coloured.

BLANCHE: You're both mistaken. It's Della Robbia blue. The blue of the robe in the old Madonna pictures. Are these grapes washed?

She fingers the bunch of grapes which EUNICE *has brought in.*

EUNICE: Huh?

BLANCHE: Washed, I said. Are they washed?

EUNICE: They're from the French Market.

BLANCHE: That doesn't mean they've been washed. [*The cathedral bells chime.*] Those cathedral bells—they're the only clean thing in the Quarter. Well, I'm going now. I'm ready to go.

EUNICE [*whispering*]: She's going to walk out before they get here.

STELLA: Wait, Blanche.

BLANCHE: I don't want to pass in front of those men.

EUNICE: Then wait'll the game breaks up.

STELLA: Sit down and . . .

BLANCHE *turns weakly, hesitantly about. She lets them push her into a chair.*

BLANCHE: I can smell the sea air. The rest of my time I'm going to spend on the sea. And when I die, I'm going to die on the sea. You know what I shall die of? [*She plucks a grape.*] I shall die of eating an unwashed grape one day out on the ocean. I will die —with my hand in the hand of some nice-looking ship's doctor, a very young one with a small blond moustache and a big silver watch. "Poor lady," they'll say, "the quinine did her no good. That unwashed grape has transported her soul to heaven." [*The cathedral chimes are heard.*] And I'll be buried at sea sewn up in a clean white sack and dropped overboard—at noon—in the blaze of summer—and into an ocean as blue as [*chimes again*] my first lover's eyes!

A DOCTOR and a MATRON have appeared around the corner of the building and climbed the steps to the porch. The gravity of their profession is exaggerated—the unmistakable aura of the state institution with its cynical detachment. The DOCTOR rings the doorbell. The murmur of the game is interrupted.

EUNICE [*whispering to STELLA*]: That must be them.

STELLA presses her fist to her lips.

BLANCHE [*rising slowly*]: What is it?
EUNICE [*affectedly casual*]: Excuse me while I see who's at the door.
STELLA: Yes.

EUNICE goes into the kitchen.

BLANCHE [*tensely*]: I wonder if it's for me.

A whispered colloquy takes place at the door.

EUNICE [*returning, brightly*]: Someone is calling for Blanche.
BLANCHE: It *is* for me, then! [*She looks fearfully from one to the other and then to the portières. The "Varsouviana" faintly plays.*] Is it the gentleman I was expecting from Dallas?
EUNICE: I think it is, Blanche.
BLANCHE: I'm not quite ready.
STELLA: Ask him to wait outside.
BLANCHE: I . . .

EUNICE goes back to the portières. Drums sound very softly.

STELLA: Everything packed?
BLANCHE: My silver toilet articles are still out.

STELLA: Ah!

EUNICE [*returning*]: They're waiting in front of the house.

BLANCHE: They! Who's "they"?

EUNICE: There's a lady with him.

BLANCHE: I cannot imagine who this "lady" could be! How is she dressed?

EUNICE: Just—just a sort of a—plain-tailored outfit.

BLANCHE: Possibly she's—— [*Her voice dies out nervously.*]

STELLA: Shall we go, Blanche?

BLANCHE: Must we go through that room?

STELLA: I will go with you.

BLANCHE: How do I look?

STELLA: Lovely.

EUNICE [*echoing*]: Lovely.

> BLANCHE *moves fearfully to the portières.* EUNICE *draws them open for her.* BLANCHE *goes into the kitchen.*

BLANCHE [*to the men*]: Please don't get up. I'm only passing through.

> *She crosses quickly to outside door.* STELLA *and* EUNICE *follow. The poker players stand awkwardly at the table—all except* MITCH, *who remains seated, looking at the table.* BLANCHE *steps out on a small porch at the side of the door. She stops short and catches her breath.*

DOCTOR: How do you do?

BLANCHE: You are not the gentleman I was expecting. [*She suddenly gasps and starts back up the steps. She stops by* STELLA, *who stands just outside the door, and speaks in a frightening whisper.*] That man isn't Shep Huntleigh.

> *The "Varsouviana" is playing distantly.*
> STELLA *stares back at* BLANCHE. EUNICE *is holding* STELLA'S *arm. There is a moment of silence—no sound but that of* STANLEY *steadily shuffling the cards.*
> BLANCHE *catches her breath again and slips back into the flat. She enters the flat with a peculiar smile, her eyes wide and brilliant. As soon as her sister goes past her,* STELLA *closes her eyes and clenches her hands.* EUNICE *throws her arms comfortingly about her. Then she starts up to her flat.* BLANCHE *stops just inside the door.* MITCH *keeps staring down at his hands on the table, but the other men look at her curiously. At last she starts around the table towards the bedroom. As*

she does, STANLEY *suddenly pushes back his chair and rises as if to block her way. The* MATRON *follows her into the flat.*

STANLEY: Did you forget something?
BLANCHE [*shrilly*]: Yes! Yes, I forgot something!

She rushes past him into the bedroom. Lurid reflections appear on the walls in odd, sinuous shapes. The "Varsouviana" is filtered into weird distortion, accompanied by the cries and noises of the jungle. BLANCHE *seizes the back of a chair as if to defend herself.*

STANLEY: Doc, you better go in.
DOCTOR [*motioning to the* MATRON]: Nurse, bring her out.

The MATRON *advances on one side.* STANLEY *on the other. Divested of all the softer properties of womanhood, the* MATRON *is a peculiarly sinister figure in her severe dress. Her voice is bold and toneless as a fire-bell.*

MATRON: Hello, Blanche.

The greeting is echoed and re-echoed by other mysterious voices behind the walls, as if reverberated through a canyon of rock.

STANLEY: She says that she forgot something.

The echo sounds in threatening whispers.

MATRON: That's all right.
STANLEY: What did you forget, Blanche?
BLANCHE: I—I——
MATRON: It don't matter. We can pick it up later.
STANLEY: Sure. We can send it along with the trunk.
BLANCHE [*retreating in panic*]: I don't know you—I don't know you. I want to be—left alone—please!
MATRON: Now, Blanche!
ECHOES [*rising and falling*]: Now, Blanche—now, Blanche—now, Blanche!
STANLEY: You left nothing here but spilt talcum and old empty perfume bottles—unless it's the paper lantern you want to take with you. You want the lantern?

He crosses to dressing-table and seizes the paper lantern, tearing it off the light bulb, and extends it towards her. She cries out as if the lantern was herself. The MATRON *steps boldly towards her. She screams and tries to break past the* MATRON. *All the men spring to their feet.* STELLA *runs out to the porch, with* EUNICE *following to comfort her, simultaneously with the confused voices of the men in the kitchen.* STELLA *rushes into* EUNICE'S *embrace on the porch.*

STELLA: Oh, my God, Eunice help me! Don't let them do that to her, don't let them hurt her! Oh, God, oh, please God, don't hurt her! What are they doing to her? What are they doing? [*She tries to break from* EUNICE'S *arms.*]

EUNICE: No, honey, no, no, honey. Stay here. Don't go back in there. Stay with me and don't look.

STELLA: What have I done to my sister? Oh, God, what have I done to my sister?

EUNICE: You done the right thing, the only thing you could do. She couldn't stay here; there wasn't no other place for her to go.

While STELLA *and* EUNICE *are speaking on the porch the voices of the men in the kitchen overlap them.*

STANLEY [*running in from the bedroom*]: Hey! Hey! Doctor! Doctor, you better go in!

DOCTOR: Too bad, too bad. I always like to avoid it.

PABLO: This is a very bad thing.

STEVE: This is no way to do it. She should've been told.

PABLO: *Madre de Dios! Cosa mala, muy, muy mala!*

MITCH *has started towards the bedroom.* STANLEY *crosses to block him.*

MITCH [*wildly*]: You! You done this, all o' your God damn interfering with things you——

STANLEY: Quit the blubber! [*He pushes him aside.*]

MITCH: I'll kill you! [*He lunges and strikes at* STANLEY.]

STANLEY: Hold this bone-headed cry-baby!

STEVE [*grasping* MITCH]: Stop it, Mitch.

PABLO: Yeah, yeah, take it easy!

MITCH *collapses at the table, sobbing.*
During the preceding scenes, the MATRON *catches hold of* BLANCHE'S *arm and prevents her flight.* BLANCHE *turns wildly and scratches at the* MATRON. *The heavy woman pinions her arms.* BLANCHE *cries out hoarsely and slips to her knees.*

MATRON: These fingernails have to be trimmed. [*The* DOCTOR *comes into the room and she looks at him.*] Jacket, Doctor?

DOCTOR: Not unless necessary.

*He takes off his hat and now becomes personalized. The unhuman
quality goes. His voice is gentle and reassuring as he crosses to* BLANCHE
*and crouches in front of her. As he speaks her name, her terror subsides
a little. The lurid reflections fade from the walls, the inhuman cries
and noises die out and her own hoarse crying is calmed.*

DOCTOR: Miss DuBois.

*She turns her face to him and stares at him with desperate pleading.
He smiles; then he speaks to the* MATRON.

It won't be necessary.
BLANCHE [*faintly*]: Ask her to let go of me.
DOCTOR [*to the* MATRON]: Let go.

The MATRON *releases her.* BLANCHE *extends her hands towards
the* DOCTOR. *He draws her up gently and supports her with his
arm and leads her through the portières.*

BLANCHE [*holding tight to his arm*]: Whoever you are—I have always
depended on the kindness of strangers.

The poker players stand back as BLANCHE *and the* DOCTOR *cross
the kitchen to the front door. She allows him to lead her as if she were
blind. As they go out on the porch,* STELLA *cries out her sister's name
from where she is crouched a few steps upon the stairs.*

STELLA: Blanche! Blanche, Blanche!

BLANCHE *walks on without turning, followed by the* DOCTOR
and the MATRON. *They go around the corner of the building.*
EUNICE *descends to* STELLA *and places the child in her arms. It
is wrapped in a pale blue blanket.* STELLA *accepts the child, sobbingly.*
EUNICE *continues downstairs and enters the kitchen where the men
except for* STANLEY, *are returning silently to their places about the
table.* STANLEY *has gone out on the porch and stands at the foot of the
steps looking at* STELLA.

STANLEY [*a bit uncertainly*]: Stella?

*She sobs with inhuman abandon. There is something luxurious in
her complete surrender to crying now that her sister is gone.*

STANLEY [*voluptuously, soothingly*]: Now, honey. Now, love. Now,

now love. [*He kneels beside her and his fingers find the opening of her blouse.*] Now, now, love. Now, love. . . .

The luxurious sobbing, the sensual murmur fade away under the swelling music of the "blue piano" and the muted trumpet.

STEVE: This game is seven-card stud.

CURTAIN

Notes

1   Hart Crane (1899–1932) was an American poet Tennessee
Williams particularly admired. This epigraph appropriately sums up the
world of the play (broken) and Blanche DuBois' elusive search for love.
3   Williams's stage directions are extremely detailed, almost
cinematic in scope. The French Quarter of New Orleans where the play
is set is poor and run down, yet Williams manages to invest it with
considerable beauty and poetry. His sensory exploration takes in strong
colours like the blue/turquoise of the sky, appropriate for spring/early
summer, and the dirty brown river; the smell of coffee and bananas
from the warehouses; and the atmospheric jazz piano, a strong leitmotif
in the play. The river and the railroad tracks (Louisiana and Nashville)
suggest transportation, an important idea, and commerce, a world only
briefly glimpsed in what is primarily a domestic play. Elysian Fields is
an appropriate name for the street, Elysium being the resting place for
the blessed in Greek mythology. It is an ironic heaven that Blanche
DuBois will be denied when she comes to stay with the Kowalskis;
death is a prominent theme in the play. Williams's comment that New
Orleans is racially tolerant might appear to jar with his own labelling of
the 'Negro Woman', but she is a minor figure who does not need to be
individualised. The term 'negro' would not have been considered
pejorative when the play was written.
3   *White frame:* a French colonial style of building: wood-frame
houses in-filled with stucco or plaster, with large windows and wooden
verandahs.
3   *She says St. Barnabas would send out his dog to lick her and when
he did she'd feel an icy cold wave all up an' down her:* we enter the play
midway through a conversation between the negro woman and Eunice
Hubbel, the Kowalskis' neighbour. Williams immediately establishes
the licentious atmosphere of this section of the city with a reference to
physical pleasure. St Barnabas (originally Joseph) was born in Cyprus
to Jewish parents. He converted to Christianity and is mentioned in the
New Testament. Williams's image is, therefore, an irreverent coupling
of sex and religion.

3   *Red hot!*: a spicy tamale (Mexican dish of meat, crushed maize and seasonings steamed or baked in maize husks) that adds to the steamy atmosphere.

3   *Don't waste your money in that clip joint!*: this refers to the already mentioned Four Deuces, a bar that doubles up as a brothel. It is the type of disreputable establishment that might be found in the Quarter.

3   *Don't let them sell you a Blue Moon cocktail or you won't go out on your own feet!*: matching the sky and the tonal colour of the piano, this potent cocktail is a combination of blue curaçao and vodka or gin.

4   *They are about twenty-eight or thirty years old, roughly dressed in blue denim work clothes*: Stanley and Mitch are immediately identified as working-class men.

4   *STELLA comes out on the first-floor landing, a gentle young woman, about twenty-five, and of a background quite different from her husband's*: Stella's gentleness contrasts with her husband's obvious brutality. Her very different social background preoccupies Blanche later when she criticises her sister's marriage.

4   *He heaves the package at her. She cries out in protest but manages to catch it: then she laughs breathlessly*: Stanley is primitive, a caveman bringing home the kill for his woman to cook. Stella's objection to his crude behaviour is soon replaced by a sense of exhilaration.

4   *Tell Steve to get him a poor boy's sandwich 'cause nothing's left here*: a large sandwich filled with simple ingredients; a further indication of the plain lives these characters lead.

4–5   The stage direction here indicates that Blanche has come with the intention of staying (she is carrying a small suitcase) but that she cannot believe her sister has moved into such a poor neighbourhood. Blanche is comically out of place, ridiculously over-dressed as if she is attending a party in the affluent Garden District of New Orleans. She is about thirty but will claim she is younger than her sister, reflecting a deep and ongoing anxiety about ageing. Dressed in white, she suggests innocence and vulnerability, two qualities she tries to cultivate. The mention of light and the similarity to a moth returns us to her age: she is attracted to brightness, to bold characters, but a naked light cruelly exposes her age. One of the working titles for the play was *The Moth*.

5   *They told me to take a streetcar named Desire, and then one called Cemeteries*: the two streetcars embody the play's interlinked themes of desire and death and, therefore, have a symbolic value. Real streetcars with these names were running in New Orleans when

Williams was working on the play.

5 *I'm looking for my sister, Stella DuBois. I mean – Mrs. Stanley Kowalski*: Blanche is unwilling to accept the fact that her sister is now a Kowalski and betrays herself here. The difficulty of the adjustment is compounded by her horror at the tenement building.

6 *Por nada*: a variant on the Spanish 'de nada', meaning 'think nothing of it/ you're welcome'. The Mexican influence in the play is strong – there are the tamale vendor, the Mexican flower seller and Pablo, one of Stanley's poker players.

6 *Belle Reve?*: the DuBois family home is an impressive plantation house architecturally defined by its columns. It will remain a picture or idea throughout the play, a symbol of a privileged existence that has been forcibly relinquished, a way of life that has been superseded. It seems almost certain that Williams wrongly assumed 'rêve' (dream) to be feminine and so his intended meaning of 'beautiful dream' should have been 'beau rêve' (the French word 'rive', meaning 'shore', is feminine). The house is a fantasy, a version of the Old South that was never quite true.

6–7 The stage direction indicates Blanche's defensiveness and her nervousness. She is easily startled by the cat's screech and then instinctively looks for the bottle of alcohol. The way that Blanche very deliberately washes up the glass implies that she is well practised in deceiving people about her drinking. Alcohol steadies her nerves and is a form of escapism.

7 *Stella for Star!*: her name literally means 'star' in Latin and, though Blanche's younger sister, she is the guiding light that has brought Blanche to New Orleans. This is another example of the light imagery in the play.

8 *Only Mr. Edgar Allan Poe! – could do it justice! Out there I suppose is the ghoul-haunted woodland of Weir*: we later discover that Blanche was an English teacher and so her literary reference is appropriate, if rather hurtful. The comparison with Poe's Gothicism brings out her sense of horror at the working-class neighbourhood and underlines her poetic imagination. The 'ghoul-haunted woodland of Weir' appears in Poe's poem of 1847, 'Ulalumé'.

9 *The wire*: the telegram.

9 *But you – you've put on some weight, yes, you're just as plump as a little partridge!*: the first indication that Stella is pregnant. She says nothing about it for fear of her sister's reaction and, because Blanche is speaking so manically, there is no clear opportunity. Desperately seeking reassurance about her own looks, Blanche tells Stella that she has not put on any weight since Stella left Belle Reve, simultaneously trying to make her sister feel guilty about leaving when their father died.

10 *Polacks?*: Stanley's Polish ancestry is repeatedly attacked by Blanche in the confrontation between the aristocratic Old South (French influenced, agrarian) and the modern working-class experience (immigrant, urban). She has earlier shown her ignorance when suggesting that Poles are 'something like Irish'.

10 *A different species*: Stella knows that Blanche will compare Stanley unfavourably with the men they used to go out with at home; Blanche will later refer to Stanley as an ape, picking up on this notion of a 'different species'.

11 *He's on the road a good deal*: Stanley's job is never specified. He works at a plant with Mitch but he also travels. Williams's father, Cornelius Coffin Williams, was a travelling salesman with the International Shoe Company before taking up a management position which took the family to St. Louis.

12 *Why, the Grim Reaper had put up his tent on our doorstep!*: Blanche claims to have suffered a whole series of deaths at first hand as the family has gradually been decimated. This image of death, the Grim Reaper, mounting a military campaign against the family will be replaced by desire in the form of army officers calling up to Blanche for sexual favours.

13 *Is Mass out yet?*: the joke depends on 'Mass' being said with such a drawl that it sounds like 'my arse'.

13 *Jax beer!*: produced at the Jax Brewing Company in Jacksonville. Interestingly, the company closed in 1956 after selling the Jax Beer copyright to the Jackson Brewing Company in New Orleans.

13–14 *Animal joy in his being . . .*: Stanley is animalistic and sexual, a Lawrentian figure (Williams was greatly influenced by the English writer, D. H. Lawrence, and wrote the one-act *I Rise in Flame, Cried the Phoenix* about the last days of his life). He seeks to control women, regarding them as objects to satisfy and impregnate.

14 *Why, I – live in Laurel:* a town in Mississippi. Williams may wish to suggest some notion of moral victory through the name.

14 *Do you mind if I make myself comfortable?*: Stanley is happy to remove his shirt in front of a woman he has just met. Though Blanche does not object, it is not the behaviour of a Southern gentleman. In the 1951 film version directed by Elia Kazan, Vivien Leigh as Blanche permits herself a lingering look at Marlon Brando's Stanley.

15 *The music of the polka rises up, faint in the distance*: another

musical motif, the polka is inextricably linked with the death of
Blanche's husband, Allan Grey.

15 *The boy – the boy died*: Blanche's husband is defined by the
youth Blanche craves. The memory of his death triggers feelings of
guilt so extreme that she is physically sick.

15 *Galatoire's*: a restaurant in the Quarter. Stanley is resentful of
Stella and Blanche's meal at a swanky restaurant, even though his poker
night requires them to leave the apartment.

16 *She's soaking in a hot tub to quiet her nerves*: Blanche makes the
bathroom her domain, a place of retreat where she can escape from
Stanley and cleanse her soul.

16 "*From the land of the sky blue water,/They brought a captive
maid!*": Blanche's song was composed by Charles Wakefield
Cadman (music) and Nelle Richmond Eberhart (lyrics) in 1909.
Appropriately, Blanche is already 'a captive maid', a prisoner in the
apartment.

17 *Napoleonic code*: New Orleans is in Louisiana, a state originally
settled by the French. Stanley likes to appear well-informed about his
rights, but, in reality, the code, which would give him ownership of
everything belonging to his wife, was probably unenforceable.

18 *He hurls the furs to the daybed. Then he jerks open small drawer
in the trunk and pulls up a fist-full of costume jewellery*: in his attempts
to get at the truth, Stanley is effectively unpacking Blanche's life.
Blanche is a consummate actress, always playing a role, and this is the
actress's wardrobe.

20 *Lay . . . her cards on the table*: as the poker party is imminent, this
is an appropriate metaphor. Though poker is a game of bluff, Stanley
likes transparency in life; he cannot bear Blanche's evasions.

20 *I like an artist who paints in strong, bold colours, primary colours*:
colour imagery is important throughout the play. Blanche claims to be
attracted to simple, dynamic, uncompromising people, but she is also
repelled by them.

20 *Now let's cut the re-bop*: Stanley is a man of action. He wants to
get back to what he sees as the central point because Blanche's words
frustrate and unsettle him. He bullies her with the volume of his voice,
knowing that her nerves are affected by any sudden sound.

21 *Atomizer*: perfume spray.

21 *If I didn't know that you was my wife's sister I'd get ideas about
you*: though women are 'the centre of his life' (p.13), Stanley here
observes the taboo about relations with his wife's sister; he reminds
Blanche that she should not be flirting with him.

22   *Our improvident grandfathers and father and uncles and brothers exchanged the land for their epic fornications – to put it plainly!*: Blanche explains that the family's property and wealth were gradually lost through paying for sex. Such a history of debauchery helps us, in part, to understand Blanche's behaviour after the death of her husband.

23   *But maybe he's what we need to mix with our blood now that we've lost Belle Reve*: survival means adapting, inter-breeding; Blanche, though appalled by Stanley's materialism and lack of refinement, understands their evolutionary priority.

24   *The blind are – leading the blind!*: Blanche realises that her bid to find sanctuary is under threat from Stanley. She is confused, directionless and throws herself on her younger sister.

24   *The Poker Night*: another working title for the play. The stage directions call for bold colours – the green baize of the Van Gogh painting, the primary colours of the men's shirts, the red and green of the watermelon, for example. The kitchen may be illuminated by '*the raw colours of childhood's spectrum*' but this is to be a game for men '*at the peak of their physical manhood*'.

24   *Portières*: curtains hung over a doorway.

24   *Anything wild this deal?*: the language of the game frequently applies to the players, particularly Stanley who, at this point, is bad-tempered because he is losing. In the game, 'wild' means the players can decide the value of the card.

24   *One-eyed jacks*: the knaves of spades and hearts in a pack of cards, which, unlike the knaves of diamonds and clubs, are seen in half-profile.

24   *Ante up*: raise the sum of money originally staked as a bet.

24   *Chips*: betting money, sometimes replaced by tokens of some sort.

25   *Spade flush*: high-scoring hand, made up entirely of spades.

25   *Hurry back and we'll fix you a sugar-tit*: a sugar-tit is a baby's teat flavoured with sugar or syrup. Though he is his friend, Stanley mocks Mitch's close, somewhat Freudian relationship with his sick mother. Williams took the character's full name, Harold Mitchell, from a roommate at the fraternity house he was living in while attending the University of Missouri.

25   *Seven card stud*: mentioned again in the last line of the play, this is a form of poker, but it also refers to the sexual attraction and potency of Stanley.

26   *Could I kibitz*: Blanche feels excluded by the men's game. With no end in sight, she asks if she can look over the shoulder of another player. Stanley rejects this idea out of hand, showing no consideration for the women who have allowed the men to continue their party all evening.

26   *It makes me so mad when he does that in front of people*: understandably, Stella does not wish to be humiliated, but there is also the insinuation that she does not mind violence in the lively sexual relationship they share.

26   *That one seems – superior to the others*: Mitch clumsily holds on to the towel as he exits the bathroom, but Blanche quickly notices a courtesy and refinement in him that makes him closer to her notion of a gentleman than any of the other poker players.

27   *Is he a wolf?*: Is he a sexual predator? Blanche ignores Mitch's closeness to his sick mother and wonders why he can be single. He will turn into a sexual predator under the influence of drink in Scene Nine.

27   *One time [laughing] the plaster – [laughing] cracked*: Stella jokes about the vigorous sex lives of the men and their large wives. We are reminded of the closeness of the apartments, the lack of privacy and the inhibiting presence of Blanche on Stanley and Stella's own sex life.

28   *Sounds like Xavier Cugat*: the Latin American music on the radio breaks the concentration required for the game and is a challenge to Stanley's selfishness. Xavier Cugat was a Catalan-Cuban-American bandleader who helped popularise Latin music in America.

28   *She returns his look without flinching*: at this point in the play, Blanche is strong enough to stand up to Stanley's physical presence.

28   *Get ants*: get ants in your pants, become restless.

28   *I'm going to the "head". Deal me out*: Mitch is going to the toilet but he appears to have lost all interest in the game, distracted as he is by Blanche's presence.

28   *Sure he's got ants now. Seven five-dollar bills in his pants pocket folded up tight as spitballs*: Mitch's restlessness is attributed to the fact that he has been winning by the other men. The folded notes suggest his excessive care with money, and this becomes another jibe about his immaturity when Stanley says that the money will eventually be deposited in a piggy bank given to him by his mother. 'Spitballs' – wads of paper chewed into small balls or pellets – also seems to anticipate the name of their next game, 'Spit in the Ocean'.

28   *Quarters*: 25-cent coins.

29   *"And if God choose,/I shall but love thee better – after – death!"*: *Sonnets from the Portuguese* (no. 43) by Elizabeth Barrett Browning. It is not surprising that Blanche recognises the quotation, but, more importantly, it establishes a shared sense of loss with Mitch and the way in which the dead still haunt the play. Though nebulous, Mitch's relationship with the 'strange' and 'sweet' girl proves that he has been able to break free from his mother.

30   *It's a French name. It means woods and Blanche means white, so the two together mean white woods. Like an orchard in spring!*: like the plantation house, Blanche's name reveals her French ancestry: she is descended from the Huguenots – French Calvinists. She is innocent and lost (in the woods). The orchard in spring also conveys youthful fertility, obviously more applicable to Stella.

30   *I can't stand a naked light bulb, any more than I can a rude remark or a vulgar action*: the paper lantern is one way that Blanche shields herself from the truth (light). It is particularly important for Blanche to continue the deception about her age (there are two references to it on this page) and to establish standards of genteel behaviour.

30   *Grade school or high school*: the American system of education is divided into grade school, an intermediate level, and high school, the final stage, possibly leading to college or university education.

31   *Bobby-soxers and drug-store Romeos*: bobby-soxers were adolescent girls who wore the contemporary fashion for ankle socks, while drug-store Romeos were the love-sick boys who hung around shops where they could buy soft drinks.

31   *Hawthorne and Whitman and Poe*: the poet and short-story writer Edgar Allan Poe has already been mentioned in connection with the apartment and the neighbourhood; Walt Whitman (1819–92) was an American poet, best known for his collection *Leaves of Grass*, and Nathaniel Hawthorne (1804–64) was a nineteenth-century prose writer, probably most remembered for his novel *The Scarlet Letter*.

31   *She turns the knobs on the radio and it begins to play "Wien, Wien, nur du allein." BLANCHE waltzes to the music with romantic gestures. MITCH is delighted and moves in awkward imitation like a dancing bear*: the lively rhumba has been replaced by a formal Viennese waltz (Rudolf Sieczynski's 1913 composition 'Vienna, City of My Dreams' or, as written here, 'Vienna, Vienna, only you alone'). This is a comic moment before Stanley explodes and throws the radio out of the window. Mitch is a buffoon, obviously incompatible with Blanche.

32   *Poker should not be played in a house with women*: Mitch repeats this line to emphasise the discrete world of the men; invading their territory leads to violence.

33   *The Negro entertainers in the bar around the corner play "Paper Doll" slow and blue*: this was a hit song for the Mills Brothers in 1943. It anticipates Stanley fondly calling Stella his 'baby doll' and serves to create a tenderer mood in which he seeks forgiveness from his wife. *Baby Doll* was the title of a later screenplay by Williams, turned into a notorious film by Elia Kazan in 1956.

33   *You whelp of a Polack, you! I hope they do haul you in and turn the fire hose on you, same as the last time!*: Eunice resorts to insulting Stanley's Polish background. She wants him to be punished while realising that this behaviour characterises the Kowalskis' marriage; it will happen again.

33   *They come together with low animal groans*: Stella and Stanley's reconciliation will be primarily sexual, animalistic, though there is tenderness and a recognition of Stella's role as a mother – both to the baby and Stanley.

34   *All quiet on the Potomac now?*: the Potomac is a river that runs into the Chesapeake Bay. On one side it borders Maryland and Washington DC; on the other, Virginia and West Virginia. Mitch's question, asked in the knowledge that these violent scenes are commonplace but short-lived, echoes the opening line of the sixth stanza of a poem, 'The Picket Guard' (1861), by Ethel Lynn Beers (1827–79): 'All quiet along the Potomac to-night'. The poem draws on telegrams sent by Major-General George B. McClellan during the American Civil War when Union and Confederate armies occupied opposite sides of the river. The line may have influenced the English title of the famous novel about the First World War, *All Quiet on the Western Front*, by Erich Maria Remarque.

34   *There is a confusion of street cries like a choral chant*: another musical variation. This conveys the busy activity of the area and suggests the chorus of Greek drama.

35   *Her eyes and lips have that almost narcotized tranquillity that is in the faces of Eastern idols*: the book of comics Stella is reading suggests her childish simplicity; an image of being drugged captures her state of post-coital bliss. Elia Kazan regarded this drugged state as the spine of Stella's character: she is under Stanley's influence.

36   *Why, on our wedding night – soon as we came in here – he snatched off one of my slippers and rushed about smashing the light bulbs with it*: another reference to light and its source. While Blanche is wary of the truth light exposes, Stanley and Stella seek darkness to enjoy their physical, sado-masochistic relationship fully.

37   *Of course you remember Shep Huntleigh. I went out with him at college and wore his pin for a while*: in her increasing desperation, Blanche clings to figures from her past. Shep is remembered as an honourable man, and the wearing of the pin as a pledge to each other recalls knights displaying their ladies' favours. Even though Blanche claims to have met him recently and to know that he is an oil tycoon, he remains an illusory saviour. His name suggests the desperate pursuit of something.

39 *Sometime today I've got to get hold of a bromo!*: a bromide tablet used to calm the nerves. Blanche's dependence on alcohol and drugs to sedate her and offer a means of escape anticipates Williams's own dependency in the sixties.

40 *What you are talking about is brutal desire – just – Desire! – the name of that rattle-trap street-car that bangs through the Quarter, up one old narrow street and down another*: the metaphorical meaning of the title is made explicit here. Stella has admitted that sex is the foundation of her relationship with Stanley and that it almost makes everything else appear irrelevant. However, she also says that she loves her husband. The noisy journey of the streetcar complements the violent passion of the couple. The sexual slang of 'bangs' will become more obvious when it is repeated.

40 *It brought me here. – Where I'm not wanted and where I'm ashamed to be*: another hint that Blanche is not as innocent as she would like people to believe. Sex with various men has characterised her recent past. However, she quickly juxtaposes her own desire with a plea for sympathy at her present circumstances.

40 *Then don't you think your superior attitude is a bit out of place?*: it is literally out of place because Blanche has been applying the standards of the Old South, those of Belle Reve. For all Blanche's misfortune, we sympathise with Stella here: her husband and whole way of life are under attack; Blanche is about to launch her most damning attack yet on Stanley's primitivism.

40 *Under cover of the train's noise STANLEY enters from outside. He stands unseen by the women, holding some packages in his arms, and overhears their following conversation. He wears an undershirt and grease-stained seersucker pants*: Williams skilfully uses the sound of the train to hide Stanley's entrance and permit his eavesdropping, so building up tension. Stanley will discover what Blanche really thinks of him and this will intensify his attempts to expose her. The packages remind us of his first entrance with the meat; and his dirty appearance will offer a further visual confirmation of Blanche's words. Stanley's trousers are made of a light fabric that puckers easily; they are probably striped.

40–1 *There's even something – sub-human [. . .]*: Blanche's long speech juxtaposes a world of primitive lust and violence with gauges of civilisation – poetry and music. Stanley reverses the evolutionary order and Blanche urges her sister not to get caught up in this atavism.

40 *In some kinds of people some tenderer feelings have had some little beginning! . . . In this dark march toward whatever it is we're approaching*: Blanche has already referred to the difficult task of nurturing an interest in literary culture among the young. Here she states the fight against ignorance rather melodramatically.

41 *STANLEY hesitates, licking his lips*: Stanley is relishing the fight to come. Appropriately, he is like a beast sizing up its prey.

41 *Them darn mechanics at Fritz's don't know their can from third base!*: Stanley's grubbiness can be explained by the fact that he had to help the mechanics at the garage. He is practical, not conventionally educated or sensitive. The baseball metaphor, 'third base', points to another sphere of male interest that might exclude women: professional sport. 'Can' has several slang meanings: a toilet; someone's backside; a car, especially adapted to get greater acceleration; and a storage battery.

41 *STELLA has embraced him with both arms, fiercely, and full in the view of BLANCHE. He laughs and clasps her head to him. Over her head he grins through the curtains at BLANCHE*: the Kowalskis present a united front. Stella may have allowed Blanche to speak at length, but she will defend what she has got '*fiercely*'. Stanley's smile is smug and threatening. Vivien Leigh, playing Blanche in the 1951 film, has a moment of panic as she realises that Stanley might have heard her tirade. Whether or not Williams intended this, the blue piano and trumpet that follow capture the high tension at the end of this scene.

42 *"Most of my sister's friends go north in the summer but some have homes on the Gulf and there has been a continued round of entertainments, teas, cocktails, and luncheons –"*: the life of the affluent Southerner, a social routine that Blanche might have enjoyed in the past but which is now just a fantasy. The palm leaf that she fans herself with further symbolises this world, but Blanche is highly conscious of her lies as she writes them.

42 *I wouldn't mind if you'd stay down at the Four Deuces, but you always going up*: the disagreements of Steve and Eunice seem intended to echo those of Stanley and Stella, though they often appear more comic by comparison. Eunice is objecting to Steve's visits to one of the prostitutes working upstairs above the bar area of the Four Deuces.

43 *Daemonic*: as if possessed by an evil spirit.

43 *I'm compiling a notebook of quaint little words and phrases I've picked up here*: Blanche's feigned ignorance of American slang is immediately seized upon by Stanley who is keen to strip away her prejudices. The battle between them will be fought on linguistic grounds: Blanche's poetic imagery versus Stanley's vivid colloquialisms.

44   *Capricorn – the Goat!*: Blanche realises that the sexually active goat is an appropriate star sign for Stanley.

44   *The Hotel Flamingo is not the sort of establishment I would dare to be seen in*: probably a brothel, the hotel adds to the colour imagery. Blanche gives telling physical reactions when both Shaw's name and the hotel are mentioned.

45   *Not in front of your sister*: Stanley makes clear just how much of a problem is Blanche's presence; he cannot be himself with his wife.

45   *I never was hard or self-sufficient enough*: now that Blanche is alone with Stella, she can hint at her recent past, a past that she fears has become common gossip. This speech really sets out Blanche's philosophy, drawing on the play's imagery of light and frailty. Soft people, like her, have got to seek protection from the likes of Stanley. They have to create the magic of illusion by glowing attractively. In stating that she had to obtain whatever shelter she could and that men only notice women when they are making love to them, Blanche gives a strong hint that she has resorted to a form of prostitution. Her comment that she does not know how much longer she can 'turn the trick' confirms this: 'trick' can mean both illusion and a prostitute's client.

46   *STELLA pours the coke into the glass. It foams over and spills. BLANCHE gives a piercing cry*: a crude image of ejaculation. The staining of Blanche's white skirt emphasises how sex has corrupted her. Her cry is probably a mixture of pleasure and pain.

47   *I want to deceive him enough to make him – want me*: Blanche considers Mitch crucial to her future, hence her continuing plan of deception. She is pretending to be a Southern belle with very strong morals. Her worry is that he will become frustrated, deterred by her not 'putting out' – making herself sexually available.

47   *Ah, me, ah, me, ah, me . . .*: in the 1951 film, Blanche touches herself quite suggestively as she says these words. Her dreamy mood is reinforced by the gathering dusk and the music from the Four Deuces.

48   *The YOUNG MAN shakes his head violently and edges hastily up the steps*: the young man immediately establishes his innocence by rejecting the advances of the negro woman.

48   *A dime*: a 10-cent coin.

48   *It's temperamental?*: in Blanche's flirtatious mood, the lighter becomes a phallic symbol.

48   *Fifteen of seven*: a quarter to seven.

48   *Don't you just love those long rainy afternoons in New Orleans when an hour isn't just an hour – but a little bit of Eternity dropped in your hands – and who knows what to do with it?*: Blanche dignifies her lust with this image of unending time. The answer to the question is clearly that they should make love.

49   *Has anyone ever told you that you look like a young prince out of the Arabian Nights?*: carried away with the overriding impression of his youth, Blanche transforms the young man into an exotic figure from literature, when the vivid detail of his drinking cherry soda has made him an archetypal American teenager.

49   *It would be nice to keep you, but I've got to be good and keep my hands off children*: an allusion to the real reason why Blanche is no longer teaching. To her (and the audience), he must seem like a child who cannot comprehend her suggestiveness, who *'stands like a bashful kid'*.

49   *My Rosenkavalier!*: Mitch's sudden entrance reminds us of Blanche's real target. He is almost as bemused but is playing the role that is expected of him: that of the romantic hero respectfully bowing before his lady. *Der Rosenkavalier* is a comic opera by Richard Strauss. The title translates as 'The Knight of the Rose'.

49   *Merciiii*: *merci* is French for 'thank you'.

50   *The utter exhaustion which only a neurasthenic personality can know is evident in BLANCHE's voice and manner*: this seems to mark a deterioration in Blanche's state. Her nervous disposition, reflected in her constant drinking and quick-fire conversation, has taken over and she is no longer able to conceal her gradual breakdown.

50   *MITCH is stolid but depressed*: it should be evident that Mitch is making the best of what has been a disappointing evening.

50 *They have probably been out to the amusement park on Lake Pontchartrain, for MITCH is bearing, upside down, a plaster statuette of Mae West, the sort of prize won at shooting-galleries and carnival games of chance*: Williams's 'probably' suggests that precisely where they have been is not as important as the mood of the evening. Located in Louisiana, Lake Pontchartrain's south shore forms the northern boundary of New Orleans. Mae West (1893–1980) was a famous American actress, a sex symbol known for her irreverent *double entendres*. The 1951 film substituted a less tacky rag doll for the statuette. The fact that the statuette is held upside down suggests that something is wrong; and the *'carnival games of chance'* are a comment on the faltering relationship between Mitch and Blanche.

50   *I'll walk over to Bourbon and catch an owl-car*: Bourbon Street, in the French Quarter, is well known for its bars and entertainment. The owl-car is a streetcar running through the night.

50 *The one that says the lady must entertain the gentleman – or no dice!*: as a lady, Blanche expects to be taken out and for everything to be paid for by the man. She realises that, in return, it is her duty to entertain him in order to make the evening and their relationship a success. The reference to dice continues the game of chance/gambling theme.

50 *No, honey, that's the key to my trunk which I must soon be packing*: Blanche's trunk contains the secrets of her past that Stanley has tried to unpack and the costumes for her role playing. She realises that her stay can only be a brief one, that she will not be able to defeat Stanley.

51 *Eureka!*: Success. The cry supposedly uttered by Archimedes when he discovered the principle of water displacement while in his bath.

51 *I'm looking for the Pleiades, the Seven Sisters, but these girls are not out tonight*: another reference to stars as guiding lights. Blanche needs direction and it is interesting to note that she makes her source of help female.

52 *Joie de vivre*: happiness, joy in living.

52 *We are going to be very Bohemian. We are going to pretend that we are sitting in a little artists' café on the Left Bank in Paris!*: another example of Blanche's ability and willingness to create a fantasy world. Mitch is entirely unsuited to an unconventional or Bohemian existence.

52 *Je suis la Dame aux Camellias! Vous êtes – Armand! Understand French?*: 'I am the Lady of the Camellias! You are – Armand!' Even if Mitch could understand French, he would be unlikely to recognise this reference to the characters from a romantic novel by Alexandre Dumas Fils (1824–95).

52 *Voulez-vous couchez avec moi ce soir? Vous ne comprenez pas? Ah, quel dommage!*: 'Do you want to sleep with me? Don't you understand? Ah, what a shame!' Blanche flirts with Mitch in the full knowledge that he will not understand. She sends out conflicting messages: they are alone in the apartment together and she wants him to relax, but she is still setting boundaries over which he must not step.

52 *I am ashamed of the way I perspire. My shirt is sticking to me*: Williams parodies romantic dialogue throughout this scene. Mitch unwisely draws attention to his physical inadequacies, and we are reminded of his clumsiness when dancing with Blanche in Scene Three.

52 *It's very light weight alpaca*: Mitch chooses to wear a coat made of light weight wool to avoid the embarrassment of perspiration stains in summer. He does not realise that this is not something you disclose to a lady.

52   *A wash-coat*: jacket of light, washable material.

53   *I was given a membership to the New Orleans Athletic Club*: Williams used this club at 222 North Rampart Street. He was a particularly keen swimmer.

52   *Samson!*: an Old Testament character whose strength lay in his hair until Delilah cut it off. Again, Mitch is unaware of romantic conventions when he asks Blanche about her weight.

54   *She rolls her eyes, knowing that he cannot see her face*: Blanche is all too aware of her hypocrisy in claiming she still has 'old-fashioned ideals'; she is giving another performance.

54   *A midnight prevue at Loew's State*: Stanley and Stella have gone to a preview showing of a film at the local cinema on Canal Street.

54   *We was together in the Two-forty-first*: Mitch refers back to the Second World War and the fact that he served with Stanley in the same regiment. This provides an important bond between the two men, one that Blanche will find hard to sever.

55   *Of course there is such a thing as the hostility of – perhaps in some perverse kind of way he – No! To think of it makes me . . .*: Blanche cannot quite bring herself to say – or pretends not to be able to bring herself to say – that Stanley's antipathy for her masks a desire that cannot be admitted. Mitch is not sharp enough to pick up on this.

55   *Why did your mother want to know my age?*: as we have seen, Blanche is sensitive about her age. She appears to sidestep the question before bringing Mitch back to it, although, tellingly, she never answers him. Mitch's closeness to his mother is both a problem for Blanche and an opportunity for mutual sympathy: her terminal illness will return Blanche to the subject of her dead husband.

56   *It was like you suddenly turned a blinding light on something that had always been half in shadow, that's how it struck the world for me*: love was a process of illumination. In Blanche's youth, intense light was associated with passion, not unwanted truth.

56   *There was something different about the boy, a nervousness, a softness and tenderness which wasn't the least bit effeminate looking – still – that thing was there....He came to me for help*: Williams has to use a form of code here because he was living and writing in homophobic times. Blanche's husband was a homosexual, something more noticeable in his gentle mannerisms than his appearance. Like many homosexuals of the time, he chose to carry on a secret life while outwardly having a conventional marriage. Feeling rejected, Blanche betrayed him.

56   *By coming suddenly into a room that I thought was empty – which wasn't empty, but had two people in it . . .*: these lines were regarded as too explicit for the first London production of the play by the Lord Chamberlain; he ordered them to be cut.

56   *A locomotive is heard approaching outside. She claps her hands to her ears and crouches over.*: another important sound effect that contributes to the psychological realism of the play. We have already been told about the proximity of the L and N tracks, so the train is not unexpected. However, its approach and impact at this key moment suggest a huge internal scar left by Blanche's treatment of her husband.

56   *Yes, the three of us drove out to Moon Lake Casino*: at this point, Blanche did not want to contemplate the reason for the presence of her husband's companion. Moon Lake Casino, now a restaurant and inn called Uncle Henry's Place near Clarksdale, Mississippi, continues the theme of gambling. Williams used Moon Lake often in his plays, especially in a sad or violent context (e.g. the destruction of Papa Romano's wine garden in *Orpheus Descending*).

57   *We danced the Varsouviana!*: this happy, lively polka tune jars with the sudden suicide of Allan Grey. It has become inseparable from the memory.

57   *And then the searchlight which had been turned on the world was turned off again and never for one moment since has there been any light that's stronger than this – kitchen – candle...*: Blanche experienced a sort of death too. She has not been able to put this experience behind her and find love again, so racked with guilt as she still is.

57   *Sometimes – there's God – so quickly!*: given the rest of the scene, Mitch appears a highly ironic God, but, at this moment of emotional vulnerability, Blanche is desperate for comfort from anyone.

58   *It is late afternoon in mid-September*: having started in early May, we are now in the autumn of Blanche's life. The play will end some weeks later, possibly in November.

58   *The portieres are open and a table is set for a birthday supper, with cake and flowers*: the attempts at celebration create further tension and expectation. Will Stanley join in? Given Blanche's sensitivity about her age, will she want to celebrate?

58   *Temperature 100 on the nose, and she soaks herself in a hot tub*: in drawing attention to the temperature, Stanley indirectly reminds us that Blanche is not just washing but attempting to purify her soul; we also get a sense of the stifling atmosphere in the apartment.

59   *BLANCHE is singing in the bathroom a saccharine popular ballad
which is used contrapuntally with STANLEY'S speech*: Williams cleverly
uses the song to punctuate (contrapuntally means in counterpoint)
Stanley's comments. It is sentimental but the words are appropriate for
Blanche and her situation.

59   *Sister Blanche is no lily*: Stanley's tone is sarcastic. Blanche is
Stella's sister but also, ironically, a nun. Stanley is attacking her claims
to a virtuous life, the white lily being a symbol of innocence.

59   *"Say it's only a paper moon, Sailing over a cardboard sea/– But it
wouldn't be make-believe If you believed in me!"*: the song is entitled
'It's Only a Paper Moon, the music was composed by Harold Arlen
and the lyrics were written by E. Y. Harburg and Billy Rose in 1933.
The song was performed by Ella Fitzgerald in 1938. The 'make-believe'
world is the one that Blanche has created as a defence mechanism; it
might not be necessary if someone truly loved and believed in her.

59   *In fact they were so impressed by Dame Blanche that they
requested her to turn in her room-key – for permanently!*: 'Dame' is
American slang for a woman but is also a title in the UK; Stanley is
attacking Blanche's superior airs, showing how she was even banned
from an establishment with such a poor reputation as the Flamingo.

59   *"It's a Barnum and Bailey world, Just as phony as it can
be –/But it wouldn't be make-believe If you believed in me!"*:
P. T. Barnum and James Anthony Bailey were famous circus
proprietors in the nineteenth century. Again, the world of performance
and illusion is alluded to.

60   *It's a honky-tonk parade!*: in this context, 'honky-tonk' means
squalid or disreputable.

60   *Regarded as not just different but downright loco – nuts*: 'loco'
means crazy. Stanley wants to prove that Blanche is not eccentric so
much as insane, and therefore needs to be locked up for everyone's
good.

60   *Which brings us to Lie Number Two*: Stanley is also giving a
performance, presenting evidence systematically in the role of a
prosecuting lawyer. Blanche has already commented sarcastically on his
'impressive judicial air' (p. 21) when explaining the Napoleonic code.

60   *No, siree, Bob!*: a colloquial American expression meaning 'No,
definitely not'. Warming to his task, Stanley's language becomes
increasingly more colloquial and colourful.

60   *A seventeen-year-old boy – she'd gotten mixed up with!*:
Blanche's absence from work is explained, as is her comment about
keeping her 'hands off children' (p. 49). The meaning of Stanley's

euphemism is made all too clear by the exclamation mark.

60   *In the bathroom the water goes on loud; little breathless cries and peels of laughter are heard as if a child were frolicking in the tub*: can Blanche hear the argument outside the bathroom? Is she trying to block it out by running more water? As Stella was with the comics, she appears childlike and vulnerable, not, at this point, the insane and promiscuous woman Stanley has tried to portray.

61   *But they had her on the hook good and proper that time and she knew that the jig was all up!*: an unpleasant image, not just of Blanche being trapped but skewered like a fish or a piece of meat. Perhaps we think of Stanley's bloody package when he first enters the play. Interestingly, 'jig' can mean a lively dance (another performance) or, in fishing, an artificial bait jerked up and down in the water; the expression 'jig is up' means that her act of deception is finally over.

61   *Yep, it was practickly a town ordinance passed against her!*: exaggerating for effect, Stanley claims that Blanche's behaviour was so grave that legislation was very nearly passed to ensure that she could not return.

61   *Possess your soul in patience!*: a commonly used line from Shakespeare's *Hamlet*. Blanche objects to the rude way in which Stanley asks her how much longer she is going to be in the bathroom.

61   *She was always – flighty!*: Stella is defending her sister but concedes that some of Blanche's behaviour has been reprehensible. Here she is searching around for the right word to describe her. 'Flighty' implies fickle and irresponsible.

62   *This beautiful and talented young man was a degenerate*: she means that he was a homosexual but the stating of this in anything other than a euphemism would not be tolerated at the time. Williams often used the word 'degenerate' with its negative connotations of immorality and corruption; it is another example of encoding homosexuality. Stanley is not very interested in Blanche's marriage to a gay man because, as he says, it is not 'recent history', and because her behaviour with heterosexual men provides him with more ammunition.

62   *Mitch is a buddy of mine*: 'buddy' implies more than simply friend. The men have bonded through their service in the army, their work and their leisure pursuits. They have a loyalty to each other which is almost more sacrosanct than any relationship with a woman. Hence, Stanley has warned Mitch off Blanche and he will not be coming to the birthday party.

63   *Maybe he was, but he's not going to jump in a tank with a school of sharks – now!*: it seems that Mitch might have considered the possibility of marrying Blanche before Stanley's revelations. This second reference to fish suggests that Blanche is very dangerous – not just one shark but a whole school of them.

63 *Her future is mapped out for her*: it is 'mapped out' in the short-term because Stanley has bought Blanche a ticket for the Greyhound bus back to Laurel, a town from which she has already been ejected. It is unclear whether he also means here that she will be committed to a mental asylum in the future.

63 *She tinkles her highball glass*: in addition to the bath, Blanche has used alcohol to calm her nerves (whisky and soda with ice).

63 *The distant piano goes into a hectic breakdown*: the piano music suddenly becomes very discordant to emphasise Blanche's increased anxiety and confusion. Williams's music again helps to create psychological realism.

64 *A torch of sunlight blazes on the side of a big water-tank or oil-drum across the empty lot toward the business district which is now pierced by pin-points of lighted windows reflecting the sunset*: the sun is setting on Blanche as Stanley closes in for the kill. The warmth suggested here contrasts with the emotional coldness of Blanche's birthday celebration, a dismal occasion. The empty lot corresponds to the vacant fourth place at the table, itself a strong visual image of Mitch's rejection of Blanche. Williams permits us another glimpse of the larger world outside the domestic environs of the play.

64 *I don't know any refined enough for your taste*: the play contains several jokes or stories. Appropriately, those told by the men are somewhat bawdy and Blanche tries to offset this with more innocent material. Her parrot joke, which barely raises a smile, mocks their situation: Stanley is the parrot who is excessively rude in the daytime and better suited to darkness; Blanche is the easily offended 'old maid' who is trying to silence him.

65 *What do you two think you are? A pair of queens? Remember what Huey Long said – "Every Man is a King!" And I am the king around here, so don't forget it!*: Stanley's somewhat uncouth behaviour at the table has borne out Blanche's criticisms of him. He spears the chop with his fork and then eats it with his fingers, covering his face in grease in the process. However, he rightly feels under attack and is stung by the persistent slur on his ethnic origins (Polack) and the suggestion that he has the manners of a pig. He believes that, as the breadwinner, he should be respected, and he cites Huey Pierce Long (1893–1935), a famous lawyer and politician (he was governor of Louisiana), in his defence. Stanley resents any challenges to his sovereignty, particularly when he sees Blanche successfully influencing his wife.

65   *My place is cleared! You want me to clear your places?*: a flamboyant gesture that, once again, highlights Stanley's physical threat. In the film, Marlon Brando cuts a slightly comic figure, with a napkin tucked into his shirt, before making a sudden and impressive outburst.

66   *God, honey, it's gonna be sweet when we can make noise in the night the way that we used to and get the coloured lights going with nobody's sister behind the curtains to hear us!*: Stanley is trying to get Stella back on side and the only way he knows how to do this is with a promise of energetic sex. Interestingly, the coloured lights symbolise this wild passion, but, on his wedding night, Stanley smashed an artificial source of light. His sexual frustration is all too clear.

66   *Oh, I hope candles are going to glow in his life and I hope that his eyes are going to be like candles, like two blue candles lighted in a white cake!*: Stella's baby, here assumed to be a boy, is the future, the promise of new life the play offers. Unsurprisingly, Blanche wants him to be soft and tender like candle light and the delicate colours she refers to. The contrast with Stanley's brash coloured lights is very marked.

67   *But what I am is a one hundred per cent. American, born and raised in the greatest country on earth and proud as hell of it, so don't ever call me a Polack*: Stanley's staunchest defence of his American identity. He is determined not to be labelled an outsider or an immigrant of uncertain status.

68   *The Varsouviana music steals in softly and continues playing*: previously associated with the death of Allan Grey and the guilt that produced, the polka tune is more closely linked with rejection here. As Allan Grey's homosexuality was a rejection of Blanche the young wife, so Stanley's 'birthday remembrance' signifies the rejection the desperate sister has long been expecting (even though she tells Stanley she was not anticipating a present). The connection is confirmed with a repeat of Blanche's convulsions.

68   *You didn't know Blanche as a girl. Nobody, nobody, was tender and trusting as she was. But people like you abused her, and forced her to change*: Stella reinforces the sympathy she (and the audience) feels for Blanche. Her sister is more sinned against than sinning, and here she seems to be a bygone culture rather than just an individual. The Old South, the epitome of civilisation and gentility, has been lost, assaulted as it has been by a ruthless modern America.

68   *I was common as dirt. You showed me the snapshot of the place with the columns. I pulled you down off them columns and how you* *loved it, having them coloured lights going!*: Stanley is proud of his working-class background and of his role as Stella's liberator. He sees the columns (significantly, he has only ever encountered them in a photograph) as a symbol of aristocratic privilege; they represent not only the plantation but also the Old South. The only way he could entice Stella away from this world was through sex, metaphorically taking her down from columns that provide safety and shelter.

68   *I done nothing to no one. Let go of my shirt. You've torn it*: Stanley feels wronged and, as if to confirm the attack on his character, one of the badges of his manhood, the *'brilliant silk bowling shirt'*, is ripped.

69   *Hoity-toity, describing me as an ape*: Stanley blames their problems on Blanche's snobbery and belittling of him as part of a lower evolutionary order. The use of the pronouns 'we' and 'she' before this shows Stanley trying to establish some distance between them. Again, he is seeking to divide and rule.

69   *The "Varsouviana" is heard, its music rising with sinister rapidity as the bathroom door opens slightly*: another rejection as Blanche is left 'twisting a washcloth' while Stanley tenderly comes to his wife's aid.

69   *El pain de mais, el pain de mais,/El pain de mais sin sal*: literally 'maize bread, maize bread, maize bread without salt'. There is a strong Mexican influence throughout the play and this folk song draws our attention to a staple of existence. There is also a Maya creation myth in which man is said to have been formed from *'masa'* or corn dough. Maize is, consequently, regarded as a gift from the gods by the Maya people. Blanche may be thinking of her own lonely life – plain and unseasoned, especially now that she is being refused any further shelter; she may be commenting on the imminent birth of Stella's child and the nourishment it will need in a difficult world.

69   *BLANCHE is seated in a tense hunched position in a bedroom chair that she has re-covered with diagonal green and white stripes. She has on her scarlet satin robe*: the contrast between Blanche's defensive foetal position and the bold colours she is now surrounding herself with is very noticeable. It is almost as if she has accepted that she is the scarlet woman or whore that Stanley has accused her of being.

69   *The music is in her mind; she is drinking to escape it and the sense of disaster closing in on her, and she seems to whisper the words of the song*: for the first time, Williams makes it clear that this is an interior soundtrack, that he is attempting to make the audience experience what Blanche is thinking. Alcohol is no longer just a relaxant but a means of banishing nightmares, of seeking oblivion.

69   *Mitch comes around the corner in work clothes: blue denim shirt and pants. He is unshaven*: Mitch's scruffy appearance is an immediate indication that he does not have romantic intentions. Blanche expects her men to be smart and well-groomed and we suspect that Mitch has complied with this on their dates.

70   *She looks fearfully after him as he stalks into the bedroom*: Stanley's influence can even be detected in Mitch's movements; there are several references to Stanley stalking aggressively in the play like an animal.

70   *No, of course you haven't, you dumb angel-puss, you'd never get anything awful caught in your head!*: Blanche mocks Mitch's lack of intelligence. She is speaking quickly and he appears not to register what she is saying, partly because he has been drinking.

70   *I won't cross-examine the witness*: Blanche desperately hopes that Mitch's presence will make the Varsouviana tune disappear. Questioning Mitch is only likely to antagonise him and, anyway, she does not want to adopt Stanley's pseudo-legal methods.

71   *A distant revolver shot is heard, BLANCHE seems relieved*: more evidence of Blanche being haunted by her treatment of her young husband. The gunshot (Allan Grey's suicide) temporarily halts the painful memory.

71   *Are you boxed out of your mind?*: Are you so drunk you cannot think or speak intelligibly? We might also think of Blanche being boxed in by both her mental condition and her physical situation.

71   *I've done so much with this place since I've been here*: Blanche prides herself on her home improvements in an attempt to show that she is a good homemaker. We remember her appalled looks and superior manner when she first arrived. Of course, Blanche's legacy will be so much more than the soft furnishings with which she seems to have bedecked the apartment.

72   *He tears the paper lantern off the light bulb. She utters a frightened gasp*: a shocking action for both Blanche and the audience. She is suddenly stripped bare and left defenceless. This clearly anticipates Scene Ten.

72   *I don't want realism*; a comment on Williams's dramatic technique, which is not straightforwardly realistic but a combination of realism and expressionism, and Blanche's inability to live with the truth

72   *I misrepresent things to them. I don't tell truth, I tell what ought to be truth. And if that is sinful, then let me be damned for it!*: Blanche talks again about the magic of invention, owning up to the deliberate deception that is symbolised by the paper lantern covering the light of

truth. Here she introduces a note of judgement from a Christian
perspective.

72 *That pitch about your ideals being so old-fashioned and all the
malarkey that you've dished out all summer. Oh, I knew you weren't
sixteen any more. But I was a fool enough to believe you was straight*:
by using the word 'pitch', Mitch implies that Blanche has been selling
herself and that he was taken in by her patter. He may have realised that
she was not in the prime of her youth, but the secrecy about her age has
troubled him, if only because his mother has asked about it. John M.
Clum notes (*Acting Gay: Male Homosexuality in Modern Drama*, p.
152) that 'straight' is part of the language of homosexuality, a subtext,
because it defines a heterosexual as well as meaning honest or
straightforward. Clum implies that Blanche represents the homosexual
(i.e. not straight) sensibility. Though Clum does not go this far, there is
a long critical tradition of viewing Blanche as Tennessee Williams in
drag.

73 *The Tarantula Arms!*: Blanche mocks Mitch's comments,
exaggerating her ability to control men and bring about their downfall.
Mitch does not seem to understand what a tarantula is; he certainly does
not pick up on her sarcasm about the way in which men try to
stigmatise her.

73 *I was played out*: she was drained of her youthful energy. Perhaps
there is also a suggestion of being out of a game of cards here.

73 *I thanked God for you . . . The poor man's Paradise – is a little
peace . . .*: Blanche's language is increasingly taking on a Christian tone.
These biblical echoes convey the modest hope of protection she had
after meeting Mitch.

74 *Never inside, I didn't lie in my heart...*: Blanche can seemingly
divorce her creation of magic from an inner integrity. The fact that she
presents herself as essentially truthful is likely to make her more
sympathetic.

74 *She is a blind MEXICAN WOMAN in a dark shawl, carrying
bunches of those gaudy tin flowers that lower class Mexicans display at
funerals and other festive occasions*: the appearance of this vendor is
timely. Blanche's spiritual death is approaching and the woman is the
symbol of this, a harbinger of doom. The fact that she is blind recalls
Tiresias, the sightless prophet of Greek legend.

74 *Flores para los muertos*: flowers for the dead. The Mexican
Spanish chant is haunting because of the subject matter but also because
of its somewhat alien quality. It sets Blanche thinking about the deaths
at Belle Reve again.

74   *Corones para los muertos*: crowns for the dead. We might think of the crown of thorns placed on Christ's head before the crucifixion.

74   *And other things such as blood-stained pillow-slips*: oblivious to Mitch at this point, Blanche has been transported back to Belle Reve and the painful deaths of her relatives. The blood represents the sin of the 'epic fornications' (p. 22), a dynasty collapsing in upon itself, as well as death. Blanche's fragmented conversations with the dead indicate a schizophrenic state.

74   *The opposite is desire*: the relationship between death (Thanatos) and desire (Eros) is one that has preoccupied Western writers. Desire is the life-force staving off death, but the insatiability of desire can only be ended with death. Blanche can no longer court desire – it was what transported her to this point – and must accept death. Williams suggests the connection between the two themes when he has Blanche talk about the two streetcars (p. 5).

74   *Later the paddy-wagon would gather them up like daisies…*: the drunken soldiers looking for sexual favours from Blanche would eventually collapse and be arrested for causing a public disturbance by police in a van. Stanley's information about Blanche creating a scandal is accurate.

75   *What I been missing all summer*: namely, sex. Now that he knows the stories about Blanche are true, Mitch can vent his sexual frustration.

75   *You're not clean enough to bring in the house with my mother*: Mitch measures women by his mother and so exhibits Freud's Oedipus complex: he secretly desires his mother but this is taboo. Of course, his mother is nearing death, another conflation of desire and death. Mitch implies that he wants to enjoy Blanche as a prostitute, rather than a girlfriend respectable enough to be presented to his family. Given that he was previously in awe of Blanche, we can see that Mitch uses a typical classification of woman as Madonna/whore.

75   *Get out of here before I start screaming fire*: to cry rape might be too sensational. A cry of 'Fire!' could refer to the force of Mitch's lust, as well as being a sure way to create an alarm and so scare Mitch off.

75   *Blanche staggers back from the window and falls to her knees. The distant piano is slow and blue*: reeling from the attack, Blanche almost falls into an attitude of prayer. The music appropriately captures this sombre mood.

75   *She has decked herself out in a somewhat soiled and crumpled white satin evening gown and a pair of scuffed silver slippers with brilliants set in their heels*: her trunk or wardrobe out in front of her, Blanche is trying to return to a world of faded glamour. The words 'soiled', 'crumpled' and 'scuffed' indicate how she has been abused, how broken and imperfect her world has been rendered.

75 *Now she is placing the rhinestone tiara on her head before the mirror of the dressing-table and murmuring excitedly as if to a group of spectral admirers*: just costume jewellery, the tiara is a symbol of the fraud Blanche has been perpetuating. She is increasingly unable to distinguish between fantasy and reality, and is haunted by the ghost of her past.

75–6 *She catches her breath and slams the mirror face down with such violence that the glass cracks*: unhappy with her appearance, probably the signs of ageing, Blanche smashes the mirror and, according to superstition, ensures seven years' bad luck.

76 *He still has on the vivid green silk bowling shirt. As he rounds the corner the honky-tonk music is heard. It continues softly throughout the scene*: the last time we saw the shirt it had been ripped by Stella. Now it again symbolises Stanley's boldness, just as the silk pyjamas will later in the scene. The music is coming from a tinny piano and helps to create a sleazy atmosphere.

76 *Does that mean we are to be alone in here?*: Blanche spells out her danger; this is ominous.

76 *What've you got on those fine feathers for?*: more bird imagery. Feathers might be a means of escape were Blanche not already trapped by Stanley.

76 *A fireman's ball?*: appropriate after the way the previous scene ended. Of course, Stanley is poking fun at Blanche's invented social invitations.

76 *ATO*: Auxiliary Territorial Officer.

76 *Gosh. I thought it was Tiffany diamonds*: Tiffany is an expensive jeweller's in New York. Stanley is being sarcastic but earlier, in scene two, he had to be told that these were rhinestones and worth nothing.

77 *The bottle cap pops off and a geyser of foam shoots up.* STANLEY *laughs happily, holding up the bottle over his head*: the phallic bottle was significant before when Blanche's dress became stained. Here it anticipates the sexual explosiveness at the end of this scene. As Stanley pours the bottle over his head, we might also be reminded of the shower being turned on over him in the aftermath of the poker party (Scene Three).

77 *Shall we bury the hatchet and make it a loving cup?*: Shall we make peace and have a celebratory drink? It is difficult to tell how sincere Stanley is being here.

77 *Well, it's a red letter night for us both*: we have both received good news. Blanche was wearing a red satin robe when Mitch visited her in Scene Nine. Of course, red is a sign of danger, a warning.

77   *The silk pyjamas I wore on my wedding night!*: we have already heard of Stanley's violence on his wedding night (the smashing of light bulbs in the apartment). The silk pyjamas are a luxury, a symbol of passion. Here their connection with marriage will extend to infidelity and rape.

78   *But I have been foolish – casting my pearls before swine!*: a biblical reference (Matthew 7:6): 'Give not that which is holy unto the dogs, neither cast ye your pearls before swine, lest they trample them under their feet, and turn again and rend you.' It is Blanche unwisely drawing once more on the image of Stanley as a pig that causes him to snap. Her 'pearls', Blanche's misplaced superiority, as Stanley sees it, and the fake jewels she wears, upset him to the point where he has to bring her fantasy crashing down. The insult is compounded by the reference to Stanley's 'buddy', Mitch.

78   *Deliberate cruelty is not forgivable*: almost Tennessee Williams's mantra. However we judge Blanche's behaviour, she does not deserve what happens to her.

79   *There isn't a goddam thing but imagination!*: Stanley has little imagination and so all that he despises is contained within this one word. Stanley's lines in this section are like a boxer's punches; Blanche is reeling on the ropes and all she can respond with each time is a shocked 'Oh!'.

79   *That worn-out Mardi Gras outfit, rented for fifty cents from some rag-picker! . . . What queen do you think you are!*: Blanche looks like something out of a carnival, possibly a freak show. Mardi Gras is on Fat Tuesday in New Orleans, a day of feasting before Lent officially begins. A rag-picker is a person who collects and sells rags, so Blanche's costume is the cheapest and tackiest that could be found. Stanley has referred to Blanche's imitation of royalty before (Scene Eight, p. 65), but 'queen' can also denote a homosexual and has been construed as coded language (see note to p. 72).

79   *You are the Queen of the Nile!*: Stanley characterises Blanche as the Egyptian queen, Cleopatra. In Shakespeare's *Antony and Cleopatra*, she is seen by the Romans as a decadent whore who has lured Antony to his doom; her world is unashamedly hedonistic.

79   *The shadows are of a grotesque and menacing form*: Blanche's worst fears and nightmares are projected onto the wall. Again, Williams is exposing the workings of her vulnerable mind.

79   *The night is filled with inhuman voices like cries in a jungle*:

auditory fears are added to visual ones. Blanche is not lost in a wood but a jungle and survival looks improbable.

79   *A prostitute has rolled a drunkard*: robbed a drunkard while he was asleep. A brief glimpse is afforded of the outside world. The prostitute takes advantage of the drunken man, just as Stanley is going to take advantage of Blanche's weakness.

80   *Some moments later the* NEGRO WOMAN *appears around the corner with a sequined bag which the prostitute had dropped on the walk. She is rooting excitedly through it*: a chain of theft is established. Because the characters have little, they greedily take from others. Stanley's materialism was obvious when he talked of the Napoleonic code in Scene Two.

80   *He grins at her as he knots the tasselled sash about his waist*: a smile of power and the ability to exact revenge. It recalls Stanley's grin at the end of Scene Four after listening to Blanche's speech about his primitivism.

80   *Then a clicking becomes audible from the telephone, steady and rasping*: a moment of high dramatic tension. The sound of the clicking phone is very insistent. It represents broken communication – both between Blanche and Stanley and Blanche and the outside world.

80   *The barely audible "blue piano" begins to drum up louder. The sound of it turns into the roar of an approaching locomotive.* BLANCHE *crouches, pressing her fists to her ears until it has gone by*: Williams uses the lugubrious piano more intensely here to build into the crashing train sound; it is ear-splitting for Blanche.

80   *Come to think of it – maybe you wouldn't be bad to – interfere with . . .*: as Stanley reaches for the right word, we are left to wonder whether this is the first time he has thought about assaulting her, whether he has always desired her but has channelled this into hostility.

81   *What are you putting on now?*: What game of deception are you trying to play now? The way this is phrased makes it sound like another costume or performance.

81   *She smashes a bottle on the table and faces him, clutching the broken top*: the loving cup has been turned into a weapon. Blanche hopes to use it to penetrate Stanley's face, but she will be overpowered and he will penetrate her violently.

81   *So you want some rough-house!*: Stanley relishes the prospect of a violent sexual encounter; he wants Blanche to offer some sort of resistance in order to make conquering her that much more satisfying.

81   *Tiger – tiger! Drop the bottle-top! Drop it! We've had this date with each other from the beginning!*: Stanley makes Blanche out to be a highly dangerous beast of the jungle, again so that he has an opponent to subdue. Interestingly, Stella portrayed Stanley as a lamb (depicting, in his remorse, the gentleness of Christ) in Scene Four after the poker night: 'He was as good as a lamb when I came back and he's really very, very ashamed of himself' (p. 36). Stanley implies an inevitability about what happens which might seem to contradict his apparent spontaneity earlier. Like two inexorable forces, Blanche and Stanley, old and new America, have been brought to this final battle of wills.

81   *He picks up her inert figure and carries her to the bed. The hot trumpet and drums from the Four Deuces sound loudly*: all resistance has been broken. The music builds to a climax, capturing the carnality of the scene. Inevitably, the film's director, Elia Kazan, encountered difficulties with the censor over this. His solution was to have Stanley's act of picking up Blanche seen through a mirror that then smashes before the shot dissolves into the next scene, so diminishing the expected rape.

81   *The atmosphere of the kitchen is now the same raw, lurid one of the disastrous poker night*: Williams revisits the world of male camaraderie and competition. By repeating the poker party, he encourages us to see both what has changed and what has remained constant.

81   *The building is framed by the sky of turquoise. STELLA has been crying as she arranges the flowery dresses in the open trunk*: the colour of the sky invites another comparison, this time with the opening scene of the play: How far has Blanche travelled metaphorically? There is the first sign of a response from Stella, though we cannot yet judge what she knows. The trunk, now being packed, is a reminder of Stanley's hostile questions and Blanche's shock at discovering him going through her belongings ('It looks like my trunk has exploded', p. 19). The flowery dresses suggest a softer, more innocent Blanche than the fake furs.

82   *Drew to an inside straight and made it, by God*: Stanley combines the idea of a race, possibly a horserace, with winning a hand of cards. His mood is far happier than when he was losing in Scene Three.

82   *Maldita sea tu suerto!*: literally 'Curse your good luck!'

82   *Put it in English, greaseball!*: Stanley, victimised as a 'Polack', does not worry about insulting his friend with this racist remark.

82   *Luck is believing you're lucky. Take at Salerno*: Stanley believes in making his own luck and, therefore, in controlling fate. Applying this to Blanche, he knew he could defeat her; he had the ultimate means of doing so. Salerno was the site of the Allied invasion of mainland Italy in the Second World War. The American forces were the Fifth Army.

82   *You ... you ... you ... Brag ... brag ... bull ... bull*: Mitch's lack of sophistication is all too clear in his conversations with Blanche. Here his anger at Stanley's insensitivity makes him particularly inarticulate.

82   *If it's not too crushed I'll wear it and on the lapel that silver and turquoise pin in the shape of a seahorse*: one of several references to the sea. Crushed herself, Blanche has to find some way through this difficult scene.

83   *I couldn't believe her story and go on living with Stanley*: Stella's moral dilemma. What Stanley has done is too appalling to contemplate; it is easier for Stella to accept that her sister is insane.

83   *She has a tragic radiance in her red satin robe following the sculptural lines of her body*: the bold colour captures Blanche's pain. Strong sympathy surrounds her at this point and she has the beauty of a work of art.

83   *At the sound of BLANCHE'S voice MITCH'S arm supporting his cards has sagged and his gaze is dissolved into space*: the first sign of Mitch's feelings of guilt. Whereas in Scene Three he could not concentrate because of Blanche's presence, here he slumps at the table with the regret that is triggered by her voice.

83   *BLANCHE stands quite still for some moments – the silverbacked mirror in her hand and a look of sorrowful perplexity as though all human experience shows on her face*: confused and shocked by the sound of Mitch's name, Blanche transcends her own situation and becomes a figure of universal suffering. Williams is gradually increasing her tragic significance. The mirror takes us back to the one that shattered at the start of Scene Ten.

84   *MITCH ducks his head lower but STANLEY shoves back his chair as if to rise*: the contrast between the two men is effectively illustrated here. Mitch is ashamed and wants to avoid a scene; Stanley is pursuing victory to the bitter end.

84   *It's Della Robbia blue. The blue of the robe in the old Madonna pictures. Are these grapes washed?*: Blanche is anxious to establish her purity and continues the reference to her being a work of art. She has been trying to wash her soul clean and now she wants assurances that everything she touches is free from dirt and sin.

84   *Those cathedral bells – they're the only clean thing in the Quarter. Well, I'm going now. I'm ready to go*: heard for the first time, the cathedral bells signify the start of Blanche's spiritual journey.

85   *"Poor lady," they'll say, "the quinine did her no good. That* *unwashed grape has transported her soul to heaven"*: typically, Blanche dreams of dying in a young man's arms. Having resisted the onset of time so assiduously, she almost seems to welcome death here. Quinine is a bitter crystalline compound found in cinchona bark and used as a tonic and to reduce fever.

85   *And I'll be buried at sea sewn up in a clean white sack and dropped overboard – at noon – in the blaze of summer – and into an ocean as blue as [chimes again] my first lover's eyes!*: Williams wanted to be buried at sea like Hart Crane, but his body was taken to St Louis for burial in the Mt Calvary Cemetery. This vignette suggests the warmth and passion of first love, not the coldness of death.

85   *The gravity of their profession is exaggerated – the unmistakable aura of the state institution with its cynical detachment*: Williams's experience of the institutions his sister Rose stayed in is evident in the thumbnail sketches we get of the doctor and the matron. They appear coldly professional until Blanche transforms the doctor into a gentleman caller. Diagnosed as schizophrenic, Rose was given a frontal lobotomy in 1943 and spent the rest of her life in institutions. Images of madness are common in Williams's plays, and Catherine Holly, a character in *Suddenly Last Summer* is even threatened with a lobotomy.

85   *STELLA presses her fist to her lips*: an obvious sign of tension.

86   *Please don't get up. I'm only passing through*: Blanche's life has latterly involved journeys; she has not been able to find a permanent shelter.

86   *There is a moment of silence – no sound but that of STANLEY steadily shuffling the cards*: a moment of tension that, together with the distant Varsouviana, suggests the threat to Blanche who still has to negotiate Stanley and the other card players.

87   *Lurid reflections appear on the walls in odd, sinuous shapes. The "Varsouviana" is filtered into weird distortion, accompanied by the cries and noises of the jungle. BLANCHE seizes the back of a chair as if to defend herself*: the distorted Varsouviana represents Blanche's most recent nightmare: the rape. The scene is re-enacted in her mind and she adopts a defensive position, this time with a chair rather than a broken bottle.

87   *The greeting is echoed and re-echoed by other mysterious voices behind the walls, as if reverberated through a canyon of rock*: Williams continues to expose the workings of Blanche's mind: she hears only a jumble of confusing voices. The canyon also represents the world falling away beneath her.

87   *She cries out as if the lantern was herself*: Stanley repeats Mitch's action of Scene Nine – essentially a figurative rape.

88   *What have I done to my sister?*: Stella understands her own involvement in the betrayal of Blanche; she knows that she has helped to destroy her.

88   *Madre de Dios! Cosa mala, muy, muy mala!*: Mother of God! This is a bad thing, a very, very bad thing! Pablo is the first of the poker players to voice his concern. By stating it here in Spanish, it seems more heartfelt.

88 *You done this, all o' your God damn interfering with things you –* : guilt-ridden as he has been throughout this scene, Mitch finally turns on Stanley. He will need to be restrained as Stanley was in Scene Three.

88   *BLANCHE turns wildly and scratches at the MATRON*: Blanche is like a feral cat or the tiger that Stanley labelled her just before the rape in Scene Ten; she does not want to be caged.

88   *Jacket*: straitjacket.

89   *He takes off his hat and now becomes personalized*: Blanche is now able to see him as a gentleman caller, though not Shep Huntleigh.

89   *Whoever you are – I have always depended on the kindness of strangers*: Blanche is in the unfortunate position of having to accept help from anyone, though she implies that she has never really known people intimately. We are reminded of her comment to Mitch at the end of Scene Three: 'I need kindness now' (p. 34).

89   *It is wrapped in a pale blue blanket*: the colour links the child with Blanche. In her delicate state, Blanche has needed to be handled like a child in this last scene.

89   *She sobs with inhuman abandon. There is something luxurious in her complete surrender to crying now that her sister is gone*: 'inhuman' echoes the jungle cries Blanche has been hearing. Only now that Blanche has left can Stella give in to the fullness of her emotions. These are self-indulgently 'luxurious', as if partly for her benefit, to foreground her own remorse rather than just what has happened to Blanche.

90   *[He kneels beside her and his fingers find the opening of her blouse.] Now, now, love. Now, love . . .*: a crude sexual gesture on Stanley's part. The repetition of 'now' emphasises his conviction that their life can return to normality. For Stanley, this means a resumption of sexual relations, even though it is only 'some weeks' after the birth of the child. The stage direction before this is *'voluptuously, soothingly'*, combining Stanley's sexual passion with his genuine love for Stella. Kazan's film version could not be seen to endorse any kind of acceptance of rape, so the ending sees Stella taking her baby and running off, promising never to return.

90   *The luxurious sobbing, the sensual murmur fade away under the swelling music of the "blue piano" and the muted trumpet*: the music and sound effects combine here in a heady mix which is both 'swelling' and 'muted'. Williams effectively smothers the emotional crescendo of the play with the music that has helped to define both the Quarter and the specific events of the play.

90   *This game is seven-card stud*: this matter-of-fact statement indicates three things: the poker players are starting a fresh game, one that they played before in Scene Three; life will continue in much the same way; Stanley, the 'stud', is triumphant, the luck that he believes in fashioning for himself signified by the number seven. At precisely what cost Stanley's victory has been achieved is a point that the audience is left to ponder.

Marlon Brando as Stanley

Vivien Leigh as Blanche

Mitch (Karl Malden) and Blanche

Blanche and Stanley

Stanley and Blanche

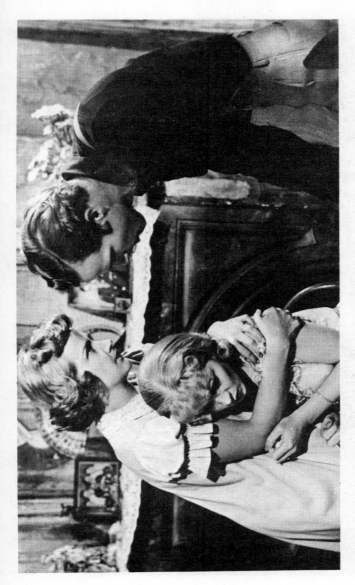

Stella (Kim Hunter), Blanche and Stanley

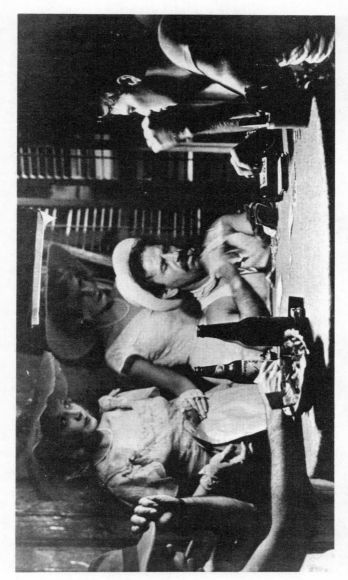

The Poker Night

Stella and Stanley

The Matron and Blanche

The Doctor leads Blanche away

Blanche and Mitch

Stanley, Blanche and Stella

The Quarter

Questions for further study

1. To what extent is Blanche the controlling force in the play?
2. Compare and contrast the attitudes of Blanche and Stella to the story of their past selves at Belle Reve.
3. How far do the audience agree with Blanche's assessment of Stanley as an 'ape'?
4. Discuss the dramatic devices which Williams uses in the play to suggest that Blanche is doomed.
5. Stanley ripping away the paper lantern represents his destruction of lies, deceit and fantasy. Explore aspects of truth and fantasy in the play.
6. 'A play must concentrate the events of a lifetime into the short span of a three-act play. Of necessity these events must be more violent than in life' (Tennessee Williams). Examine the creation of tension as it is developed through the eleven scenes of the play.
7. In his directorial notes on the play Elia Kazan suggests that through watching the decline of Blanche '[the audience] begin to realise that they are sitting in at the death of something extraordinary [. . .] and then they feel the tragedy'. Discuss the fall of Blanche in the play.
8. Explore Williams's use of colour as it impacts upon the changing atmosphere of the play.
9. The 'visual projection of Blanche's inner life' is a key aspect of Williams's dramatic technique. How is it used?
10. The 'infusion' of lyricism in the atmosphere of Elysian Fields is created using a range of visual and aural devices. Examine Williams's creation of environment within the play.
11. 'If Blanche belongs to the crumbling grandeur of the Southern plantations, Stanley is a new American, an immigrant man of the city.' How does the play express the conflict between traditional values and the new world?

12. 'The blind are leading the blind' (Blanche, Scene II). Examine the twinned themes of sight and blindness as they are expressed through character and dramatic incidents.

13. 'Don't hang back with the brutes' (Blanche, Scene IV). Discuss the development of the character of Stanley as it is revealed, both through his own words and actions, and the perceptions of others.

14. 'The relationship between Stanley and Stella is based on his need for domination and her need for protection.' Discuss.

15. The relationship between Blanche and Mitch offers an interesting perspective on the nature of gender relations in the play. Focusing on clear examples of at least two of the relationships, explore the issues which arise.

16. 'He acts like an animal, has an animal's habits' (Blanche, Scene IV). Explore the conflicts between gentility and animal brutality in the play.

17. 'I lived in a house where dying old women remembered their dead men [. . .] Death . . . [. . .] the opposite is desire' (Blanche, Scene IX). Examine Williams's use of this theme to affect the audience.

18. The lurid reflections which fall across the walls in the final scene are a potential manifestation of Blanche's terrors and fears. Discuss the dramatic devices used by Williams in the final scene.

19. 'The language of the play is shaped by two needs: character-identification and thematic development.' Explore this statement.

20. Stella's apparent betrayal of Blanche offers the audience a clear insight into her character. Discuss the complexities of the relationship between the sisters in the light of Stella's final act.

21. *A Streetcar Named Desire* appears to be a hybrid drama: naturalistic, symbolic and poetic. Do you agree?

22. Blanche's response to the figure of the doctor in the final scene of the play is characteristic of her deep-rooted perception of the role of men in her life. Explore the range of Blanche's attitudes towards the men in the play.

23. 'To hold front position in this rat-race you've got to believe you are lucky' (Stanley, Scene XI). To what extent does Williams emphasise the role of luck in dictating the course of the lives of his characters?

24. Is *A Streetcar Named Desire* a moral play?